# Forecasting with Judgment

# Forecasting with Judgment

*Edited by*

**George Wright**

*Strathclyde Graduate Business School, UK*

*and*

**Paul Goodwin**

*University of the West of England, UK*

JOHN WILEY & SONS

Chichester · New York · Weinheim · Brisbane · Singapore · Toronto

*Other Wiley Editorial Offices*

John Wiley & Sons, Inc., 605 Third Avenue,
New York, NY 10158-0012, USA

VCH Verlagsgesellschaft mbH, Pappelallee 3,
D-69469 Weinheim, Germany

Jacaranda Wiley Ltd, 33 Park Road, Milton,
Queensland 4064, Australia

John Wiley & Sons (Asia) Pte Ltd, 2 Clementi Loop #02-01,
Jin Xing Distripark, Singapore 129809

John Wiley & Sons (Canada) Ltd, 22 Worcester Road,
Rexdale, Ontario M9W 1L1, Canada

***Library of Congress Cataloging-in-Publication Data***

Forecasting with judgment / edited by George Wright and Paul Goodwin.
    p.   cm.
  Includes bibliographical references (p.    ) and index.
  ISBN 0–471–97014–X
  1. Business forecasting.   2. Forecasting.   3. Judgment.
  4. Decision-making.   I. Wright, George, 1952–    .  II. Goodwin,
Paul.
  HD30.27.F688   1998
  338.5′442—dc21                                      97-18364
                                                          CIP

***British Library Cataloguing in Publication Data***

A catalogue record for this book is available from the British Library

ISBN 0-471-97014-X.

Typeset in 11/13pt Times by Mathematical Composition Setters Ltd, Salisbury, Wiltshire
Printed and bound in Great Britain by Biddles Ltd, Guildford and King's Lynn
This book is printed on acid-free paper responsibly manufactured from sustainable forestry, in which at least two trees are planted for each one used for paper production.

# Contents

# Contributors

J. SCOTT ARMSTRONG
Wharton School, University of Pennsylvania, Philadelphia, PA 19104, USA

PETER AYTON
Department of Psychology, City University, Northampton Square, London EC1V 0HB, UK

FERGUS BOLGER
Faculty of Business Administration, Bilkent University, Bilkent 06533, Ankara, Turkey

GLENN J. BROWNE
College of Business Administration, Texas Tech University, Lubbock, TX 79409-2101, USA

FRED COLLOPY
The Weatherhead School of Management, Case Western Reserve University, Cleveland, OH 44106\displaylines{7325, USA

SHAWN P. CURLEY
Carlson School of Management, University of Minnesota, Minneapolis, MN 55455, USA

ANIL GABA
INSEAD, Boulevard de Constance, 77305 Fontainbleu Cedex, France

PAUL GOODWIN
Department of Mathematical Sciences, University of the West of England, Coldharbour Lane, Frenchay, Bristol BS16 1QY, UK

NIGEL HARVEY
Psychology Department, University College London, Gower Street, London, UK

MICHAEL LAWRENCE
School of Information Systems, University of New South Wales, Kensington, NSW 2052, Australia

SPYROS MAKRIDAKIS
INSEAD, Boulevard de Constance, 77305 Fontainbleu Cedex, France

MARCUS O'CONNOR
School of Information Systems, University of New South Wales, Kensington, NSW 2052, Australia

DILEK ÖNKAL-ATAY
Faculty of Business Administration, Bilkent University, 06533 Ankara, Turkey

GENE ROWE
Department of Psychology, University of Surrey, Guildford GU2 5XH, UK

KEES VAN DER HEIJDEN
Department of Management Science, University of Strathclyde, 40 George Street, Glasgow G1 1QE, UK

# Preface

This book is a follow-up to an earlier collection of writings on the judgmental aspects of forecasting which was published by Wiley as *Judgmental Forecasting* in 1987. That book was edited by George Wright and Peter Ayton. Since then there has been a growth in the study of the role of judgment in forecasting by both psychologists and management scientists. Indeed, in March 1996 a special issue of the *International Journal of Forecasting* was devoted to the topic. Like the 1987 book, the present volume contains specially commissioned chapters from a mix of contributors who are based in either psychology departments or business schools. Our renewed objective is to present an up-to-date overview of current research and practice in forecasting with judgment—in a format that is accessible to a broad-based multi-disciplinary audience of forecasting practitioners and academics.

All forecasting involves judgment, whether it be in the selection of the forecasting method or the formulation of the forecasting model. Indeed, even sophisticated statistical methods such as Box–Jenkins and multiple regression (cf. Makridakis & Wheelwright, 1989) rely heavily on judgment—the former in the model identification phase, the latter in the selection of independent variables.

More commonly, however, the term "judgmental forecasting" is associated with forecasts which are made wholly on the basis of judgment, or with judgmental adjustments to statistical forecasts. There is much evidence that these judgmental approaches are widely used in business and other organizations to forecast variables like sales or costs (Dalrymple, 1987; Sanders & Manrodt, 1994). Often, forecasters have access to the past history of the forecast variable (time series information) and usually the forecasts are expressed as single values, or point forecasts (e.g. "we forecast sales of 230 units next month"), so that there is no indication of the level of uncertainty that is associated with the forecast. Judgmental forecasting where time series information is available has attracted an increasing amount of attention in the decade since the volume by Wright & Ayton was published. While the early focus of research was on the relative accuracy of judgmental and statistical forecasting, interest has now broadened to embrace the study of how judges arrive at their forecasts and how forecast accuracy can be improved by providing appropriate support (Goodwin & Wright, 1993, 1994).

Another major role of judgment in forecasting is in the subjective estimation of probabilities. These probabilities can be subsequently used to guide people's decisions, either informally or through formal methods like decision analysis (Goodwin & Wright, 1998). This area has continued to be subject to the greatest amount of research activity. The Wright & Ayton volume contained much debate about the quality of human probability judgments. One view characterized humans as "intellectual cripples, whose intuitive judgments in the face of uncertainty violated the fundamental principles of optimal behavior" (Slovic, 1982). An alternative view was that poor judgment was a peculiar outcome of paper-and-pencil tasks carried out in the psychological laboratory (Beach, Christensen-Szalanski & Barnes, 1987). Since this research generally involved student subjects carrying out contrived tasks with which they were unfamiliar on a day-to-day basis, the predominance of poor judgment was, perhaps, not surprising. In the real world, it was argued, there is considerable evidence of high quality judgment. As many of the chapters in this volume document, the debate has continued and broadened, with some researchers (e.g. Gigerenzer, 1991, 1994) now arguing that many biases evident in subjective probability estimation do not apply when people are asked to assess frequencies instead. For example, an assessment of the *subjective probability* of a randomly selected company failing in the next year is likely to be less accurate than an assessment of the *number* of companies in a random sample of 100 who will fail in the next year.

All of these aspects of forecasting with judgment are addressed in the current volume.

In Chapter 1, Spyros Makridakis and Anil Gaba analyze the thought processes of chess grand masters and compare their performance with that of top executives in business organizations. Makridakis & Gaba analyze the role of judgment in strategy development and summarize the various heuristics that are used in assessing the likelihood of future events. These authors propose that for strategy to be successful it must be foresighted, creatively unique, and sustainable. Foresight requires numerous predictions about the industry within which the organization operates, e.g. the economy, technology, competition, social and demographic trends, consumer needs and attitudes, and other factors. Statistical methods, which rely on extrapolating historical patterns, are unlikely to capture changes that will occur in the future. On the other hand, judgmental forecasting, in the form of point forecasts or subjective probabilities, may be negatively influenced by judgmental heuristics that can lead to bias. By contrast, successful foresight is underpinned by an understanding of the nature of economic, social, technological and political forces which will drive the future. Makridakis & Gaba provide a set of questions which strategists can use as a framework to facilitate creative discussions about the nature of the future.

Such a focus is at the heart of scenario planning, where no attempt is made to forecast the future. Instead, multiple plausible futures are constructed which bound the critical uncertainties and trends that are seen to have an impact on the future. Subjective probabilities are not attached to individual scenarios—since each scenario has an infinitesimal likelihood of actual occurrence. Instead, an organization's current strategy can be tested for "robustness" against the scenarios in a way analogous to that in which the design of a new airplane is tested in a variety of wind conditions in an experimental wind tunnel. Kees van der Heijden has labeled this approach to strategy evaluation "wind-tunneling". The essential differences between forecasting and scenario planning are discussed in Chapter 2, by Kees van der Heijden. Here, van der Heijden notes that the paradigm of rationalistic decision making contends that subjective probabilities *can* be assessed for the occurrence of unique events. However, as Makridakis & Gaba have documented, heuristics are used in such assessments and these heuristics can lead to bias. Van der Heijden argues that non-probabilistic scenario thinking contains an iterative, process methodology to overcome such potential biases in ill-defined situations. His chapter analyzes the processes involved in the practice of scenario planning. The focus is on how groups interact and how this interaction can be facilitated to aid development of causal insights into the nature of plausible futures.

Marcus O'Connor and Michael Lawrence begin Chapter 3 by illustrating the processes at work in a product forecasting meeting. They conclude that, in practice, such meetings are not focused on the historic time series. Instead, the focus is evaluating the causal influences that are seen, by the meeting participants, to exert an influence on future sales. Such non-time-series information has been shown by academic researchers to produce judgmental forecasts (or adjustments) that are superior to the predictions of statistical models. O'Connor & Lawrence's chapter looks at the way in which people use non-time-series information in sales forecasting and considers the degree of use of this information where time-series information and related statistical modeling tools are also available. In reviewing empirical evidence from a range of studies, the authors suggest that non-time-series information tends to be used inefficiently by judgmental forecasters, despite the importance that it can have in improving forecast accuracy. They suggest that further research is needed to establish how people use "hard" statistical information in combination with softer information, such as that relating to special events which will occur in the future.

In Chapter 4, Paul Goodwin outlines the variety of tasks that judgmental forecasting can involve and considers how research can best support people who carry out these tasks in practice. The laboratory has often been criticized for not being a suitable environment for obtaining research results that can generalize to the real world. In contrast to the laboratory tasks, real world forecasting has usually been perceived as involving highly motivated and expert forecasters, with ready access to appropriate information sources. However, Goodwin cites studies which show that the practice of forecasting in many organizations is a low priority activity conducted by inadequately supported, poorly trained and poorly motivated personnel. Moreover, targets, plans and decisions are often misrepresented as forecasts. In the light of this, Goodwin argues that the laboratory offers an environment that can play a pivotal role in identifying the conditions which will lead to judgmental forecast improvement. He argues that, while changes in organizational attitudes towards the role and status of forecasting are essential if the quality of judgmental forecasting is to improve, discoveries of what can be achieved under appropriate conditions in the laboratory may help to spur these changes.

In Chapter 5, Fergus Bolger and Nigel Harvey revisit Scott Armstrong's (1985) differentiation of stages in the forecasting process: choice of method; application of method; comparison and combination of forecasts; adjustment of forecasts; and evaluation. Bolger & Harvey note the prevalence of judgmental inputs at each stage and then marshall evidence for heuristics—and possible biases—at each stage. In terms of the application of a forecasting strategy, the heuristic that has received most attention is that of anchoring and (insufficient) adjustment. Here, a supplied or salient forecast is taken as an anchor and a final judgment is made by adjusting away from this anchor. Documentation of the prevalence of this heuristic is most evident in studies of the judgmental extrapolation of time series where forecasters may anchor on recent values, or other characteristics, of the series. Bolger & Harvey analyze the extent to which choice of anchor is adaptive and appropriate to the series being forecast. Next, Bolger & Harvey describe the biases that have been found in the subjective assessment of probability. Generally, individuals have been shown to be "over-confident"—in that assessed probabilities are more extreme than is justified by the actual occurrence of events.

In Chapter 6, Dilek Önkal-Atay documents the prominent role that judgment has in financial forecasting. Judgmental predictions can be point-event forecasts (e.g. value of an exchange rate), categorical-event forecasts (e.g. increase in a stock price) or subjective probabilities attached to these events. Önkal-Atay describes and analyses research on each of these forecast types. Most of the empirical research has focused on point and categorical forecasts of earnings given by security analysts. This focus of attention is because of the real-world importance of such forecasts. A general conclusion is that of the superior accuracy of judgment, despite the prevalence of heuristic processes, but that potential improvement *may* result from combination of judgment with statistical forecasts. Önkal-Atay argues that apparently conflicting and ambiguous information will continue to dominate volatile financial markets such that the future role of judgment will be accentuated rather than attenuated. She concludes that research focused on understanding the factors which contribute to the accuracy of domain experts and on the successful communication of their forecasts to end-users is critical, given the prominent role of judgment in financial forecasting.

In Chapter 7, Glenn Browne and Shawn Curley focus on the reasoning processes that underpin unique subjective probability forecasts. Until recently, the focus in probability forecasting has been on measuring the quality of such judgmental forecasts and on identifying situational factors that are linked with high and low quality, or validity, of such forecasting. Early research on the validity of probability assessment was labeled "dust-bowl empiricism" (cf. Lichtenstein, Fischhoff & Phillips, 1982) but, more recently, theoretical accounts of the causes of judgmental quality have been developed and evaluated (cf. McClelland & Bolger, 1994). Browne & Curley's approach is innovative in that it extends investigation of the reasoning processes that act to produce judgments of probability. In their chapter, they develop a number of testable propositions about the selection and use of information for judgmental forecasting.

Chapter 8 is devoted to the analysis of techniques to aid small-group-based forecasting. Here, Gene Rowe compares and contrasts the ways in which the judgment of groups of individuals can be enhanced by structuring the way in which these individuals interact in their exchange of information. Theoretically, structured group techniques, such as Delphi, should produce a judgment that is at least as good as, and often better than, that of an individual chosen at random from the grouping. Rowe focuses on the rationale of the Delphi technique and evaluates empirical studies of its effectiveness in comparison to other techniques that have sought to enhance group judgment. The general finding is that Delphi sometimes leads to higher accuracy and sometimes does not. Rowe traces this pattern of mixed results to differences in the application of the Delphi procedure. A major research focus should now be on understanding the processes underpinning opinion change such that (a) the success, or not, of interventions using group decision support systems can be understood, and (b) the design of technological systems and techniques to support group decision making or forecasting can be refined.

In Chapter 9, Peter Ayton considers the degree to which judgment is subject to the biases that Makridakis & Gaba introduced and which subsequent chapters have analyzed in detail. Is judgment massively flawed? If so, do individuals realize this? Ayton reviews the work of Gerd Gigerenzer and his colleagues, who have shown that whilst people are poor at making judgments in some laboratory tasks that have been devised by psychologists, if the tasks are restructured by the experimenter then evidence for excellent judgment can be produced. For example, under some task conditions over-confidence can be made to disappear. Ayton argues that biases which can be overcome by such simple interventions cannot illustrate fundamental limitations of human judgment. Nevertheless, recent research continues to demonstrate that subjective probability judgments do not obey the laws of probability theory. Ayton concludes that such judgments, if used as the basis for actions, will lead to poor decision-making.

In Chapter 10, J. Scott Armstrong and Fred Collopy focus on how judgment and statistical methods should be integrated for improved time-series forecasting. In their chapter, they identify 46 empirical studies which have focused on this issue and identify five separable integration procedures: revising judgment; combining forecasts; revising extrapolations; rule-based forecasting; and econometric forecasting. As Armstrong & Collopy note, integration procedures can be expected to be successful if judgments and statistical forecasts are independent of one another—such that double-counting is avoided. Armstrong & Collopy argue that domain knowledge can help identify the direction of causal forces on the series of interest. For example, forecasts for petroleum reserves have *increased* over the last decades because of improvements in exploration technology. As O'Connor & Lawrence note, in practice the search for such causal forces is prevalent in many unstructured forecasting situations. Indeed, as van der Heijden has documented, recognition and structuring of such causal forces is a key component of scenario construction. However, note that in the scenario-construction process, the *systemic* interplay between such causal driving forces is a major issue of concern. This is because an appreciation of systemic effects can lead to insight into, say, subsequent self-limiting processes underpinning an initial increase or decline in a target variable. Such process-orientated methods for capturing and enhancing insights into causality are, as yet, undeveloped in putative techniques to enhance judgmental interventions in time-series models and subjective probability forecasting. In conclusion, although Armstrong & Collopy find that much research has recently been conducted on the relative roles of judgment and statistical modeling in forecasting, it is too early to specify exact principles for integration. Nevertheless, these authors outline conditions under which various integration procedures are likely to be effective. These procedures involve the forecaster making judgmental inputs to statistical methods *rather* than revising model output.

## REFERENCES

Armstrong, J.S. (1985) *Long-range Forecasting: From Crystal Ball to Computer*. Wiley-Interscience, New York.

Beach, L.R., Christensen-Szalanski, J.J.J. & Barnes, V.E. (1987) Assessing human judgment: has it been done, can it be done, should it be done? In G. Wright & P. Ayton (eds) *Judgmental Forecasting*. Wiley, Chichester.

Dalrymple, D.J. (1987) Sales forecasting practices: results from a United States survey. *International Journal of Forecasting*, **3**, 379–91.

Gigerenzer, G. (1991) How to make cognitive illusions disappear: beyond heuristics and biases. In W. Stroebe & M. Hewstone (eds), *European Review of Social Psychology*, vol. 2. Wiley, Chichester.

Gigerenzer, G. (1994) Why the distinction between single-event probabilities and frequencies is important for psychology (and vice versa). In G. Wright and P. Ayton (eds), *Subjective Probability*, Wiley, Chichester.

Goodwin, P. & Wright, G. (1993) Improving judgmental time series forecasting: a review of the guidance provided by research. *International Journal of Forecasting*, **9**, 147–61.

Goodwin, P. & Wright, G. (1994) Heuristics, biases and improvement strategies in judgmental time series forecasting. *Omega International Journal of Management Science*, **22**, 553–68.

Goodwin, P. & Wright, G. (1998) *Decision Analysis for Management Judgment*, 2nd edn. Wiley, Chichester.

Lichtenstein, S., Fischhoff, B. & Phillips, L.D. (1982) Calibration of probabilities: the state of the art to 1980. In D. Kahneman, P. Slovic & A. Tversky (eds) *Judgment under Uncertainty: Heuristics and Biases*. Cambridge University Press, Cambridge.

Makridakis, S. & Wheelwright, S.C. (1989) *Forecasting Methods for Management*, 5th edn. Wiley, New York.

McClelland, A. & Bolger, F. (1994) The calibration of subjective probabilities: theories and models 1980–94. In G. Wright and P. Ayton (eds) *Subjective Probability*. Wiley, Chichester.

Sanders, N.R. & Manrodt, K.B. (1994) Forecasting practices in US corporations: survey results. *Interfaces*, **24**, 92–100.

Slovic, P. (1982) Towards understanding and improving decisions. In W.C. Howell & E.A. Fleishmann (eds), *Human Performance and Productivity*, vol. 12, *Information Processing and Decision Making*. Erlbaum, Hillsdale, NJ.

# Chapter 1

# Judgment: Its Role and Value for Strategy

Spyros Makridakis and Anil Gaba

*INSEAD, Fontainbleu, France*

*Many times what are described as today's implementation failures are really yesterday's foresight failures in disguise (Hamel & Prahalad, 1994, p. 75)*

## SUMMARY

Judgmental biases and limitations have been extensively studied for repetitive decisions when inputs can be quantified and compared to those of corresponding decision rules. Judgmental inputs for strategy, however, are neither repetitive nor quantifiable, yet their importance is crucial to the success of whole countries and business firms. This chapter describes this critical role of judgment, concentrating on its value in strategic forecasting. Furthermore, it discusses the implications of judgmental biases and limitations on the future success of strategy and proposes ways of reducing their negative impact.

*Forecasting with Judgment.* Edited by G. Wright and P. Goodwin.
© 1998 John Wiley & Sons Ltd.

## 1.1  INTRODUCTION

Chess is an intellectually demanding game played by millions of people around the world. Yet unlike tennis or other competitive sports, there are few changes in the rankings of chess players. There have only been 12 World Chess Champions (see Table 1.1) since the official title was first established in 1886. Emanuel Lasker held the title for 27 years (1894–1921), Aleksandr Alekhine for 17, and Mikhail Botvinnik for 13. The last World Champion, Anatoly Karpov, held the title for 10 years between 1975 and 1985. In 1985 the current Champion, Gary Kasparov, was the youngest player, at the age of 22, to win the world chess title, which he has successfully defended since. Below the World Champion there are grand masters, masters, and many levels of chess experts, in addition to the great numbers of ordinary people playing

**Table 1.1**  Chess World Champions: 1886 to today

| Name | Becoming champ: year | Becoming champ: age | No. of years as World Champion |
|---|---|---|---|
| W. Steinitz | 1886 | 50 | 12 |
| E. Lasker | 1894 | 26 | 27 |
| J.P. Capablanca | 1921 | 33 | 6 |
| A.A. Alekhine (died Champion) | 1927 | 35 Lost the title 1935–37 | 17 |
| Vacant title | 1946–48 | – | – |
| M. Botvinnik | 1948 | 37 Lost the title 1957–58 and 1960–61 | 13 |
| T. Petrosian | 1963 | 33 | 6 |
| B. Spassky | 1969 | 32 | 3 |
| B. Fischer (he relinquished the title) | 1972 | 29 | 3 |
| A. Karpov | 1975 | 23 | 10 |
| G. Kasparov | 1985–today | 22 | 12+ |

chess. Yet grand masters (including the World Champion, who is the top among the grand masters) consistently win against all other chess players.

The popular view is that grand masters are highly intelligent people with a photographic memory and the ability to calculate the implications of various moves with amazing speed. Yet research has shown that the intelligence of grand masters is not different from that of other people of the same education and socio-economic background. Moreover, grand masters do not have a better or more photographic memory than the general public, while their power of calculation is not faster than that of other people. Finally, the number of moves ahead considered by grand masters and masters, as well as chess experts, is the same. They all usually examine two to three moves ahead, with a maximum of five (de Groot, 1965; Chase & Simon, 1973). The interesting questions are, then: why do they consistently win, and why have there only been 12 World Champions in the more than 110 years of the official title championships?

Grand masters possess two interrelated talents: the first permits them to *effortlessly and speedily* recognize chess patterns *correctly*; the second allows them to know *the best* move *intuitively and instantly*. Chess experts and novices do not have these talents, while masters possess them to a lesser degree (de Groot, 1965; Chase & Simon, 1973).

Grand masters can reconstruct a chess board, after they have looked at it for only 5 seconds, with 90% accuracy. In the other 10% of cases the mistake(s) involved is (are) usually small—involving minor pieces such as pawns. However, they cannot reconstruct boards where the pieces have been put randomly. The board must be that of an actual game between, say, grand masters after the twentieth move when the starting game had ended and few pieces had been won or lost (this makes the arrangement of the pieces on the board the most complex, while it cannot be asserted that the pattern can be "remembered" from memory because it is that of an opening game).

Related to this great ability of instant pattern recognition, chess grand masters possess an additional ability that allows them to intuitively know the best next move. In order to study and understand the way grand masters play chess, researchers have placed cameras below the chess board which capture, among other things, all eye movements. Using such cameras it has been shown that once the opponent has made his move the grand master's eyes *start*, three out of four times, at the best move, which he begins examining. Consequently, he then evaluates alternative moves to return and play (three out of four times) the move he considered first. Remembering that in games between grand masters every single chess move must be highly creative (whatever is obvious can be seen by even novice players) and powerful, it is hard to explain scientifically or rationally how grand masters can intuitively and instantly know which is the best move the great majority of the time.

Furthermore, grand masters are capable of playing simultaneous chess games against as many as 50 expert opponents and they win the great majority of them. This is a considerable achievement, as their opponents have ample time to analyze and carefully evaluate a great number of moves, while the grand master is playing against each of the remaining opponents he is simultaneously facing. The grand masters' two unique talents of *effortlessly and speedily* recognizing patterns *and* of *intuitively and instantly* seeing the best move overcome the ample time available to their opponents and prove the limitations of pure analytical evaluation or thinking. Finally, although a minimum of approximately 50 000 hours (or about 10 years) of knowledge acquisition and intense practice is required to become a grand master (Simon, 1985), there are many chess experts who have also spent equal or longer periods playing chess. Thus, the ability of grand masters to win consistently in chess games cannot be explained rationally; somehow, they possess, and/or have cultivated, at least *two* unique talents which provide them with the ability to stay at the top, very often for extended periods of time that cover more than one decade.

At the other extreme from grand masters are financial market professionals whose actual decisions (judgments) or recommended choices for buying stocks, bonds or other investment instruments are, on average, worse than random selections of similar portfolios (Bernstein, 1996; Glassman, 1997; Graham & Harvey, 1995; Rothchild, 1988). Obviously, such random selections do not require any knowledge or experience/expertise, yet they beat, on average, those of "professionals" who use their judgment, which incorporates their knowledge and experience/expertise of many years. Are there some financial professionals who, like the grand masters, significantly beat the market over long periods of time? The answer to this question is probably "No" (Graham & Harvey, 1995), although there are many people who think otherwise. The interesting question then becomes, "Why cannot the majority of knowledgeable 'professionals' with many years of experience do better than random choices?" The implications of answering this question correctly are considerable for understanding better the role and value of our judgment.

Evaluating the performance of CEOs and other top executives in business organizations is not as easy as that of chess players or investment analysts. Success and failure in business can be the outcome of many factors, making it difficult to pinpoint the isolated contribution of judgment in such success or failure. However, if we study the performance of many firms and associate it with the ability of their CEOs we can definitely identify some CEOs who have performed considerably above average over long periods of time, others who have consistently been below average, and some who started and stayed well above average for long time spans and then underperformed or even bankrupted their firms. There are, in addition, some CEOs who have succeeded after many setbacks, or even bankruptcies. However, the great majority of firms and CEOs perform to an average standard, by definition, over the long run. As CEOs are mainly concerned with the strategy of their firms, and as their good or bad judgment is the primary factor determining the success or failure of these firms, it is not clear how CEOs succeed or fail and when there is a reversal from success to failure or *vice versa*.

The purpose of this chapter is to study the role and value of human judgment and its contribution to strategy. Is human judgment a "...superb piece of work! Noble in reason! Infinite in faculty!" as Shakespeare believed, or are "errors of judgment ... often systematic rather than random, manifesting bias rather than confusion", causing us to "suffer from mental astigmatism as well as myopia" (Kahneman & Tversky, 1979)? Answering, or even better understanding, whether (or under what circumstances) Shakespeare or Kahneman & Tversky are right or wrong is critical for strategic decision-making, as obviously Shakespeare's view of human judgment holds in the case of grand masters, while that of Kahneman & Tversky prevails in the case of financial analysts.

This chapter is organized as follows: first, the role of judgment, in particular as it relates to strategy, is examined; second, the ability of human judgment to assess the likelihood of forthcoming events is discussed, together with the various judgmental biases and limitations that negatively affect it; third, various dimensions of developing a strategy are proposed. Finally, we discuss the need for future research in developing better foresight and improving the judgmental processes required in formulating and evaluating successful strategies.

## 1.2 THE IMPORTANCE OF JUDGMENT IN STRATEGY

Strategy, whatever definition we accept (Makridakis & Héau, 1987), deals with future events and requires predictions about them. If the predictions (or lack of them) do not correctly identify important forthcoming events or critical changes in the business environment, there is little chance that strategy will be successful. Examples abound. The inability of American automobile firms in the early 1970s to foresee the changes in consumer attitudes towards smaller, oil-efficient cars opened the door to their West European and Japanese rivals to take a big chunk of the American market (Magaziner & Patinkin, 1989). The inability or unwillingness of IBM to recognize the revolutionary changes being brought about by the personal computer resulted in the end of its dominance of the computer industry and in huge losses that brought this giant close to bankruptcy (Makridakis, 1997a). Similarly, the high rate of unemployment in the great majority of EU nations, which started in the early 1990s, has been the consequence of not anticipating the negative repercussions of the welfare state on the long-term ability of their economies to adapt to technological and other changes. European nations opted, therefore, to save jobs in the short term, but in doing so they increased long-term unemployment a great deal as job security laws, market and labor regulations, as well as numerous bureaucratic obstacles, halted the creation of new business firms and reduced the number of new jobs. Finally, even Japan, the superstar of the 1970s and 1980s, found itself in serious trouble as its firms and politicians did not predict the obvious: that is, that other nations and firms would learn and imitate the successful practices of Japanese businesses and apply these to compete on more equal terms against them. Many current problems are, therefore, the consequence of yesterday's failures of foresight, as the quotation at the beginning of this chapter indicates.

We must be extremely careful when studying the implications of good or bad forecasts. Predictions are different from explaining what has happened in the past, after the fact. Explaining the past is easy (Makridakis, 1997a). Predicting the future is an extremely difficult task, in particular when strategic events are involved. The most important lesson we have probably learned in the field of forecasting in the last two decades is that the model that best fits historical data (the equivalent of explaining the past) is not necessarily the most accurate one for predicting the future that is beyond available data (Makridakis, 1997a).

Such a lesson has serious implications for strategy, for two reasons. First, real predictions cannot be based simply on extrapolating the past, or alternatively on just historical information. Second, studying and imitating past successes is not enough to guarantee future ones. This means that to succeed in the future we must go beyond recipes, models, and/or theories that provide a procedure, or sequence of steps, for formulating or implementing a successful strategy (Micklethwait & Woldridge, 1996). Examples abound: from companies discussed in *In Search of Excellence* (Peters & Waterman, 1982), a book that provided advice from America's best-run companies (these companies found themselves in serious trouble not long after the book was published— Makridakis, 1990) to Japan, which after four decades of spectacular success has found itself with very serious economic and competitive problems—including a recession and slow growth for the last 6 years.

In the field of business strategy one of the authors of this chapter (Makridakis, 1997b) has, for instance, identified 18 theories that have appeared during the last 30 years. All of these theories have attempted to provide analytical tools to deal with strategy and have, with no exception, all failed. Strategy must be, among other things, unique. Otherwise a large number of firms can apply it, thus minimizing its value and reducing the benefits from its successful implementation to "average", as it is usually impossible for everyone to succeed in a big way. This means that above-average success requires something "unique" which can only be based on judgmental inputs (including creative thinking) that, among other things, must correctly anticipate forthcoming events and changes, and then do something to exploit their potential benefits or avoid their negative consequences.

At present there is a great deal of debate about the future of the Internet and the potential benefits, as well as dangers, it holds for business firms, and even whole nations. At the level of computer firms, if the Internet and the NC (Network Computer) prevail there will be billions of dollars of revenues shifting from Intel and Microsoft to firms like Netscape and Sun (Schlender, 1996). Beyond the computer firms, huge opportunities for teleshopping, telework, and all sorts of entertainment over the Internet can open up as the price of computers and communications will continue to fall. The big question is, therefore, whether or not these predictions about NC, which costs the same as a color TV set, and global communications over the Internet, which cost the same as a local call, will materialize. Moreover, timing is critical so that it can be decided when a practical strategy can be formulated and then implemented. Obviously, success cannot be guaranteed by accurately predicting the future implications of low-cost, or even practically free, computing and communications. At the same time, we can say with near certainty that many of the existing firms will lose their dominant position if they do not follow the new developments in computers and telecommunications and do not manage to adapt themselves to the new reality of the Internet. Today, however, the timing with which Internet communications will flourish is not known. Some say it will take a couple of years, while others estimate a couple of decades. Thus, making the vast investments required to harness the benefits of NCs and the Internet is a hard strategic choice with much uncertainty involved.

In one or two decades, by which time what has already happened will be clear, it will be easy to go back and explain why the winners won and to say that the losers lost because of their inability to foresee forthcoming changes and take bold actions to exploit their benefits and/or avoid the dangers involved. Today, however, neither the evolution of computers and the Internet nor the exact timing of such evolution are obvious. This makes it difficult for firms to formulate a strategy that exploits the opportunities and avoids the dangers that will develop. Moreover, neither is the extent of the potential competition clear, nor is the way that firms will maintain competitive advantages known, even if such advantages can be gained through large initial investments (Grove, 1996).

There is an irony surrounding accurate forecasts and their practical value to business firms. For a forecast to be useful it must provide firms with the opportunity to exploit potential benefits and/or stay clear of forthcoming dangers. But if people can correctly predict the future they will definitely develop strategies and take steps to gain from these predictions. Yet this will certainly affect the course of future events and in many cases alter or even invalidate the forecasts. For example, the prediction that the NC will replace the PC will definitely draw reactions from Intel and Microsoft, who will be the major players to lose from the NC. They have already started to formulate their own strategies for substantially reducing the price of PC computers and that of related softwares. They offer such software (often free of charge) over telecommunications networks, including the Internet, and even offer their own versions of the NC, which will be a stripped-down version of a PC, offering everything an NC can do while still possessing some of the most desirable features of a PC—but at a price not much higher than that of an NC. At the same time, those pushing NC will react to the anticipated moves of Intel and Microsoft by attempting to maximize their own benefits while reducing those of their opponents.

There are many other players besides just computer firms. Telecommunication companies, entertainment outfits, news organizations, travel, insurance and brokerage firms, just to mention a few, will also be involved as they can gain a big market by doing business over the Internet. As there are billions of dollars of potential profits or losses at stake, there is no doubt that anticipations will play a critical role and that through such anticipations the various players will attempt to change the course of future events to fit their own purposes. As a matter of fact, the more certain it is that the forecasts will materialize, the greater will be the attempt by companies to take concrete steps to invalidate these by developing and implementing strategies that will attempt to change the course of future events to fit their own purposes and achieve their goals. In a strategic setting, where many people are involved as decision-makers, there is never certainty about the future. The final outcome depends on the natural course of events and on actions, reactions and counter-actions. Successful strategies must take all these factors into account, necessitating judgment of the kind possessed by grand masters rather than financial analysts.

## 1.3 HUMAN JUDGMENT: ITS BIASES AND LIMITATIONS

Not many of us can remember the telephone numbers of our favorite restaurants, what we ate for lunch a month ago, or all of our appointments for next week. However, we are well aware of the limitations of our memories. We know we cannot remember everything, so we take steps to avoid the negative consequences involved. We write down the names of people and businesses in alphabetical order, along with the addresses and phone numbers in order to be able to retrieve them easily. For appointments we use an organizer or a calendar to enter the names of people to see, telephone calls to make, or meetings to attend, along with the times, under the correct date. A simple glance at the calendar reveals the day's schedule.

The fact that we do not entrust these things to memory and take remedial action to compensate for its deficiencies and limitations does not mean that our memory is deficient. On the contrary, the human memory is an exceptional organ, of infinite value. Even the most sophisticated computer cannot achieve a fraction of its marvelous workings. The human memory's complexity is estimated to be roughly the equivalent of 60 times that of the US telephone system, and its capacity 500 times that of the entire *Encyclopaedia Britannica* (or 500 000 times if redundancies are counted). Yet even this enormous capacity would be filled in a few days if everything were indiscriminately stored. Thus, one of the most important functions of our memory (and mind) is to know what is important to remember and what can be ignored. Furthermore, it can determine when something stored has to be pushed back or be forgotten to accommodate new, more important information. It is because the memory is such sophisticated mechanism that we should write down all the things that can be easily retrieved. The more it is relieved of the burden of storing trivial facts, the greater its capacity to store and easily retrieve more important information.

The ability of our brains to process information and make decisions is very similar to memory, on which it depends a great deal. There are many tasks our minds can do extremely well. But, as with memory, there are other tasks they cannot accomplish as well or cannot do at all. Think, for instance, of finding the square root of 53 591 468 115. Unless one is a computational genius, or perhaps an *idiot savant*, the task cannot be achieved directly by the brain alone. As with memory, our mind must make compromises in order to accomplish many different and often conflicting tasks. For instance, novel problem-solving and creativity require abilities at the opposite extreme from those needed to make computations or deal with routine, repetitive situations. Similarly, learning requires trial and error (it therefore necessitates making mistakes), which is dysfunctional in stable situations when no change is involved.

The big difference between memory and judgment is that while we accept the deficiencies and limitations of our memory (and so write down useful addresses or things we want to remember later on), we rarely do anything to remedy the deficiencies of our judgment, mainly because we are unaware or unwilling to accept that our judgment can be faulty or biased. Because they are almost never presumed to exist, it is extremely important to expose judgmental biases. Empirical evidence demonstrates, beyond all reasonable doubt, their existence and their negative, damaging consequences (Dawes, 1988; Dixon, 1976; Goldberg, 1970; Kahneman, Slovic & Tversky, 1982; Meehl, 1954). Research shows that judgmental biases do not mean stupidity, for their presence is clearly discernible among highly intelligent people. Rather, they result from the way the mind operates and reflect its endeavors to achieve the optimal reconciliation of conflicting objectives.

Clearly, business executives, like everybody, are not free from biases (Hogarth & Makridakis, 1981). Thus, a great deal of attention is required to deal with judgmental biases and limitations as they affect strategy (and decision-making in general) whose success or failure can have a substantial impact on the well-being of organizations. In the remainder of this section those biases relevant to forecasting and strategy are described and ways of minimizing or neutralizing their negative impact are proposed.

One of the judgmental biases that we often encounter is inconsistency. It happens when we change our minds (or decisions) when there is no need to do so. Consider, for instance, a production manager who must decide how much to manufacture for each of 10 products in the coming month. Bowman (1963) found that production managers' decisions about how much to produce fluctuated from month to month for no apparently good reason, and that making their decisions consistent improved profitability. Bowman's findings have been reproduced in a great number of studies. The conclusion is always the same. Repetitive, routine decisions can be improved if inconsistency is removed. People are often unable or unwilling to apply the same criteria or procedures when making similar decisions. Sometimes they forget; other times they are influenced by their mood at the time (think of a decision made the morning after a quarrel with one's spouse and a sleepless night); still other times they might be bored and want to try something new; finally, they might believe that conditions have changed when they actually have not.

Production managers are not the only ones whose decisions are inconsistent. Meehl (1954), in a small but influential book, concluded that decision rules using a few variables to predict do better than people, mostly because the models can consistently apply the same variables and decision criteria, while people are inconsistent in their choice of variables on which to base their decisions and in the criteria they employ.

Meehl's conclusions have been confirmed by hundreds of additional studies. Decision rules in the form of simple statistical models have been found to out-perform expert judges when repetitive, routine decisions were involved. These decisions included medical diagnosis, psychological predictions about people's personality traits, selection of students to be admitted to colleges or universities, predicting future earnings of companies, and so forth. There is hardly any evidence showing that expert decision-makers do better than decision rules. Obviously, these studies refer to repetitive, routine decisions, but even then their conclusions are surprising, as in the case of medical diagnosis. Garland (1960), for instance, reported a study in which experienced X-ray specialists, when examining X-rays, failed to recognize the presence of lung disease that was definitely visible on the X-ray film about 30% of the time. Similarly, studies found that radiologists changed their minds about 20% of the time *when given the same X-ray on two different occasions.*

Inconsistency can be avoided by formalizing the decision-making process (in our day it is called "building expert systems"). This would require deciding, first, what factors are important to consider in making a certain repetitive decision; second, how such factors should be weighted (one might be twice as important as another); and third, what objective should be optimized. The usefulness of decision rules derives from the fact that several people can get involved in determining them, thus making it possible to select the best factors, an optimal weighting scheme, and a viable objective. Since the rule will be used again and again, it makes sense to devote effort and resources to come up with the best one possible. The rule can subsequently be applied on a routine basis, freeing considerable human resources. Consider, for instance, when credit officers decide on a case-by-case basis whether or not a purchase by an American Express cardholder should be approved. This takes numerous credit officers and becomes an expensive operation. Now consider finding all-important factors that are used by credit officers to decide whether or not to approve a credit request. Since many such officers can be consulted and a great deal of effort can be devoted to the process, the most relevant factors can be found and included in a statistical model, which would determine whether such factors are indeed important and how much weight should be given to each. A decision rule will thus be established, allowing a clerk to enter the required information and let the model reach a decision. Credit officers would be consulted only in the exceptional case where the model indicates a gray area and cannot decide. Fewer officers are required, and decisions will be consistent (based on the decision rule accepted) and objective. Given today's computer technology and telecommunications capabilities, decision models of the type just described can be economically developed and profitably applied on a routine basis. American Express has indeed applied one such decision-making model (called an expert system) and has reported considerable improvements in efficiency and profits.

Similarly, a decision rule that to some extent selects stocks at random can considerably improve the performance of the great majority of professionally managed investment funds (Dawes, 1988). As such selection is trivial, it will result in a substantial cost reduction of a fund's expenses as no highly paid investment professionals will be needed. This would mean charging consumers less money for administering the investments while providing them with higher returns (a win/win situation). Richard Branson's Virgin Funds select stocks randomly and charge very low management fees to their clients.

Obviously, decision rules can neither be used indefinitely nor be always appropriate for strategic purposes. The environment changes, as does competition; new objectives might be set, and so on. In addition, decision rules that can be applied by everyone become competitive requirements which offer no strategic advantages in the long run. Too much consistency in strategy can be even more dangerous than inconsistency, for it excludes learning and leads to another more critical bias that affects strategy, that of conservatism. Such conservatism arises when organizations become incapable of recognizing (or unwilling to recognize) that the changes in the environment are affecting them and that they must do something to deal with these changes.

This is the problem with biases—in trying to avoid one we might cultivate another. A bias in this case exists precisely because our minds must ensure consistency, but must also allow for learning. The challenge facing all of us, therefore, is to be consistent while at the same time introducing mechanisms to ensure learning, and eventually changes in the decision rules to adapt to new conditions.

Another prominent example of a judgmental bias is recency (remembering more vividly recent events, which consequently influence our judgment to a greater extent than less recent events). Consider the oil prices between 1950 and 1988. During that period basic economic facts were ignored and many mistakes were made because of this recency bias, as organizations and governments overreacted to the latest price levels and developed strategies assuming first that decreasing real oil prices between 1955 and 1973 and then increasing ones between 1973 and 1981 were going to last for very long periods of time, if not for ever. The negative consequences of this recency bias for strategy were enormous. Utility companies, for instance, switched in the late 1960s or early 1970s from burning coal to burning oil to generate electricity, while whole countries like France undertook huge investments in nuclear energy, whose financial costs (not to mention the environmental ones) have been considerably higher than conventional utility plants using coal or oil.

Searching for supportive evidence is another bias (often called the confirmation bias) which can have serious negative consequences. Wason & Johnson-Laird (1972), cognitive psychologists, made it their lives' goal to learn more about how people search for and use information. They found that as much as 90% of all the information we are searching for aims at supporting views, beliefs or hypotheses that we have long cherished. Thus, if a CEO thinks that a certain strategy will be beneficial she/he will look for supportive evidence to prove that that belief (or, more precisely, that hypothesis) is correct. Unfortunately, however, it is practically impossible to prove the hypothesis that the strategy being considered will work, since it will take many years, if not decades, to do so and there are many factors, including luck, involved which cannot be isolated.

Moreover, we tend to remember information that confirms our beliefs far better than information that disproves them. In experiments, believers have tended to remember confirming material with 100% accuracy, but negative material only about 40% of the time. Thus, not only do we search for supportive evidence, but once we find it we tend to remember it more accurately. Consider the implications of these facts. If we believe something, we tend to search for information that proves our point of view. If we come across conflicting evidence, we are inclined to disregard it as irrelevant. Furthermore, our memories retain supportive evidence better than disconfirming evidence. Finally, the higher up a manager is in an organization, the more the information he/she receives is filtered by several levels of subordinates, assistants and secretaries. They know, or think they do, what the manager wants to hear and selectively present such supportive information.

It is possible to minimize or avoid confirmation biases, that is, the search for and selective remembering of supportive evidence. This can be done by setting up procedures in an organization that encourage the search for disconfirming evidence. First of all, disconfirming, rather than supportive, evidence must be collected. This is not always a practical thing to do. For example, one cannot stop implementing a certain strategy to find out whether or not one's firm will go bankrupt.

However, there are ways of getting round the problem. In meetings, for instance, disconfirming evidence must also be deliberately elicited when new projects, ideas or strategies are considered, e.g. by encouraging someone to play the role of devil's advocate, or always including people with opposing views in the same meeting. Or, an executive can pretend that his/her choice is the opposite of what he/she really wants. If he/she can be convinced he/she is wrong, this would be an effective way of obtaining disconfirming evidence to prove that his/her belief or hypothesis is correct.

Describing all the known judgmental biases is beyond the scope of this chapter, as much of this is covered in other chapters of this book. However, Table 1.2 describes biases that mainly affect forecasting and strategy, or future-oriented decision making in general. Also listed in Table 1.2 are some suggestions for avoiding these biases.

**Table 1.2** List of judgmental biases, their description, and ways to avoid their negative impact

| Type of bias | Description of bias | Ways of avoiding or reducing the negative impact of bias |
|---|---|---|
| Inconsistency | Inability to apply the same decision criteria in similar situations | Formalize the decision-making process<br>Create decision-making rules to be followed |
| Conservatism | Failure to change (or changing slowly) one's own mind in light of new information/evidence | Monitor for changes in the environment and build procedures to take actions when such changes are identified |
| Recency | The most recent events dominate those in the less recent past, which are downgraded or ignored | Realize that cycles exist and that not all ups or downs are permanent<br>Consider the fundamental factors that affect the event of interest |

*continued*

**Table 1.2** (*continued*)

| Type of bias | Description of bias | Ways of avoiding or reducing the negative impact of bias |
|---|---|---|
| Availability | Reliance upon specific events easily recalled from memory, to the exclusion of other pertinent information | Present complete information<br>Present information in a way that points out all sides of the situation being considered |
| Anchoring | Predictions are unduly influenced by initial information which is given more weight in the forecasting process | Start with objective information (e.g. forecasts)<br>Ask people to discuss the types of changes that are possible; also ask for reasons when changes are being proposed |
| Illusory correlations | Belief that patterns are evident and/or two variables are causally related when they are not | Verify statistical significance of patterns<br>Model relationships, if possible, in terms of changes |
| Selective perception | People tend to see problems in terms of their own background and experience | Ask people with different backgrounds and experience to independently suggest solutions |
| Regression effects | Persistent increases might be due to random reasons which, if true, would increase the chance of a decrease. Alternatively, persistent decreases might increase the chances of increases | Explain that when errors are random the chances of a negative error increase when several positive ones have occurred<br>*Continued* |

**Table 1.2**  (*continued*)

| Type of bias | Description of bias | Ways of avoiding or reducing the negative impact of bias |
|---|---|---|
| Attribution of success and failure | Success is attributed to one's skills while failure to bad luck, or someone else's error. This inhibits learning as it does not allow recognition of one's mistakes | Do not punish mistakes, instead encourage people to accept their mistakes and make them public so they and others can learn to avoid similar mistakes in the future. (This is how Japanese companies deal with mistakes) |
| Optimism, wishful thinking | People's preferences for future outcomes affect their forecasts of such outcomes | Have the forecasts made by a disinterested third party. Have more than one person independently make the forecasts |
| Searching for supportive evidence | People search for and remember information which is in accord with their beliefs and opinions | Collect disconfirming evidence. Have someone play devil's advocate |
| Underestimating uncertainty | Excessive optimism, illusory correlation, and the need to reduce anxiety result in underestimating future uncertainty | Estimate uncertainty objectively. Consider many possible future events by asking different people to come up with unpredictable situations/events |

Another class of biases that can threaten the effectiveness of strategy arise from conventional wisdom. We have grown up in a culture where we accept certain statements as true, even though they may not be. For instance, we believe that the more information we have, the more accurate our decisions will be. Empirical evidence does not support such a belief. Instead, more information merely seems to increase our confidence that we are right without necessarily improving the accuracy

**Table 1.3** Conventional wisdom, empirical findings, and ways to avoid negative consequences

| Conventional wisdom | Empirical findings | Ways to avoid negative consequences |
|---|---|---|
| The more information we have, the more accurate the decision | The amount of information does not improve the accuracy of decisions, instead it increases our confidence that our decision will be correct | We must make sure that our sources of information are *not* redundant (that is, come from similar sources) |
| We can distinguish between useful and irrelevant information | Irrelevant information can be the cause of reducing the accuracy of our decisions | All information must be checked for its accuracy and relevance, even when coming from "reputable" sources |
| The more confident we are about the correctness of our decision, the more accurate our decision will be | There is *no* relationship between how confident someone is and how accurate his/her decision is | Weigh equally the information provided by various people/sources |
| We can decide rationally when it is time to quit | We feel we have invested too much to quit, although the investment is a sunk cost | Accept sunk costs and introduce objective procedures to end a project, even if large investments have been made, when the chances of success become small |
| Monetary rewards and punishments contribute to better performance | Human behavior is too complex to be motivated by monetary factors only | Introduce a variety of rewards that recognize human aspirations and the need for self-esteem |

*continued*

**Table 1.3** (*continued*)

| Conventional wisdom | Empirical findings | Ways to avoid negative consequences |
|---|---|---|
| We can assess our chances of succeeding or failing reasonably well | We are overly optimistic and tend to downgrade or ignore problems and difficulties | Provide assessment of the chances of succeeding by a third, objective, party. If the assessment is negative, accept it, even if large sunk costs are involved |
| Experience and/or expertise improve the accuracy of decisions | In many repetitive, routine decisions, experience and/or expertise do not contribute more value to future-oriented decisions | We need a minimum level of experience and/or expertise but we do not need the best guru or the highest paid consultant |
| We really know what we want, and our preferences are stable | Slight differences in a situation can change our preferences (most people, for instance, prefer a half-full to a half-empty glass of water) | Always look at preferences from at least two points of view and make sure that they do not change when, for instance, we see a glass as half-empty or alternatively as half-full |

of our decisions. This is a conclusion reached by Oskamp (1965) and many other researchers, who warn against devoting energy and resources to gathering a lot of information. In reality, the information found is usually redundant and provides little additional value. Another example of conventional wisdom is that we are capable of discriminating between useful and irrelevant information. Empirical research (Kahneman, Slovic & Tversky, 1982) indicates that this is rarely the case. In experiments, subjects supplied with "good" and "bad" information are not capable of distinguishing between the two. In addition, the irrelevant information is often used to decrease the effectiveness of decision making.

Table 1.3 summarizes relevant biases that arise from conventional wisdom. As with the judgmental biases discussed earlier, the biases linked to conventional wisdom can greatly influence our decisions and negatively affect the success of our strategy. Attempts must therefore be made to avoid such biases. Table 1.3 also lists suggestions for trying to overcome the negative influences of conventional wisdom.

Can biases be avoided if decisions are made in groups? Unfortunately not—in fact there is evidence (Janis, 1972) suggesting that groups amplify bias by introducing groupthink (a phenomenon that develops when group members become supportive of their leader and each other, thus avoiding conflict and dissent during their meetings). Moreover, group decisions are more risky, as responsibility for the decisions cannot be attributed to any single individual (Janis, 1972).

## 1.4  THE THREE ASPECTS OF STRATEGY

In certain dimensions, today's supercomputers are not even comparable to a small child. Among other things, they cannot exhibit even elementary intelligence or reasoning, leave alone superior cerebral functions such as imagination or creativity. Moreover, computers are not capable of learning, not to speak of adjusting their behavior to temporary changes or adapting it to permanent ones. Computers are capable of storing billions of pieces of information but they cannot turn this information into useful knowledge or use it for higher-level decision making. They can calculate with literally the speed of light but cannot demonstrate common sense or understand humor. At the same time practically all humans possess the above-mentioned abilities and apply them a great many times each day, effortlessly and unconsciously. There are also some talented humans who exhibit superior abilities to those of the average. Great artists, superb philosophers, distinguished politicians, and first-rate CEOs, in addition to the chess grand masters mentioned at the beginning of this chapter, display outstanding abilities, often lasting a lifetime, that distinguish them from the rest of the people.

Yet all people, from the greatest artists to the World Chess Champion, display the judgmental biases and limitations described in the previous section. Computers, on the other hand, are super-rational, exhibiting no biases or computational limitations. This human contradiction of phenomenal cerebral abilities coupled with numerous biases and serious limitations is something that must be accepted and dealt with, in particular in the case of judgmental inputs required for strategy. It becomes of paramount importance, then, to exploit our judgment's unique abilities while minimizing its biases and limitations exposed in the earlier section.

There are two main criticisms that can be levied against academics and business consultants working in the field of strategy. First, they have attempted to formalize and standardize its use through their attempts to develop tool boxes that could be applied across various firms and industries; and second, they have emphasized the intended outcome rather than the judgmental process involved while developing and/or modifying a certain strategy. In this section we describe strategy as a high-level judgmental process that requires a combination of both intuitive and analytical inputs. In the final analysis it is the quality of this process and the worthiness of these inputs that determine its overall value and eventual success. It is essential, therefore, to look at both such processes and inputs in order to discuss their role and value to a sound strategy.

For strategy to be successful it must be *foresighted, creatively unique* and, of course, *sustainable*. Such characteristics require a combination of intuitive and analytical skills: intuitive and creative in coming up with imaginative alternatives, and analytical in evaluating predictions and strategies for their practicality and profitability. We strongly believe, therefore, that successful strategies exclude recipes, algorithms or any kind of "canned" theories that can be applied across many firms and industries (Weisberg, 1986). Such strategies cannot, by definition, be imaginative, creative or unique. Consequently, we suggest that strategy development is a multifaceted judgmental process that can be based neither in pure intuition nor in elaborate analysis. Rather, we need to combine the two to develop strategies which are company-, industry- and time-specific. Grand masters, as we discussed at the beginning of this chapter, combine in a sophisticated manner such intuitive and analytical judgmental skills.

Grand masters have developed an exceptional ability of pattern recognition. Furthermore, they are capable of coming up with highly creative, effective moves and, most importantly, of doing so in an intuitive, effortless manner. However, they also possess strong analytical skills that allow them to evaluate a number of pertinent and critical moves for both their uniqueness and greatness—because in games among grand masters good or simply satisfactory moves lead to defeat. Finally, they develop and pursue a game plan that is based on an overall strategy of simultaneous defense and attack (de Groot, 1966). As the match progresses, they develop an overall game plan (see below for more details) which they pursue with great insistence, even after having to abandon it temporarily (Znosko-Borovsky, 1980).

Good business strategists must go a step beyond grand masters because the environment within which they operate constantly changes, while this is not the case with chess, where the rules of the game are well known and fixed. Moreover, in chess games there is a single opponent who is well known and whose moves are restricted within those allowed by the rules. This is not, however, the case in business situations, where there can be many competitors who are not obliged to follow established rules as long as their actions are not illegal. This brings business strategy closer to that of generals in war (Liddel Hart, 1957; Beaufre, 1985) than to chess playing. Finally, strategy and its success depends a great deal upon the goals of the CEO and his/her top executives (Makridakis, 1990). If the goals are set low, a certain strategy can be more easily achieved. At the same time, the benefits are of lesser significance. This tradeoff between demanding and easier goals is not different from that of athletes who must set the level (local, regional, national, international) at which they want to compete and then strive to develop the appropriate competences required to succeed at such a level.

Below we describe the three aspects of strategy we consider essential for its eventual success. Two of these three aspects are mainly intuitive (foresight and creative uniqueness) and the third (sustainability) is mostly formal or analytic.

### 1.4.1 Foresight

Strategies must be future-oriented, spanning the long term. As such, they require numerous predictions about the industry, economy, technology and competition, as well as social and demographic trends, consumer needs and attitudes, and similar factors that may affect the course of future events and, therefore, strategy. However, these predictions can rarely be found by extrapolating historical information. By now it is clear that the future will in all probability be different from the past, making it necessary to go beyond known or popular predictions to insightful ones that are based on an understanding of forthcoming changes, a grasp of the timing with which such changes will start affecting the industry, and an awareness of the implications involved for the firm. Most importantly, executives must be capable of forming their foresight as well in advance of their competitors as possible and of using such foresight to create a clear vision of where their industry is heading and, subsequently, to develop a strategy for their firm which will be capable of making such a vision a reality. It is by doing so that they can become the industry leader, shaping its progress and directing its advancement.

Correct and useful foresight is not trivial, requiring much more than technical skills in formal, analytical forecasting. Analytical forecasting is based on the extrapolation of established patterns and relationships and as such cannot predict changes from such patterns/relationships. At the same time, historical patterns and relationships are seldom stable, thus making intuitive judgments crucial for predicting the future.

Intuitive judgments can be negatively influenced by the biases of conservatism, availability and recency. Conservatism predisposes people towards the status quo. They feel secure and comfortable at the present and are not willing to consider future changes, in particular when such changes are threatening. Moreover, the more threatening the change, the greater people's unwillingness to contemplate it. It is like hiding one's head in the sand and believing that the danger is not there. Availability influences people to over-weigh information that is easily recalled from memory, that we read about in business publications or the general press. This information, however, is readily available to practically everyone, and as such it is of little value in the development of foresight, which ought to consider the future in an imaginative and distinctive manner. We can say that by the time a story or idea has made headlines it is too late to consider it in a foresighted manner. Instead, its only use should be to examine its possible implications for defending a firm against others which will have already sought to exploit the potential advantages involved. Finally, recency induces people to utilize more recent information, which they tend to remember more easily. This information, however, may not be the most appropriate for strategy, which is concerned with the long term. Figure 1.1 shows the huge danger of recency. By not using Figure 1.1(d) which contains information about the long-term behavior of real copper prices, we can draw the wrong conclusions about the trend in such prices, depending upon how recent the information we are using is. The worst case is to use Figure 1.1(c) which, although it covers a time-span of more than 30 years, is still not

(a)

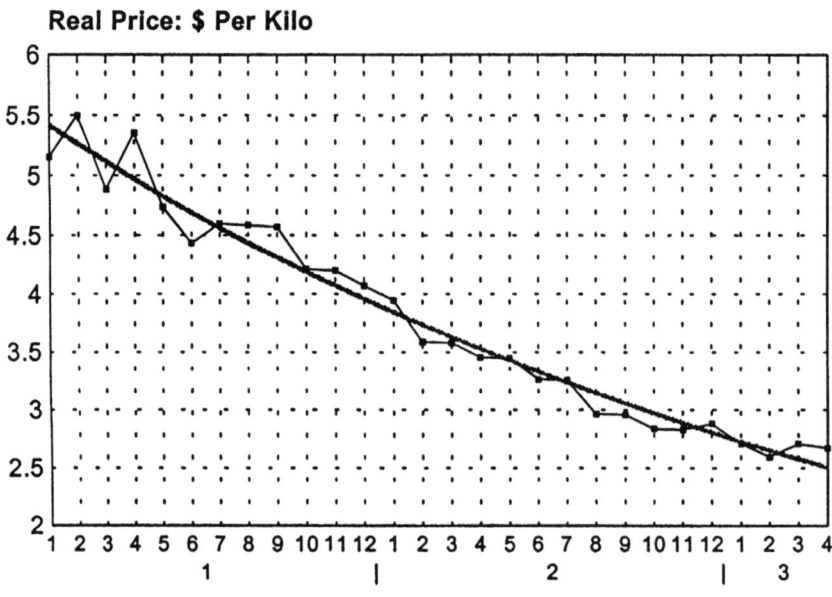

(b)

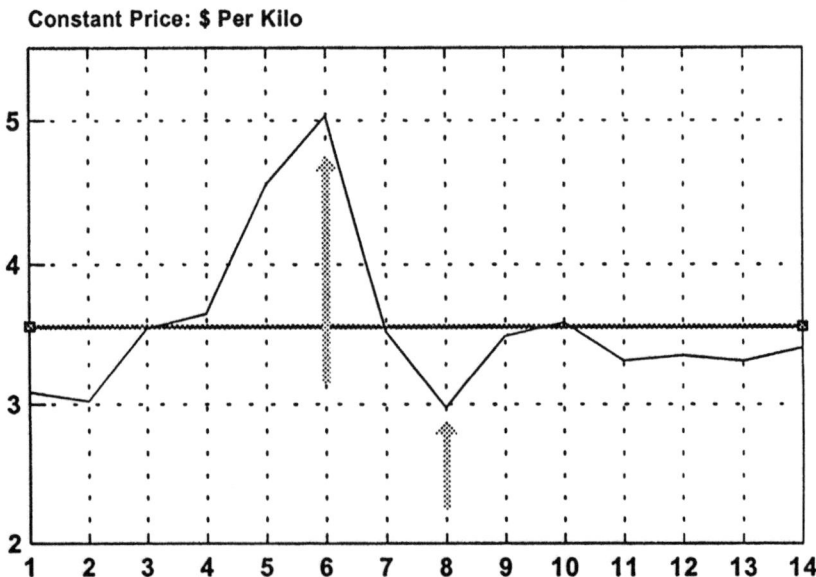

(c)

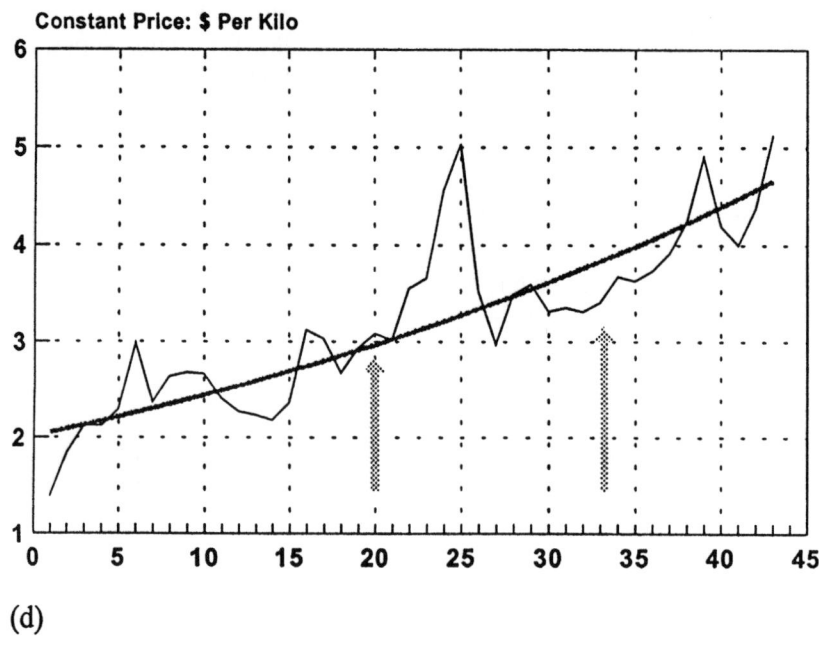

(d)

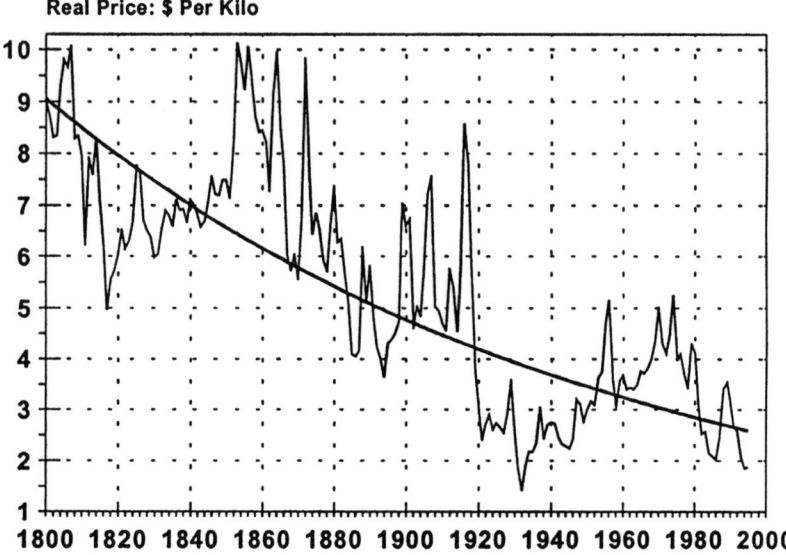

**Figure 1.1** Real 1997 copper prices. (a) monthly; (b) yearly; (c) yearly; (d) in constant 1997 dollars

appropriate, as business and economic data are greatly influenced by cycles whose length sometimes extends to more than 60 years.

Foresight must be both imaginative and commonsensical. In addition to looking at the future with an open mind, the following types of commonsensical questions need to be considered and answered:

(1) Where will our industry be in 10 years' time, or will there even be an industry as we know it today? Will there be banks, for instance, or book and music stores, or will we use smart cards for money and the Internet (or some other network) to do our financial transactions and to order, or even download to our computer, books or music from suppliers located in any part of the world?

(2) What will our customers want and how will we best be able to satisfy their needs, particularly when their freedom of choice will be enormous as they can buy products or receive services from around the world? What services, for instance, will a bank have to offer to attract customers to its branch if people can do all their transactions through the Internet?

(3) Where will our firm be in 10 years' time if we continue on our established course?

(4) Where do we want our firm to be in 10 years' time? Moreover, if we had the chance to start from scratch without any constraints, how would we organize and how would we operate our firm? What would be the major differences between the present and the brand new firm started from scratch without any of the constraints we are facing at present when we want to introduce change?

(5) Which of the predicted, popular forthcoming changes would we adopt?
   • Provide our customers with as wide a freedom of choice as possible.
   • Supply our products and/or offer our services as speedily as possible.
   • Offer our customers the lowest cost with the best service.
   • Customize our products and services for each of our customers.

(6) In which of the predicted, popular directions would we go?
   • From products to services.
   • From satisfying existing needs to identifying and fulfilling new ones.

- From mass markets to niche markets.
- From traditional organization to virtual organization.
- From a single business entity to a network of global alliances.

(7) Which of the popular management tools/ideas would we follow?
- Continuous improvements.
- Empowerment and self-directed teams.
- Groupware.
- Reengineering.
- Benchmarking.
- Core competencies.
- Value chain analysis.
- Shareholders value added.

(8) As there is a very high chance that our competitors will be using the majority of the forthcoming changes mentioned above, how would we distinguish ourselves and gain or maintain competitive advantages?

(9) What new tools/ideas would we utilize before or better than our competitors so that we can gain and/or maintain some competitive advantages?

Answering, or even carefully thinking about, the above questions can provide organizations with a framework for their discussions about the future and a guide to come up with practical foresight about major, forthcoming changes and their implications, and help them develop a consensus about the future.

### 1.4.2 Creative Uniqueness

No strategy can be developed in a vacuum. It must be based on individual organizations with their particular cultures, specific goals, values and needs, special resource and other constraints, and definite conceptions about risk taking. Moreover, the place where a firm operates, its size, its existing and potential competitors, as well as the timing of intended strategy, are critical factors. It is inconceivable, for instance, for a medium-sized firm operating in Greece or India to have the same strategy as a Japanese or an American one. Further, successful strategies of even the early 1990s are obsolete today. Strategies must be unique and specific. Most importantly, as the following quotations show, they must emerge gradually and must take into account the latest information about the present and the organizational foresight about the future (Znosko-Borovsky, 1980).

> It is impossible to play a satisfactory game without following a strategic plan, which sooner or later will have to be evolved. To settle on a plan too late means an advantage to the opponent, who will be ahead of us in his threats; to have no plan at all would render our play inconsistent— without logic and therefore without strength. ... It must not be thought that a plan will occur to us fully worked out in all its details at a given moment, like Pallas Athene arising fully armed from the head of Zeus. Step by step, after the tentative maneuvers of the opening, it takes shape in our mind, at first in vague outlines, gaining gradually in definition and character.
>
> Where the position is simple and the advantage well defined, there is no difficulty in formulating at once a suitable strategic plan. But it is not possible to do this at will in obscure and complicated positions of no definite character, where both sides have equal chances, or, worse still, where the formations are symmetrical.

Creativity is the single most important prerequisite for coming up with a unique strategy, one that is not only distinct from that of the competition but is also consistent with one's goals, risk attitudes and constraints. The biases of conservatism and selective perceptions can become serious barriers. While these biases have to be avoided, creativity must play an important role in strategy formulation.

Creativity is exciting but also elusive; moreover, it is not always in harmony with the more mundane, everyday operational tasks required for running a business firm. Operational effectiveness and efficiency demand consistency, conformity to standards and time pressures, while creativity calls for ample time to think and to go beyond (or even reject) traditional thinking and conventional wisdom. Yet creativity is an ordinary judgmental process, as the following quote indicates (Simon, 1985):

> It is not necessary to surround creativity with mystery and obfuscation. No sparks of genius need be postulated to account for human invention, discovery, creation. These acts are acts of the human brain, the same brain that helps us dress in the morning, arrive at our office, and go through our daily chores, however uncreative most of these chores may be.

The big challenge for developing a successful strategy is to come up with a commonsensical, but also creative and practical, strategy that utilizes the organizational foresight developed about the future and also takes into account the uniqueness of the situation of a firm (goals, attitudes towards risk, constraints, competition, etc.).

The subject of creativity is huge and beyond the scope of this chapter. The interested reader ought to turn to the vast literature on the subject for further reading. In this chapter we are mainly interested in stressing the need for novel, creative strategies that can be successfully applied against tough and determined opponents who have their own strategies and who are also determined to win, as the following quotation from another grand master (Kotov, 1985) indicates:

> There is probably no other strategic concept which the student of the game has dinned into him as much as the concept of conceiving a plan. ... when you meet a strong, inventive opponent and he counters every one of your intentions, not only by defensive but also by counter-attacking measures, it is far from simple to carry out a simple strategic plan.

Although creativity cannot be taught, there are certain necessary prerequisites for becoming more creative, even though such prerequisites cannot, by any means, guarantee high-quality creative output.

### The acquisition of a knowledge base and substantial experience

Simon (1985) and other researchers (de Groot, 1966) suggest that a prerequisite for substantial creative output is the acquisition of considerable knowledge and experience. Simon cites studies estimating that at least 10 years are required to acquire such knowledge or experience and to develop appropriate skills that increase one's chances of producing high-level creative output. For instance, Simon writes, no world-class expert has reached his/her level without at least 10 years of intensive effort.

### High motivation and persistence

Knowledge and expertise are not enough. In addition, creative breakthroughs require considerable motivation in the form of hard work and complete immersion in the task or problem at hand. James Gleick (1987) describes the work habits of a scientist who discovered a major theory in physics: "He worked for two months without pause. His functional day was 22 hours. He would try to go to sleep in a kind of buzz, and awaken 2 hours later with his thoughts exactly where he had left them" (Gleick, 1987). Similarly, Levy describes how a computer terminal was completed, "that took 6 weeks of 14–17-hour days, 7 days a week" (Levy, 1984).

The same is true of great artists. Great art is rarely produced in flashes of imagination. A detailed monograph on Van Gogh or Picasso would reveal that a multitude of drawings, studies, and unfinished paintings are done in preparation for the final version of a great work. Moreover, great scientists, artists or creative thinkers must be self-motivated, because money, competition or fame alone can never adequately explain their hard work and desire to excel.

## Taking risks

It might be possible to systematize incremental creativity by designing procedures that contribute to small increases in creative output. Marginal improvements in products or production processes, or slight variations in existing services, can be achieved through R&D, engineering or "creative" departments. However, breakthroughs can rarely be systematized or planned for (Nayak & Ketteringham, 1986; Von Hippel, 1987). As our previous examples show, moreover, not all creative ideas succeed. The more far-fetched the idea, the greater its chance of failure will be.

## Thinking differently from the crowd

It is possible that people who do not like to follow tradition, have no taste for formal education, or take little interest in the work of others, can come up with new ideas. Their thinking is virginal and not influenced by conventional wisdom, so they can follow paths no-one else has discovered and hit upon new solutions. Although the chances of failure might be higher among rebels or unconventional thinkers, so is their chance of coming up with new creative ideas.

## Adopting an "open-minded" attitude

Important creative ideas or solutions and creative breakthroughs require adopting an open-minded attitude whereby assumptions are questioned, unusual or even improbable solutions are considered, stereotypes are avoided, and reverse thinking is used. An open-minded attitude also encourages learning about how similar problems are dealt with outside the area of one's expertise, and in general being capable of

**Table 1.4**  Factors that facilitate creativity

1. Thinking in abstractions, conceiving ideas in images
2. Examining all (or as many as possible) combinations of basic ideas and/or existing products/services
3. Avoiding stereotypes
4. Searching outside one's area of business or field of study for fresh ways of looking at old things
5. Questioning assumptions
6. Rejecting conventional wisdom
7. Disliking to:
   (a) Be supervised or told what to do
   (b) Be criticized or told to hurry up
   (c) Be promised rewards for accelerating current progress

thinking in different ways from the majority of people. That is a key element of novelty; ideas are regarded as new and original because the majority of people have not been able to discover them through conventional thinking.

*Creative accidents*

A great deal is made of the occasional creative ideas or discoveries made by accident. However, recognizing accidents and exploiting their significance also requires an open mind and the ability to accept that conventional wisdom does not always hold. Even accidents favor the prepared and the open-minded, who can recognize their implications and use them to come up with original ideas or discover novel solutions.

Finally, Table 1.4 summarizes some of the factors that facilitate creativity and which become important if we are to escape conventional thinking and manage to look at the world with a different pair of glasses which would allow us to both look further away and, at the same time, more clearly.

## 1.5  SUSTAINABILITY

Whatever strategies have been formulated must be carefully evaluated, preferably by a person or team other than that responsible for their development. Such an evaluation must systematically advance disconfirming evidence as the most appropriate form of testing the long-term viability of the strategies being advanced. Illusory correlations, underestimation of uncertainty, confounding of forecasts by wishful thinking, and anchoring and availability biases must be avoided.

In this aspect of strategy, certain decision-analytic tools such as *decomposition* (Webby & O'Connor, 1996; Goodwin & Wright, 1993; MacGregor & Armstrong, 1994; Holloway, 1979) can play a very useful role. Decomposition is best illustrated by a simple example. Suppose that top management is considering whether to undertake a large promotional campaign to increase market share of a product. A key judgment then required is about the likelihood of market share going up, or not going up, given the promotional campaign. The simple tree diagram in Figure 1.2 shows two branches with these possibilities. The tree in Figure 1.3 decomposes the two possibilities, making them conditional on various other events—the state of the economy, the movement of the overall market for the product, and the actions of the competition. In any case, attempts to elicit opinions from someone about the two possibilities directly (market share going up and not going up, as in Figure 1.2) would in most cases lead to conditional statements of the type, "It depends on what the competition does, and on what happens to the economy...", and so on. Decomposition merely formalizes this process.

Such decomposition has two main advantages (MacGregor & Armstrong, 1994). First, it reduces a complex task of judging an event into smaller and cognitively more manageable parts. It should be easier to think about whether the market share of the company will increase or not increase conditional on, for example, the economy improving, the overall market increasing, and there being no increase in promotional campaigns by the competition. This also makes the

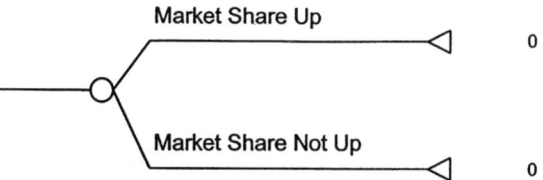

**Figure 1.2** Tree without decomposition

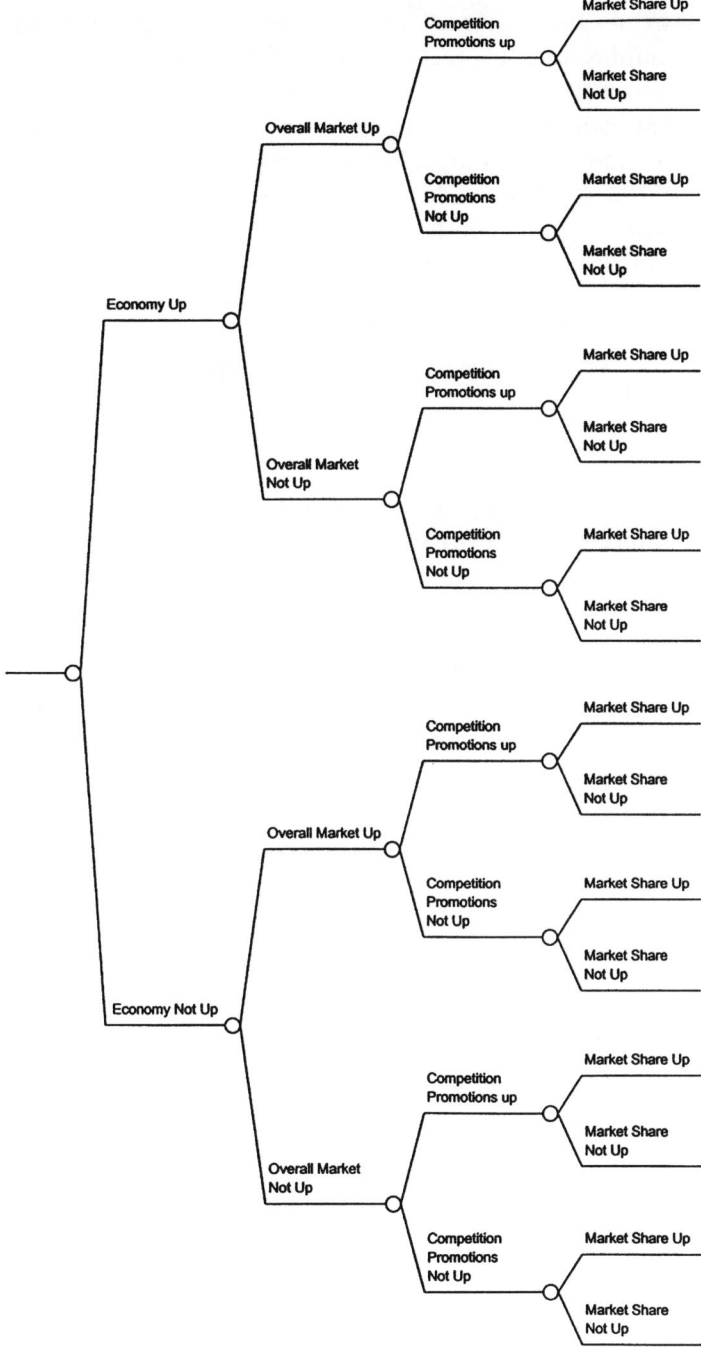

**Figure 1.3** Tree with decomposition

dependence between the various events more explicit. Second, decomposition enables one to receive input from more than one expert, from each according to his/her ability. In the example presented here, one can use an economist to give a judgment about the economy, an industry analyst in the company to generate judgments about the overall market of the product, and someone who follows the moves of the competition to make a judgment about the likely actions of the competition. Such a break-up of the problem would ensure that all available expertise is used and, in each case, for the appropriate judgments.

There remain, however, some further issues regarding how the decomposition should be done. For example, what should be the scale of the decomposition, i.e. how much conditioning should one do? Clearly, there cannot be any universal rule. Too much conditioning might make the tree very bushy, thus increasing the chances that a disproportionate share of the effort will be on events which ultimately have minor influence on the event of interest. On the other hand, inadequate decomposition might not simplify the judgmental problem into intuitively manageable parts and might not enable, in a clear manner, full use of the information and expertise that is available. In general, decomposition, at a minimum, should be adequate to enable full use of in-house expertise and use of information from external sources that is readily available at a low cost. Working with a select team of diverse experts, and brainstorming about a list of major events on which the event of interest might be dependent, would surely be helpful.

Another issue that might arise is the sequencing of the events in the conditioning. Consider the example given above. Should the state of the economy precede the state of the overall market, or *vice versa*? The sequencing would depend on what is easier to think about intuitively. For example, it might be easier to make judgments about the state of the overall market, given that the economy does well or does not do well, rather than to think about whether the economy will do well, given that the overall market for the product increases or does not increase (of course, this might not be true in all contexts).

Nevertheless, decomposition can serve as a very useful tool for generating judgments and evaluating the sustainability of different strategies, by breaking up a complex task into more manageable parts and by enabling the use of different experts within an organization.

## 1.6 CONCLUSIONS

This chapter has looked at strategy as a high-level, multifaceted judgmental process. Human judgment presents us, however, with a big contradiction. On the one hand, it exhibits some sophisticated capabilities such as those of the grand masters; on the other hand, it is plagued by numerous biases and serious limitations, as in the case of the investment professionals, which diminishes its value and endangers the development of successful strategies. In this chapter we argue that we must accept this contradiction and use our judgment to come up with intuitive strategies. At the same time we must do our utmost to first eliminate or minimize the negative consequences of the biases/limitations, while at the same time subjecting the strategies being formulated to as vigorous analytical evaluation as possible.

The multifaceted character of strategy was expressed in the three aspects of foresight, creative uniqueness and sustainability. Each of these aspects of strategy was discussed and their necessity and contributions, as well as dangers, to successful strategies elaborated. It was emphasized that strategy cannot be standardized, expressed in recipes, or be formulated from tool boxes. Sound strategies must be powerful and unique and, at the same time, space- and time-specific, taking competition and forthcoming events into account. This is why we strongly believe that a great amount of research is needed to advance the field of strategy and make it relevant, useful and practical. Equally important, we think that it is dysfunctional to assume that all strategies could be successful, in particular when they include direct competitors. Moreover, we must accept that the fruits of successful strategies will come in the long run. It may even be necessary "to lose a few battles to win the war".

Another consideration is that strategy cannot be conceived in its totality at one point in time. Instead, it must evolve by making corrections, adjusting or even adapting to the changing environmental conditions as they unfold. Finally, it may indeed be necessary to abandon a long-held strategy and ignore even large sunk costs when it becomes obvious that it cannot succeed. This is why it is indispensable to make sure, as part of the strategic process, to collect feedback, at prespecified times, so that an evaluation of accomplishing the set strategy can be made. Such feedback and evaluation can consequently be used to correct course, learn, or even abandon a given strategy if it becomes necessary.

Research on strategy must extend to both the intuitive and analytical aspects of our judgment, as strategy is a high-level judgmental process whose soundness, overall effectiveness and ultimate success depend upon the worthiness of such judgment. It is imperative to understand better the role and value of human judgment in high-level future-oriented decision making like that involved while considering and developing business strategies.

## REFERENCES

Beaufre, A. (1985) *Introduction à la Stratégie*. Economica, Paris.

Bernstein, P.L. (1996) *Against the Gods: The Remarkable Story of Risk*. Wiley, New York.

Bowman, E.H. (1963) Consistency and optimality in managerial decision making. *Management Science*, **10** (1), 310–21.

Chase, W.G. & Simon, H.A. (1973) The mind's eye in chess. In W.G. Chase (ed.), *Visual Information Processing*. Academic Press, London.

Dawes, R.M. (1988) *Rational Choice in an Uncertain World*. Harcourt Brace Jovanovich, New York.

de Groot, A.D. (1965) *Thought and Choice in Chess* (translated from *Het denker van der schaker*, 1946). Morton, The Hague.

de Groot, A.D. (1966) Perception and memory versus thought: some old ideas and recent findings. In B. Kleinmuntz, (ed.), *Problem Solving*. Wiley, New York, pp. 19–50.

Dixon, N. (1976) *On the Psychology of Military Incompetence*. Jonathan Cape, London.

Garland, L.H. (1960) The problem of observer error. *Bulletin of the New York Academy of Medicine*, 569–84.

Glassman, J. (1997) In a random universe, the case against funds, *Washington Post Service*, January 4.

Gleick, J. (1987) *Chaos: Making a New Science*. Viking, New York.

Goldberg, L.R. (1970) Man vs model of man: a rationale, plus some evidence, for a method of improving on clinical inferences. *Psychological Bulletin*, 422–32.

Goodwin, P. & Wright, G. (1993) Improving judgemental time series forecasting: a review of the guidance provided by research. *International Journal of Forecasting*, **9**, 147–61.

Graham, J.R. & Harvey, C.R. (1995) Market timing and volatility implied in investment newsletters' asset allocation recommendations. Working Paper. Fuqua School of Business, Duke University, Durham, NC.

Grove, A.S. (1996) *Only the Paranoid Survive: How to Exploit the Crisis Points that Challenge Every Company and Career.* Doubleday, New York.

Hamel, G. & Prahalad, C.K. (1994) *Competing for the Future.* Harvard University Press, Boston.

Hogarth, R. & Makridakis, S. (1981) Forecasting and planning: an evaluation. *Management Science,* **27**, 115–38.

Holloway, C.A. (1979) *Decision Making Under Uncertainty: Models and Choices.* Prentice-Hall, Englewood Cliffs, NJ.

Janis, I.L. (1972) *Victims of Group Think.* Houghton Mifflin, Boston.

Kahneman, D., Slovic, P. & Tversky, A. (1982) *Judgment Under Uncertainty: Heuristics and Biases.* Cambridge University Press, Cambridge.

Kahneman, D. & Tversky, A. (1979) Intuitive prediction: biases and corrective procedures, *TIMS Studies in Management Sciences,* **12**, 313–27.

Kotov, A. (1985) *Think Like a Grandmaster.* Dover, New York.

Levy, S. (1984) *Hackers: Heroes of the Computer Revolution.* Dell, New York.

Liddell Hart, B.H. (1957) *Strategy.* Faber & Faber, London.

MacGregor, D.G. & Armstrong, J.S. (1994) Judgmental decomposition: when does it work? *International Journal of Forecasting,* **10**, 495–506.

Magaziner, I. & Patinkin, M. (1989) *The Silent War: Inside the Global Business Battles Shaping America's Future.* Random House, New York.

Makridakis, S. (1990) *Forecasting, Planning and Strategy for the 21st Century.* The Free Press, New York.

Makridakis, S. (1997a) Forecasting: its role and value for planning and strategy. *International Journal of Forecasting,* **12**, 513–39.

Makridakis, S. (1997b) Metastrategy: learning and avoiding past mistakes. *Long Range Planning Journal,* **30**, 133–5.

Makridakis, S. & Héau, D. (1987) Strategic planning and forecasting. In W.R. King & D.S. Cleland (eds), *Strategic Management and Planning Handbook.* Van Nostrand Reinhold, New York, 3–21.

Meehl, P. (1954) *Clinical Versus Statistical Prediction: A Theoretical Analysis and a Review of the Evidence.* University of Minnesota Press, Minneapolis.

Micklethwait, J. & Woldridge, A. (1996) *The Witch Doctors: Making Sense of the Management Gurus.* Random House, New York.

Nayak, P.R. & Ketteringham, J.M. (1986) *Breakthroughs!* Rawson Associates, New York.

Oskamp, S. (1965) Overconfidence in case-study judgments. *Journal of Consulting Psychology,* **29**, 261–5.

Peters, T.J. & Waterman, R.H. (1982) *In Search of Excellence: Lessons from America's Best-Run Companies.* Harper & Row, New York.

Rothchild, J. (1988) *A Fool and His Money: The Odyssey of an Average Investor.* Viking, New York.

Schlender, B. (1996) Sun's Java: the threat to Microsoft is real. *Fortune,* November 11, 87–92.

Simon, H. (1985)   What we know about the creative process. In R.L. Kuhn (ed.), *Frontiers in Creative and Innovative Management*. Ballinger, Cambridge, MA.

Von Hippel, E. (1987)   *The Sources of Innovation*. Oxford University Press, Oxford and New York.

Wason, P.C. & Johnson-Laird, P.N. (1972)   *Psychology of Reasoning: Structure and Content*. Batsford, London.

Webby, R. & O'Connor, R. (1996)   Judgmental and statistical time series forecasting: a review of the literature. *International Journal of Forecasting*, **12**, 91–118.

Weisberg, R.W. (1986)   *Creativity: Genius and Other Myths*. W.H. Freeman, New York.

Znosko-Borovsky, E.A. (1980)   *The Middle Game of Chess*. Dover, New York.

# Chapter 2

# Scenario Planning: Scaffolding Disorganized Ideas about the Future

Kees van der Heijden
*University of Strathclyde, Glasgow, UK*

## SUMMARY

This chapter argues that thinking about the future follows one of two basic paradigms, the rationalistic or the processual. The rationalist's view of the world can be called a variance theory, where the world exists independent of the observer, all relations are basically unequivocal, and uncertainty is due to measuring and computing constraints, leading to "error" which can be minimized to any degree desired by investment in time and resources. The processualist adopts a process theory, which includes relationships which are indeterminate by nature. Prediction is not possible, the future is uncertain in a fundamental way, and can only be expressed in multiples, called scenarios. Vygotsky's theory of proximal development is introduced as a way to make sense of the processualist's approach. Concern about the future is related to lack of understanding of past/current experiences. Through engagement with the social group the planner tries to "scaffold" the many seemingly

*Forecasting with Judgment*. Edited by G. Wright and P. Goodwin.
© 1998 John Wiley & Sons Ltd.

unrelated experiences into a coherent causal model, maximizing well-defined structure but allowing for irreducible indeterminate relationships. Perception becomes the focus of attention, and tacit knowledge and intuition become crucial elements of future exploration. On the basis of the newly acquired understanding the decision maker can move forward, collecting new experiences on the way which requires the process to be repeated.

## 2.1 CONCEPTUALIZING THE FUTURE

At the start of the well-known film *Lawrence of Arabia*, about 15 minutes into it, is a scene with Lawrence (Peter O'Toole) and a fellow-traveller taking a rest at a well during an arduous trip through the desert. An unusually long shot, a dyspeptic-looking Peter O'Toole and his guide, sitting out in the sun. And a long, long way away, just perceptible on the horizon, a speck. It grows, something is approaching from a far corner of the screen. It is moving toward them forever. The horizon seems so far away and the whole vision shimmers in the heat of the desert. What is it? Long looks toward the horizon ..., is it a band of horsemen ...? Turks? Bedouins? They can't make it out. They watch. They wait. They hardly speak. Two men just standing there, not knowing what to do about an approaching unknown. The shot keeps rolling: what's visible, finally, is a man galloping in on a camel. Who is this man? The camera still rolls on this one long, long shot. Mesmerized, they stand and watch, not knowing what this is or what to do. Finally, the dude with O'Toole suspects something really bad is about to happen, runs towards his camel, grabs his revolver, lifts it and BAM, from this desert spectre, a rifle retort and O'Toole's guide falls to the ground. The camera is still rolling on the dead man. Omar Sharif dismounts his camel, rifle in hand, walks over, looks and says, "He's dead". O'Toole says, "Yes ...... why?"

Having identified an approaching speck on the horizon the decision makers try to relate it meaningfully to their known world. In the film the two people work hard at it. Various hypotheses are suggested. However, it is not clear how these can be explored. Resources for gathering additional data are extremely limited. Nothing much is done in terms of response while they are trying to develop a more substantiated theory about what the future will bring. This is needed in order to work out what needs to be done. As the "speck on the horizon" develops, new data come in and old bits of incomplete theory are thrown out. While they are trying to keep up with the dynamics of the situation, paralysis has set in as no theory sticks long enough to be used for decision making. Their intuition is letting them down. Meanwhile things continue to develop and the time available for deciding on a suitable response becomes shorter and shorter. Finally, further inaction intuitively feels intolerable, something just needs to be done. There is no more time left for thinking. Panic sets in, and the first action that presents itself is pursued. With disastrous consequences, as so often with panic actions.

The film shot is a vivid illustration of paralysis that can result from facing uncertainty in a "predict and control" frame of mind, leading to sub-optimal panic reactions when time is up. Compare this with the approach chosen by the "scenario thinker". He will be trained to follow two lines of attack simultaneously:

- Explore the situation in order to discover as much as possible of what is predetermined.
- Look out for the point in time beyond which expending energy on trying to work out what will happen produces diminishing returns.

In any decision-making situation there is a point in time when energy needs to be refocused from the question, "Will this happen?" to a different question, "What will we do if this happens?" and, following that, "What does this mean for what we do now?" (De Geus, 1988). It requires keeping more than one future simultaneously operational in the mind. Although this seems only common sense it is surprisingly seldom that it is practised explicitly in organizational settings. Many people in a "problem-solving" frame of mind find this explicit facing up to uncertainty difficult and uncomfortable. The scenario-thinking methodology tries to address these problems (van der Heijden, 1996).

## 2.2  DECISIONS AND INTUITION

It is often argued that one-line decision makers account for uncertainty intuitively. To substantiate this one only has to consider how intuitive we normally are in taking many rather crucial decisions in our personal lives. In fact, it is by no means obvious what leads to better decisions, intuition or rational reasoning. It may well be that explicit articulation can not match the way in which intuition can evaluate a situation by tacitly integrating a multitude of experiences.

However, even if this is the case, it can be so only up to a point. Logically there are limitations to the use of intuition. Tacit knowledge can only be useful to one individual. Articulated knowledge, on the other hand, can be shared and analysed. It allows two things to happen that intuition alone cannot accomplish:

- It allows the experiences of more than one individual to be taken into account in evaluating the situation.
- It allows focused and organized search for additional, supporting or contradicting information.

Intuition cannot integrate the experiences of more than one person. This is important if we assume that multiple perspectives will lead to a more accurate assessment of the situation and therefore to better (more purposeful) decisions. It seems reasonable to assume that if a number of people spend time together in a situation, they will all have different but overlapping perceptions about it that have the potential of contributing to a richer shared analysis of the situation (Eden, 1992).

Such integration takes place through a process based on language. The use of language requires the decomposition of one's intuition into categories, creating constructs which become common property of the group (Kelly, 1963). These can be used to express one's individual perceptions for others to take in and comprehend. The ensuing conversation allows each participant to contribute their insights, based on their own perceptions, for others to comment on and judge.

The opening case of this chapter illustrates that intuition cannot function unless it is fed by information. Having been unsuccessful in collecting much information about the situation, one of the characters nevertheless feels intuitively that something needs to be done. This intuition proves fatal, because in retrospect essential information was lacking. Effective collection of information is something that all decision approaches, including intuition, rely on. Bringing to bear the perceptions of more than one person on the process of sense making leads to the appreciation of differences and the need to search for additional information to explore these.

## 2.3 ARTICULATION OF STRATEGY

The problem of deciding on the best decision-making process fundamentally revolves around uncertainty. However, if everything were uncertain the whole idea of spending energy on improving decision making would not make sense. We therefore start from the premise that there are elements in any situation which are to a degree predictable. These are known as the predetermined elements in the situation. An effective scenario-thinking methodology therefore does two things:

- It aims to maximize knowledge and understanding of what is predetermined.
- It aims to develop awareness of what is not predetermined, and therefore fundamentally uncertain.

Scenario planning is premised on the assumption that it is only in the full light of these two aspects of the situation that trying to improve the effectiveness of decisions makes sense.

The degree to which uncertainty affects decisions can vary considerably. A useful concept in this context was introduced by Ackof (1974) in what he calls the "futurity" of decisions. By this he means the degree to which the decision affects how the future will unfold. A decision on what you will eat today has low futurity—there will not be much effect (normally) on what happens tomorrow and thereafter. On the other hand, the decision about which school to select for your son has higher futurity—this decision will stay with him, and therefore with you, for the rest of your life.

The further out one looks into the future the less is predetermined and the more uncertainty has to be faced up to. In fact, thinking about uncertainty raises the question of why anything would be predictable. One important source of predictability in the world is inertia, either physical or psychological. After the laws of nature it is the most important source of predetermined elements. The effect of inertia wears off with time. Therefore, decisions with high futurity, i.e. those of the highest impact, have to be taken in the light of high uncertainty.

Decisions with high futurity are also called strategic decisions. Strategy tends to relate to unique issues that have not been seen before. Indeed, a strategy must have unique features in order to lead to success. Success requires that the strategist can appropriate some of the value created by the strategy. If a strategy has nothing that is unique this will not be possible, as any value created will quickly be competed away with others following the same strategy. Therefore, strategy relates to the big fundamental dilemmas faced by organizations. They involve choice.

Mintzberg & Waters (1985) argue that little of our planning effort affects what actually happens. They suggest that most strategy can only be understood in retrospect, when we are able to analyse and see patterns in what has actually happened. I have found that most managers do not consider this an intuitively appealing view. They would find it highly unsatisfactory to accept that good thinking would not make a difference. They believe there must be a constant pattern connecting the quality of their thinking, strategic choices made and resulting success or failure.

The next sections analyse these strategic choices and alternative approaches towards strategic decision making (Whittington, 1993).

## 2.4 RATIONALISTIC STRATEGIC DECISIONS

The prevailing paradigm can be called rationalistic decision making (Simon, 1983). The rationalistic tradition essentially involves the decision maker in the following steps:

- Predicting the future environment (within a margin of forecasting error, if appropriate).
- Identifying the basic aims of the "self" (individual or organizational), and related measures of success.
- Identifying the capabilities (strengths/weaknesses) of the "self".
- Developing a list of optional action plans, based on these capabilities.
- Evaluating the performance of each optional plan in terms of the established measure of success, in the predicted environment.
- Selecting the highest-scoring option.
- Implementing the selected option.

As we argued above, most decisions do not follow such a process but are made intuitively. The rationalist decision process does not (mostly) characterize an individual's decision-making process. However, it is typical of the way people explain their decisions to each other (van der Heijden, 1993). We have already suggested that strategic conversation can improve decision making. In the process differences in views will come to the surface. The conversation will then turn towards trying to evaluate the relative merits of different interpretations of the situation.

Access to multiple perspectives is the crucial feature of this process. This leads to participants trying to convince each other. In most organizational conversation the principle underlying this is rationality. The human mind is capable of changing the way it organizes its insights by an alternative logic contributed from the outside. The organizational strategic conversation is mostly based on rationality (van der Heijden, 1993). Because of the nature of the strategic conversation, organizations are more rational in their decision making than individuals.

## 2.5 UNCERTAINTY

In the context of this chapter we are particularly interested in the way the rationalistic paradigm handles uncertainty. Three approaches are possible:

- It can be ignored. The argument often used is that there is nothing much we can do about things we don't know. Therefore, the best way forward is to develop a "most likely" prediction, by using the intuition of the most expert individuals we can get access to, and use this as the basis of decision making.
- Each variable can be annotated with a margin of error. These are carried through the evaluation of the value of all optional action plans. The preferred option has the highest score on the basis of a statistically derived measure such as "mean value". (The use of the word "error" is indicative for the philosophical underpinning: there is a true value, but we cannot measure it accurately—yet.)
- A number of alternative futures are generated, a probability is assigned to each, and the value of each option is calculated by averaging the values for each future, weighted on the basis of these probabilities.

Each of these approaches will lead to one unequivocal answer, by either ignoring uncertainty or dealing with it on the basis of probability. The question remains, how to establish the requisite probabilities?

The concept of probability has meaning only if two conditions are fulfilled:

- We are considering events which belong to a set of similar events; and
- We can get hold of behavioural characteristics of the whole set.

The latter can be done by bringing to bear one of three frameworks:

- First principles, such as symmetry (e.g. each side of dice has equal chance).
- Laws of nature (e.g. uncertainty principle).
- Empirical observation (e.g. weather statistics).

In this chapter we are dealing with questions of strategy. Strategy tends to relate to unique issues that have not been seen before. Indeed, we have argued that a strategy must have unique features in order to lead to success. This seems at variance with the underlying principle of probability as set out.

At this point the strong rationalist introduces the notion of "subjective probability". It is left to "the expert" to decide how to assess the probabilities. However, the fact remains that the notion of the probability of a unique event is internally inconsistent (van der Heijden, 1994). This is not the same issue as the dichotomy between the frequency interpretation of probability and single-event probability (Gigerenzer, 1994). Gigerenzer shows how biases and illusions in subjective probabilities seem to disappear as soon as single-event probability problems are reformulated on a frequency basis. The events we are looking at here are those which cannot be looked at from a frequency perspective, simply because there is no set to which they can be logically related. Why is it that managers nevertheless often seem prepared to come up with an answer to the probability question? One possibility is that managers, if asked to make such an assessment, make a metaphorical link with another area of human endeavour they know, for which they feel they have some historical evidence. However, the validity of the analogy cannot be assessed; metaphors have no assessable predictive value. Another, possibly more likely, explanation is that the word "probability" is not being interpreted in a statistical sense at all.

There is strong evidence that people use the word "probable" for events which can be explained through a heuristic called "scenario availability", which considers how easy it is to construct or imagine a scenario that leads from known history through articulated chains of cause and effect to the event under consideration (Wagenaar, 1994). If no such chain can be thought of, the event is called "unlikely". Specifically, the version of what is known as the "conjunction fallacy", in which people increase their assessment of the likelihood of an event after having been confronted with a logical causal chain ("I can see it now"), shows that in this area the colloquial use of words related to probability contradicts basic principles. The conjunction fallacy provides evidence that thinking is not probabilistic but causal (Tversky & Kahneman, 1983).

Ideas about the future are based on causal theories about how phenomena come into being in the world. Such theories are based on explicit or implicit assumptions concerning causal relationships. Even if we use statistically established relationships to say something about the future, we imply that underpinning these are causal relationships. For example, for a long time it was argued that the correlation between smoking and lung cancer did not imply that the one would be caused by the other. The possibility was argued that both were caused by a third variable. One does not hear these arguments any longer: we now believe that in addition to the statistical correlation we have been able to show causality through direct experimentation.

## 2.6 UNCERTAINTY AND THEORIES ABOUT THE WORLD

Depending on the philosophical assumptions one makes about the chain of causality, different theories result with respect to the degree of predictability of the future. These basic assumptions can be classified in three categories (adopting a somewhat modified framework proposed by Mohr, 1982):

- *Variance theory.* The underlying assumption is that events are caused by efficient causes, in the nature of a "clockwork" world. If the total system were known it would be possible to identify the set of causes that would together completely explain the variable of interest, and knowing the total set would be the necessary and sufficient condition to determine future behaviour of the predicted variable. If we are unable to predict a variable in complete detail, this is the result of our limited knowledge of the system, and the resulting uncertainty is interpreted as "error". The logical consequence of this is that there is always the possibility to improve one's forecasting ability by finding out more about the system and improving measuring effectiveness. In the final analysis the truth is out there somewhere, and the challenge is to get as close as possible.
- *Probabilistic process theory.* The underlying assumption is that there is a causal chain explaining events, but some steps in the chain

are probabilistic relationships. An example would be the prediction of an epidemic of malaria. While it is possible to explain in detail how malaria is spread, it is not possible to predict whether a particular individual will be affected as not everyone would be subject to mosquito bites capable of transferring the disease. However, by studying the behaviour of mosquitoes it is possible to collect data which establish the probability that a particular individual will be affected. Whether this will in fact happen cannot be predicted. The theory describes necessary causes, but it is not a sufficient explanation in an individual case—two scenarios remain valid. However, as a consequence of the law of large numbers, the government can use the theory at the level of the total population, e.g. to prepare an adequate and sufficient medical system. A probabilistic process theory can be used to predict the future (in fact it becomes a variance theory) at a sufficient level of aggregation of the predicted variable.

- *Indeterminate process theory.* As we saw, assigning a probability to a causal link can be done in three ways: (a) on the basis of the historical performance of the statistical set of similar events; (b) on the basis of laws of nature; or (c) on the basis of first principles, such as symmetry. However, it may not always be possible to assign a probability in this way. This is the case especially when we consider unique events, related to emergent behaviour of highly complex systems, for which no statistical set is known (Wagenaar, 1994). For example, even if it was possible in 1990 to develop a causal process theory on how apartheid in South Africa might end peacefully, there was no way of assigning a probability (in the statistical sense of the word) to such an event happening over the next 5 years. Or, looking forward, there are causally convincing process theories about how global warming might create conditions under which the Gulf Stream would "switch off", turning Western Europe into a Siberian climate. Even so, I have not been able to find an expert yet who was prepared to assign a probability to this event happening in our life-time. One finds a similar situation around the development of understanding of new diseases such as BSE, where new process theories are generated, with essential links remaining indeterminate due to a lack of statistical evidence. Even if such theories may eventually become probabilistic process theories, they remain indeterminate as long as sufficient statistical data has not yet been collected.

In order to predict the future, one needs a variance theory containing the necessary and sufficient conditions to describe outcomes. In contrast, an indeterminate process theory, which contains necessary but not sufficient conditions, can be used retrospectively to explain why things have happened and prospectively what could happen. It does not predict. Newton's laws are examples of a variance theory, Darwinian evolution is an indeterminate process theory.

Rationalistic decision making is based on a variance theory of the world. Underpinning the rationalist view is the assumption that ultimately there is one and only one best answer to any strategy question. It may be hidden from our view due to poor measurement or lack of resources to carry out the analysis necessary to discover it. But behind our uncertainty there exists one "clockwork" future and the art of strategy design is to get as close as possible to it, i.e. to minimize the "error" term in our variance theory.

There is an alternative view. This is that there are aspects of the future which are fundamentally uncertain, unknowable and indeterminate. This is the thinking world of process theories. In this view the future is fundamentally plural, which means that the "best strategy" does not exist. As time moves on, confronting us with events which could not have been foreseen, what the rationalist may consider "best strategy" is subject to continuous change.

There is no way to determine objectively whether the behaviour of a system should be understood in terms of a variance theory or a probabilistic or indeterminate process theory. The choice reflects one's philosophical outlook on the world. A preference for a variance theoretical view of the world leads to future thinking based on forecasting and control. A preference for indeterminate process theory will logically lead to rejection of the idea of forecasting, and point towards the use of multiple scenarios in future thinking.

Scenario planners have a philosophical outlook which makes them describe the world by means of indeterminate process theories. It is important to stress that this does not absolve them from analysing the situation in the greatest depth possible. There is a lot predetermined in any process theory, and it is the task of the scenario thinker to surface as much of this as possible. You cannot understand malaria unless you have discovered the way of propagation, the role of mosquitoes, and so on. Surfacing these predetermineds is essential to develop useful malaria scenarios. Similarly, useful scenarios about the future of the Gulf Stream require understanding of the system which creates the underlying sea movements, and the influence of melting polar ice on it. Good scenario work requires a lot of rational analysis.

## 2.7  FORECASTING AND SCENARIO THINKING

As we saw, the forecaster thinks in terms of variance theory, the scenario thinker in terms of process theory. The forecaster looks for a model of reality containing the necessary and sufficient conditions to pin down the future, the scenario thinker is satisfied to work with only necessary conditions, and is happy to explore the multiple possibilities these lead to.

What this difference can lead to is interestingly illustrated by Godet (1982), who compared the characteristics of these two ways of future thinking as shown in Table 2.1. There are many aspects to be considered in this comparison. Forecasting seems indicated in predictable situations which, on the basis of experience, can be adequately described by variance theory. As we saw, everything else being equal, short-term events will be more predictable than long-term events, due to the influence of inertia. However, even in many short-term situations variance theory may be considered inappropriate, due to the assumption of probabilistic or indeterminate causal links. This view will tend to prevail in long-term, high-impact theories, such as those relating to strategic decisions.

The hard rationalist, exemplified by the typical "energetic problem solver" finds it intuitively difficult to see how one can perform in such an indeterminate situation. The dominant model in organizations still projects the person who, being confronted with a problem, aims to solve it as soon as possible, in order to be able to move on to the next one. Problem-solvers extrapolate the rationalistic approach used in problem solving to strategy, leading to premises such as:

- Thinking can be separated from action.
- There is one right answer to each strategic question.
- Implementation follows the discovery of strategy.

Problem solvers require approaches that simplify and reduce the problem situation, not make it more complex by the introduction of indeterminates and multiple scenarios. This difficulty will not be resolved until it becomes clear that a decision process based on a

**Table 2.1**  Forecasting and scenario thinking—two ways of future thinking

|  | Classical forecasting | Scenario approach |
| --- | --- | --- |
|  | Piecemeal | Overall approach |
| Viewpoint | "Everything else being equal" | "Nothing else being equal" |
| Variables | Quantitative, objective and known | Qualitative, not necessarily quantitative, subjective, known or hidden |
| Relationships | Static, fixed structures | Dynamic, evolving structure |
| Explanation | The past explains the future | The future is the *raison d'être* of the present |
| Future | Single and certain | Multiple and uncertain |
| Method | Deterministic and quantitative models | Intentional analysis. Qualitative (structural analysis) |
| Attitude to the future | Passive or adaptive (future comes about) | Active and creative (future brought about) |

process theory will be fundamentally different from the "forecast and control" approach based on variance theory. The logical consequence of describing the world with a process theory containing unknowable uncertainty is that there is *not* one and only one best answer to any strategy question. In the light of multiple equally plausible futures, the underpinning of the typical rationalistic decision process discussed above collapses.

It is replaced with something more akin to an ongoing learning process (van der Heijden, 1996). In the multiple futures view, both thinking and action continue over time. What may seem "best" today may be far from the optimum tomorrow. A process theory cannot predict the future. What is a "best strategy" continuously changes over time. Developing strategy becomes an ongoing activity, in which perception, theory building and action work closely together over time in a continuous learning loop.

## 2.8  SCENARIO PLANNING AND LEARNING PROCESSES

Having discussed the approach of the forecaster, let us now follow a scenario planner developing a project. The scenario planner is facing a situation which he considers can only be suitably described by a process theory, and therefore needs to be characterized by not one but multiple equally plausible futures. How does this lead to a learning approach to decision making?

As we saw, the idea of scenario thinking cannot be combined with the notion of strategy making as a one-time strategic decision. Instead it considers strategy making as an ongoing process. Scenario thinkers are continuously aware that there is a point beyond which increasing analysis does not any longer improve the predictability of the outcome of actions undertaken. A strategic decision does not remove the underlying issue or situation from the agenda. Every strategic decision remains with the decision maker until it is overtaken by another bigger, more urgent issue (Colin Eden (1987) calls this "problem finishing").

The first difference to observe, comparing the scenario planner with the "problem solver", is that the starting point is not any longer a problem to be solved. Contrary to the forecaster, the scenario planner is not given a problem to solve. Instead the situation to be looked at will be an area of activity about which decision makers feel uncertain and uncomfortable, an area of concern in need of better understanding. The concerns will be related to the opportunities and threats the situation may seem to contain. The scenario planner will try to express this situation, possibly in terms of an organizing question. The scenario planner will need to define a focus for the project, like the rationalist, but instead of pinning this down as "a decision to be taken" or "a problem to be solved" he will prefer to define it as a "situation requiring understanding".

Like the rationalistic forecaster, the scenario planner will try to find out as much as possible about the situation of concern. However, his search will be less focused and wider. The forecaster knows what he needs to forecast, the scenario planner does not know yet where the boundaries of the situation, and therefore of the scenarios, are. Therefore, he will start with making a preliminary outline, in terms of themes and sub-themes that seem intuitively relevant. But relevance needs an anchor. This leads the scenario planner to give high priority to a clear identification of a scenario "client", the person or the group of people struggling with one or more puzzling aspects of the situation on whose behalf the work will be done. Clients determine success or failure of the project and therefore are the ultimate arbiters of what needs to be considered relevant. They need to remain connected to the scenario project.

Initially the scenario planner will engage in an open-ended conversation with the client to obtain as accurate a picture as possible of what is worrying in the situation faced by the client. This leads to an initial delineation of the territory to be considered, e.g. in the form of a short list of scenario themes. This provides some initial guidance on the boundaries of the scenario project, within which proper process theories have to be developed, describing the predetermineds and indeterminates. The scenario methodology builds this up through an iterative process, alternating between:

- Mapping areas of predetermineds and indeterminates, in the form of a scenario framework; and
- Systemic analysis filling in the gaps in the knowledge of the knowable system, as a basis for developing the scenario story-lines.

## 2.9 FINDING PREDETERMINED ELEMENTS

The scenario planner starts with a set of unrelated concerns of the client, on the basis of which he has developed a preliminary scenario agenda. In an area of concern, ideas are not very well linked into existing cognitive structures. The search for predetermined elements helps in creating more structure around the area of puzzlement of the client.

Some predetermined elements are self-evident, and may be clearly relevant. In that case they need to be included in the first analysis phase. One can think of the obvious inertias in the world, e.g. demographics, economic development, cultural beliefs, and so on. But it is likely that these will produce a very incomplete picture of the driving forces in the situation considered. The reason is that most predetermined elements are emergent properties of the slow-changing causal structures of the systems studied. In order to map these out, the scenario planner needs to identify as many causal links as possible. He will search the history of the system's behaviour for evidence of this, by looking for "cues for

**Box A—Articulation**

We can divide our knowledge of the world into two categories, a codified part and a tacit part. The codified part is operationally available for decision making. Elements are well connected and integrated and are understood in context; they have meaning. However, we also have tacit knowledge, which we cannot articulate well. These elements consist of isolated observations and experiences that we have not yet been able to conceptualize and integrate with our codified knowledge. They are isolated bits of knowledge which seem intuitively important but puzzling, the meaning of which we do not yet understand very clearly.

It is difficult for us to make our poorly connected constructs explicit on our own. In order to learn, one needs to relate new experiences to existing cognitive structures. Articulation of tacit knowledge requires an outside agent to confront the individual's unconnected bits of empirical knowledge with the knowledge structure in the wider group or society. This is the role of a "teacher" or "sounding board". Vygotsky (1986) suggests that learning occurs as the result of social interaction. He introduces the term "the zone of proximal development" around a person's existing cognitive structures. It is here that an individual's empirically rich, but disorganized tacit mental constructs interact with the logic of the causal reasoning expressed in the language of the social group. As a result of this interaction, the weaknesses of spontaneous reasoning are supported by the strength of the group logic. The process is known as "scaffolding" the thought processes of the learning individual. As a result, unconnected bits of insight become part of the overall structure of the individual's domain knowledge (become meaningful) and in this way enrich the mental model used to consider the future operationally. This process of making sense can take place only in the zone of proximal development.

Scenario development is essentially a process of invention. It needs to go beyond codified knowledge, and must involve linking in unconnected insights that have so far remained tacit. This means that the process takes place in the zone of proximal development. Scenario development can be seen as a process of scaffolding new insights about the environment.

causality". Einhorn & Hogarth (1982) suggest the following as cues for causality:

- Temporal order; events organized on a time line, e.g. trends in events over time.
- Co-variance; different variables follow similar patterns over time.
- Spatial/temporal closeness; one thing always follows another, indicating a link.
- Similarity, in any form or pattern.

The scenario planner will initially search widely for such relationships. In the early stages any idea is considered as a potential building block. In the process of this the area of analysis will be continuously redefined, depending on factors that enter the causal equation, while elements may be removed which have become secondary in any relevant explanation.

This phase of the analysis is sometimes called the "breathing-in" phase. While the situation is being opened up everything is highly dynamic and ever-changing, while more and more findings of possible relevance are "put on the table".

The research activity involves linking into the societal knowledge pool to extract elements of already articulated knowledge which are relevant to the situation. In Vygotsky's (1986) terms, the scenario planner looks for a "teacher" with whom to engage in a dialogue (see Box A).

As a result of this process the scenario planner develops a new causal framework, linking in (scaffolding) some of the tacit knowledge which initially made the situation puzzling. Some of this will now be capable of being understood. A number of causal relationships will have become clear, but many relations will still seem uncertain and unpredictable. More and more effort can be invested in pushing this area back further. But in the analysis a point of diminishing returns will be reached. At this stage the scenario planner needs to take stock, organize his current understanding in a scenario framework, which in turn may indicate new lines of productive analytical attack.

## 2.10  BUILDING A SCENARIO FRAMEWORK

Why is the process of analysis as described above not enough? Why is it necessary from time to time to stop the analysis *per se* and build scenarios around the findings of the analysis?

Initially the problematic situation is ill-defined. Through open-ended interviewing the scenario planner can obtain some idea of the nature of the concerns of the client, but this will be poorly structured and only vaguely outlined. Uncertainty in the perception of the scenario planner will be due more to lack of knowledge of the system than genuine indeterminates. At the end of the project this needs to be transformed into a clear understanding of the predetermineds and indeterminates of the situation. And the more predetermineds that can be discovered, the more the client will feel he/she has been helped to get on top of the situation. Basically, the process is a search for as many predetermineds as we can find. This process has to be "bootstrapped". In the early stages of a scenario project there is no easy way of distinguishing between predetermineds and indeterminates (in fact, it can be philosophically argued that the distinction is fundamentally subjective). Structure will not automatically jump out of the situation description embodied in the scenario themes. Initially the situation facing the scenario planner is extremely ill-defined, there are no obvious points to start analysing. Where to begin? A scenario framework can be a powerful organizing device in this situation.

The process of creating a scenario framework should be seen as a way of organizing insights, in order to:

- Indicate the direction of further analytical enquiry; and/or
- Communicate the results of the analysis.

The scenario framework phase forces the scenario planner to reflect the findings of the analysis so far in a number of stories about the future, which express the discoveries made. The stories will need to overlap in terms of the established and predictable causal structures (predetermineds) but differ in terms of how the uncertainties will be assumed to pan out. At the early stages of the process the uncertainties will indicate both areas of lack of understanding as well as genuine indeterminates. At the later stages one hopes that all uncertainties left are indeterminates.

The principle involved is similar to that of action research carried out on a system that is too complex to understand by reductionist methods. Action research is based on the creation of a deliberate perturbation in an only partially known system. The system may behave as was expected, in which case not much is learned. But if the behaviour deviates from expectations, research into the reason for the deviation from expectation will create new understanding of the system's underlying structure. The activity of scenario building carries out a similar process on one's mental model of the situation under consideration. A good scenario framework process challenges the existing mental models of the scenario planners. This can be done by the discipline of designing a number of significantly different scenario end-states in a future "horizon year", which then need to be linked to the recent past and the present by causally logical, internally consistent, story lines. The process is effective in bringing out the areas where understanding is lacking, and research needs to be done.

There are various ways of approaching the task of creating a scenario framework. Detailed description of these methods goes beyond the scope of this chapter, but can be found in the literature (van der Heijden, 1996). Multiple intuitions play a crucial role in the process. For this reason the project requires a scenario team working interactively. The basic principle involved is for a group of people to brainstorm on what they feel is predictable and what is uncertain in the situation being confronted. All participants, building on their own perceptions, will use their own categories to express what they see as having high impact while being unpredictable. A degree of implicit uncertainty will also surface through the range of views expressed in the group.

The process will initially be bedevilled by different conceptualizations being used in the group. However, multiple scenarios allow projection both of predetermineds that everyone agrees upon, as well as the range of different views expressing the perception of uncertainty and ambiguity in the group. Things do not have to be argued out—the approach provides scope for intuitive input. The ensuing discussion will lift some of the conceptual fog, but many uncertainties remain. In most cases what is initially seen as uncertainty later proves to be a difference in the way people conceptualize a situation. This has to surface through further analysis at a later stage. This is not problematic as long as analysis and scenario building are seen as two phases of an iterative process, with analysis resolving conceptualization problems and scenario building pointing the way for further analysis.

The scenario framework will indicate how the results of these deliberations can be expressed in a limited number of different and challenging futures. The process of trying to create a causal chain of events which explains these futures, based on what is known about the history and the present state of the system, will bring to light areas where further knowledge is lacking. For this process to work well the futures must create a significant perturbation in the team members' mental model; they must force thinking beyond the conventional and well-known. At this stage one is looking for a small number of challenging images of the future, based on high-impact driving forces which will stretch the scenario building into the zone of proximal development. This means that intuition needs to play a crucial role in their generation. This explains the use of creativity techniques such as brainstorming. If this is done well this step will provide clear indications for input into the next analytical phase, in the form of a number of well-formulated research questions.

The next phase of the scenario project is research into causal relationships which the framework has identified as insufficiently understood. During this time a new causal map will be produced which underpins the scenario framework developed. However, in doing so new relationships will be discovered which throw new light on the structure of the framework, so that eventually this becomes less suitable for containing the knowledge the team is developing. At that point another iteration is required, developing a new framework on the basis of the knowledge the team has at that time (creating another "generation" of scenarios).

This process is illustrated by the example quoted by Pierre Wack in his well-known *Harvard Business Review* article (Wack, 1985). For example, he describes a scenario framework for the French oil industry, based on two dimensions which were initially selected as the most important and the most uncertain. These were the attitude of the French government towards regulating the industry ("laissez-faire" or "dirigiste") and the discovery (or not) of significant indigenous gas reserves in France. These two dimensions produced four scenario end-states, which were at that time considered "first-generation", i.e. in need of further analysis. During the process of fleshing out the story lines, a number of important discoveries were made. One was the realization that with abundant gas supply available from elsewhere in Europe (The Netherlands and Norway, and very large reserves waiting to be developed in Russia), indigenous availability was secondary to the (predetermined) desire of the French consumer to tap into the convenience and environmental benefit of natural gas in determining the size of the market. The second discovery was that underlying driving forces would eventually force the French government to liberalize the industry, the only indeterminate being when this would happen. At this time a lot had been learned about the situation driving the industry, but the initial framework had become obsolete. One uncertainty dimension had been removed altogether and the other had collapsed into a predetermined event happening early or late. Time had arrived to arrange another framework workshop with the scenario team. The first-generation scenarios had done their work, but now had to be replaced with a new generation.

## 2.11 SCENARIO BUILDING, AN ITERATIVE PROCESS

In summary the scenario framework serves the following functions:

- Structuring existing knowledge about the situation.
- Indicating directions in which to search for information leading to enhanced understanding of predetermineds.
- Providing a medium in which acquired knowledge can be communicated effectively.

A fully-fledged scenario project iterates between framework construction and analysis of individual scenario story-lines until the results obtained stabilize and further work produces diminishing returns. At that point the framework is finalized and the story-lines completed. The process is shown diagrammatically in Figure 2.1.

The process iterates between scenario building and research, between intuition and analysis. In this way it uses the power of people's intuition while overcoming the problems of a purely intuitive approach. The measure of success of the project as a whole is the degree to which conceptual uncertainty and ambiguity have been replaced by a set of clearly defined predetermined elements and irreducible indeterminates. For the scenario client this will be manifested in the degree to which ill-defined concerns about the future are scaffolded into understanding and purposefulness.

If the process is to lead to significant discoveries of predetermined elements, it will take time and resources. Unfortunately, such discoveries are not guaranteed and depend on the structure of the situation studied and the quality of the approach adopted. However, it is seldom that the scenario team does not learn a lot about the situation that proves helpful to the client in getting on top of the situation. Because the finished scenarios will have incorporated a lot of what was initially tacit knowledge in a coherent framework, the activity is often felt as an important and empowering learning experience. The scenario planner

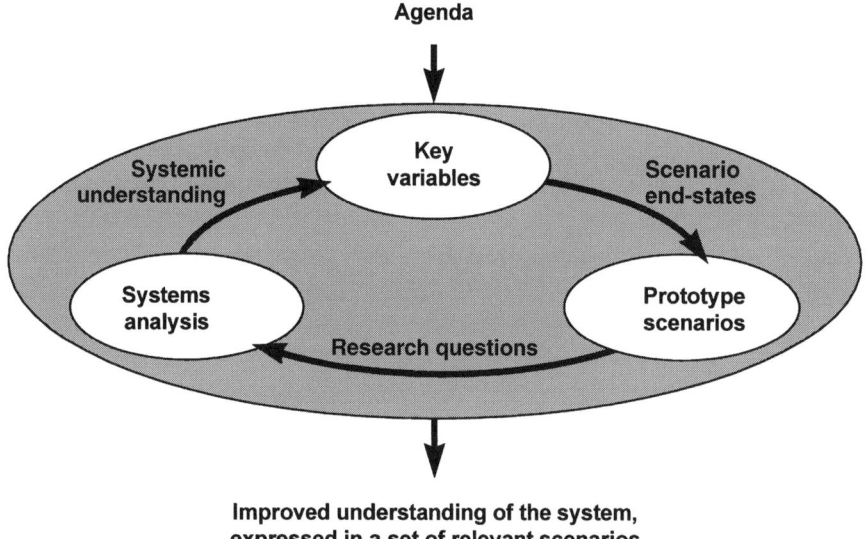

**Figure 2.1** The scenario-building process

now feels more in control of the situation, simply because sense can be made out of something that earlier seemed opaque and troubling. For this reason the trip can be a rewarding one, creating a lot of positive energy. As a consequence, scenario planners are often keen to share their scenarios with others, and experience disappointment with the lukewarm reception from those who have not been connected with the situation studied.

The Vygotsky theory explains why scenarios which were so highly meaningful to their authors are generally of little consequence to a general audience. A positive learning experience can take place only in the zone of proximal development. This will be highly specific to a particular individual or group, reflecting their specific experience and history. Another group will have had another history, and their zone of proximal development will be somewhere else. Someone else's scenarios will be experienced either as boring (if their discoveries were already part of one's articulated knowledge) or as "science fiction", maybe fun but not very important (if their discoveries are outside the audience's zone of proximal development).

Pierre Wack tells a story of an imaginary mayor of Dresden who, being new to the job in 1925, asked to be given a forecast for the city over the next 20 years, in order to be able to make better decisions. Imagine that he had managed to find a forecaster who really knew the future. This person would tell him about a major stock exchange crash in 1929, that the world would be thrown into an unrecoverable depression with unprecedented unemployment, that despair would bring a group called "the Nazis" to power, who would rev up the military machine, making Germany embark on an episode of geographical expansion, leading to World War II and eventually to the complete destruction of the city. Having produced this forecast, imagine that the mayor would be asked what he was going to do with this forecast. The only possible answer to this question would be "nothing". The scenario would deviate so much from his model of the world that it could not possibly be a trigger for action. The projected future would be well outside his zone of proximal development. On the other hand, if someone would have predicted the destruction of the city in 1940, this would have been a completely different matter. At that time the possibility of another world war had firmly entered people's tacit knowledge, so that a major act of destruction could be credibly scaffolded into one's mental model.

Vygotsky's theory of "proximal development" clarifies why scenario planning is a customized activity. Scenario planners must be very clear in their minds about the identity of their client, and stay close to them while the process unfolds. While the scenario team iterates between scenario frameworks and analysis, there is a real danger that the content of the work gradually diverges from the zone of proximal development of the client. If this is allowed to drift it becomes increasingly likely that the final product is not any longer connected, as a result of which the project comes to be seen as a failure. A wise scenario planner will touch base with the client during every iteration. In this way he will ensure that every discovery by the scenario team is also a discovery for the client.

## 2.12 CONCLUSIONS

In this chapter we argue that mental representations of the world can be categorized as either variance theories or process theories. People who have learned to interpret the world through a process theory, with its intrinsic indeterminates, cannot any longer plan ahead in the traditional "predict and control" mode. The process world-view will lead them inevitably to scenario planning and strategy making in the form of continuous learning, linking perception, theories and action in an ever on-going interwoven process.

Vygotsky's theory of "proximal development" is introduced to argue that such learning processes can take place only in a limited area of attention, called the zone of proximal development.

The realization that scenario planning is a logical outcome of a process world-view leads to a number of principles underpinning the effectiveness of the scenario project, including:

- The need to identify a client as the relevance anchor.
- The need for thorough analysis of the situation to identify as many predetermined elements as possible, based on causal relationships and inertia.
- The need to identify the zone of proximal development of the client, as an indication of how far the scenarios should/can be taken.
- The use of scenario framework design, as an intuitive way to map the zone of proximal development of the client.
- The need to alternate scenario framework design with analysis.
- The need to stay with the evolving zone of proximal development of the client as the project develops.
- Scenario development is a team activity.

## REFERENCES

Ackoff, R.L. (1974)  *Redesigning the Future.* Wiley, New York.

de Geus, A.L. (1988)  Planning as learning. *Harvard Business Review,* March/April, 70–74.

Eden, C. (1987)  Problem solving/finishing. In M. Jackson & P. Keys (eds) *New Directions in Management Sciences.* Gower, Aldershot.

Eden, C. (1992)  Strategic management as a social process. *Journal of Management Studies,* **29**, 799–811.

Einhorn, H.J. & Hogarth, R.M. (1982)  Prediction, diagnosis and causal thinking in forecasting. *Journal of Forecasting,* **1**, 22–36.

Gigerenzer, G. (1994)  Why the distinction between single-event probabilities and frequencies is important for psychology (and *vice versa*). In G. Wright & P. Ayton (eds), *Subjective Probability.* Wiley, Chichester.

Godet, M. (1982)  From forecasting to "la prospective": a new way of looking at futures. *Journal of Forecasting,* **1**, 293–302.

Kelly, G.A. (1963) *A Theory of Personality: The Psychology of Personal Constructs.* Norton, New York.

Mintzberg, H. & Waters, J. (1985) Of strategies, deliberate and emergent. *Strategic Management Journal,* **6**, 257–72.

Mohr, L.B. (1982) *Explaining Organizational Behavior: The Limits and Possibilities of Theory and Research.* Jossey-Bass, San Francisco, CA.

Simon, H.A. (1983) *Reason in Human Affairs.* Blackwell, Oxford.

Tversky, A. & Kahneman, D. (1983) Extentional versus intuitive reasoning: the conjunction fallacy in probability judgments. *Psychological Review,* **30**, 293–315.

van der Heijden, K. (1993) Strategic vision at work: discussing strategic visions in management teams. In J. Hendri & G. Johnson (eds), *Strategic Thinking, Leadership and the Management of Change.* Wiley, Chichester.

van der Heijden, K. (1994) Probabilistic planning and scenario planning. In G. Wright & P. Ayton (eds), *Subjective Probability.* Wiley, Chichester.

van der Heijden, K. (1996) *Scenarios, the Art of Strategic Conversation.* Wiley, Chichester.

Vygotsky, L.S. (1986) *Thought and Language.* MIT Press, Boston, MA.

Wack, P. (1985) Scenarios: uncharted waters ahead. *Harvard Business Review,* Sept–Oct, 73–90.

Wagenaar, W.A. (1994) The subjective probability of guilt. In G. Wright & P. Ayton (eds), *Subjective Probability.* Wiley, Chichester.

Whittington, R. (1993) *What Is Strategy and Does It Matter?* Routledge, London.

# Chapter 3

# Judgemental Forecasting and the Use of Available Information

Marcus O'Connor and Michael Lawrence

*University of New South Wales, Kensington, Australia*

## SUMMARY

In the light of evidence that judgemental approaches are extensively used in practice, this chapter examines the performance of judgemental approaches in the context of sales or product forecasting. It examines the performance of people under controlled laboratory conditions where they were provided with time-series information only, and also with varieties of additional information (including causal information). It also examines the way people engage in the practice of product forecasting using the plethora of information available to them, describes the process by which product forecasts are derived, and comments on the efficiency with which the information is used.

## 3.1  INTRODUCTION

The following is an edited version of the discourse at a monthly sales forecasting meeting to decide on the forecasts for company products

*Forecasting with Judgment*. Edited by G. Wright and P. Goodwin.
© 1998 John Wiley & Sons Ltd.

over each of the next 6 months. The company was in the food industry and had undergone a strong growth of its products over the last 5 years. It was perceived by the industry to be a successful company and excellent at marketing and finding niche products.

It is 8 am on the last Thursday of the month, the regular time for the monthly sales forecasting meeting. By the end of the meeting the individual forecasts for all 35 products need to be set in concrete for the next month and established with varying degrees of accuracy for the other 5 months. The convenor of the meeting is the Marketing and Sales Director. Other attendees are the Director of Production, the Marketing Manager (responsible for the forecasting process), the three Product Managers, the Purchasing Manager and the Sales Manager.

*Marketing Director*   Welcome to the meeting. Let's see if we can push this through in an hour—not like last time when we talked for over 2 hours! As usual, Glenda (the Marketing Manager) has prepared for us the results of the computer-produced statistical forecasts— although it seems to me that we spend little time talking about them! Glenda, let's have it.

*Marketing Manager*   OK. I've produced the forecasts for each product. As usual, we have lots to discuss for several of the products. So I suggest we get the easy ones out of the way first.

*Marketing Director*   Should we just leave the forecasting of these easy low-profile products to Glenda, or would you like to discuss them in turn? I'm not sure we are not wasting our time discussing them.

*Sales Manager*   I don't think we should just accept the computer output. We can quite quickly go through them, and then we know we've had some input in the process.

*Marketing Director*   OK. But let's not waste too much time on them. We need to focus on the key products.

(After about 40 minutes)

*Marketing Director*   Good, the non-key products are out of the way. But it has taken us too much time again. We'll have to do something about this in future. Lets deal with P1 (the first of the key products). Glenda?

*Marketing Manager*   I've produced a forecast of 120 000 units for next month. This was a bit of a guess. The computer forecast was only

87 566 units. But I know we have some marketing efforts that need to be taken into account.

*Marketing Director*    Yes, Glenda. A national TV advertising campaign will begin next month. This is the first time we have done this. I have managed to convince the major distributors to increase their orders accordingly. In addition to this, I have decided to appoint a different distributor in Queensland (a state of Australia). I'm sure this will lift our disappointing game in Queensland considerably. Moreover, the forecast temperature (a major causally related force) for the next month is extraordinarily high and this means that sales will increase commensurately. The danger, if I can pre-empt Production, is that we may have a potential stock-out problem. All in all, I feel we are looking at about a 50% increase in the level of sales.

*Production Director*    That's all very well for the Marketing people, but we are already stretched to the limit in our productive capacity. There is no way we can deal with this unless we begin to work 24 hours a day (from the current 18 hours). This would also introduce more maintenance problems and personnel issues that I choose not to even think about at this stage. We can't do it with our current procedures and set-up!

*Marketing Director*    Bob, I've committed to it! Geoff (the CEO) has committed to it! We, as Directors, have discussed it! This is a great opportunity to significantly increase our profile with the supermarket chains. It's that once-in-a-lifetime window of opportunity. If we are successful in this one, I'm sure the chains will look favourably on other promotions we have in the future. At the moment, we are seen as too small to be taken seriously. If we can show that we can drive the demand higher and supply the stock, the supermarket chains will accept more of our product line.

*Production Director*    I can see your arguments. But it's to no avail if we can't get the product. I may be able to increase to a 24-hour production schedule. But, I need a new baking oven. You will have to talk to Geoff (the CEO) about this. He wasn't convinced about it when I spoke to him last. So a word from you will help. He won't believe me alone. Also, if I pull out all stops for P1, I will need to cut production in P2 (another product). I can't do them both.

*Purchasing Manager*    If I can add a point here—it still can't be done. Drought conditions in the last 2 months have meant that the quality of the blueberries is very poor. I have to investigate getting them from overseas. I can't do that quickly. Quality is paramount, as you know.

This edited extract of the discourse at a product forecasting meeting reveals a number of issues that remain to be the subject of concentrated research in forecasting. First, much of the process of forecasting is inextricably mixed with the setting of targets. Sometimes it may be impossible to isolate the two processes. Clearly, the issue of performance appraisal is also relevant. However, we know relatively little about how the process of forecasting and target setting are intertwined.

Second, almost all the discussion concentrates on factors other than the time series. At most, the time series is considered only in passing. In our experience it was just considered for seasonal influences—and then only by comparing against the same period last year. In fact, one of the lasting impressions gained from this study of product forecasting (to be described in detail in a later section) was the general lack of a detailed examination of the time series. When asked about this, a number of people indicated that they were interested in the future, not the past. However inappropriate this viewpoint may be, the point remains that people believe that the past may not be a good predictor of the future— a point confirmed from the M-Competition data (Makridakis et al., 1982; see Carbone & Makridakis, 1986).

Third, the overwhelming consideration of these product forecasting meetings was on the influence of the (so-called) non-time-series information on the sales. In the extract cited above, we see the importance of marketing efforts, advertising, distribution channels and the limits of production and purchasing. If the whole discourse had been reproduced, we would have seen the issues of labour relations and the preferences of the CEO being discussed. We would also have seen the Director of Production refusing to accept a low forecast for a product and threatening to withdraw from the regular monthly forecasting process. In this case, whilst the marketing people saw a reduction in the market for the product due to competitor action, the subsequent lack of sales would have resulted in an excess in inventory levels, leading to Production being chastised by the CEO. This forced the marketing people to agree to shift some of the product via special deals. Clearly, the final forecast was not the product of the time series!

In general, the overwhelming focus of these monthly meetings was not the time series, but the causal influences that drive the sales. The underlying assumption of academic time-series forecasting, that the past data can predict the future data, may not be accepted in sales forecasting, at least for key products. Consideration is concentrated on those pieces of information that are seen to drive the behaviour of the variable. A number of studies have recognized the importance of this non-time-series information (Edmundson, Lawrence & O'Connor, 1988; Sanders & Ritzman, 1992). Others have stressed the importance of managerial adjustment of statistical forecasts for this additional information (Willemain, 1989; Mathews & Diamantopolous, 1992, 1996). In general, the common conclusion of these studies is that knowledge of this information is a major contributor to the superior accuracy of judgemental forecasts (Webby & O'Connor, 1996).

This chapter examines the way in which people use non-time-series information in the context of product/sales forecasting. After reviewing background literature, it reports on two groups of studies that focus on the contribution of this additional information to forecast accuracy. The first group of studies are concerned with the way people are able to utilize additional causal information in the production of their final forecasts. These were undertaken in controlled laboratory conditions. The second group reports the results of a large field survey of the process of product forecasting and examines the contribution of this causal information in practice.

## 3.2 BACKGROUND LITERATURE

The previous section has demonstrated that non-time-series information is viewed by practitioners as important to the sales-forecasting process. This section reviews the literature on the ability of people to utilize such information. It considers not only the literature on forecasting, but also the literature from cognitive psychology on the ability of people to use causal or contextual information. The first part of this section reviews the effects of labels on performance at a decision task; the next part reviews the forecasting literature on the importance of non-time-series information; and the final section reviews the ability of people to use contextual or causal information.

### 3.2.1 Label or Context Effects

The traditional focus of most judgemental forecasting research has purposefully eliminated the context of the time series or data provided to the subjects (Lawrence, Edmundson & O'Connor, 1985). Whilst there were very good reasons for the elimination of this information, it must be remembered that a knowledge of this information may be vitally important to performance of the task. In the forecasting arena, Armstrong showed how this knowledge could change the judgemental forecasts. Armstrong (1983) demonstrated that people made different forecasts when presented with a graph of US production of automobiles, compared to those with a graph that was labelled "Production of product X in Transylvania". Similarly, it was found that different forecasts were estimated for expenses than for sales. These differences are particularly relevant for medium- to long-term forecasts.

In general, a well-documented theory of cognitive decision making—prospect theory (Kahneman & Tversky, 1979)—suggests that people make different decisions when faced with different task contexts. When faced with a prospect of losses, people make different decisions than when they are faced with the prospect of gains. Thus, the nature or context of the series may need to be considered. In general, the cognitive decision-making literature has also concluded that the nature of the variable of interest makes a difference to the decisions. Adelman (1981), Brehmer & Kuylenstierna (1980) and Koele (1980) found that a meaningful label or context on the variable of interest was beneficial to decision performance. Sniezek (1986) also confirmed the effect of meaningful labels—and they also assisted in the encoding and retrieval of information. However, people are slow at learning to utilize the label information effectively. Miller (1971) suggested that, whilst labels are beneficial, some people are better at the task than others (students are not particularly good at the tasks!).

Thus, a knowledge of the nature of the time series will in general be beneficial to the judgemental forecasts. Whilst this may seem self-evident and even trite, it is important to establish that people can use such information and that this information will affect the estimation of the forecasts.

### 3.2.2 Contextual Information in Forecasting

Several studies have demonstrated the importance of contextual information in forecasting. Edmundson, Lawrence & O'Connor (1988) examined the short-term forecasts of product forecasters (the *product knowledge group*) and compared them with those of students without the contextual information (the *no knowledge group*) and the product forecasters themselves, who had the same series which were transformed so they could not be recognized (the *industry knowledge group*)—note that this latter group had the benefits of labelling. Results indicated clearly that the forecasts of the product knowledge group were superior to those of the other groups (there being no difference in accuracy between the industry knowledge and no knowledge groups). But this result was only true for the products that were considered as key to the Marketing department. For the non-key products, there was no difference in the accuracy of the forecasts of the three groups. This study clearly shows that a knowledge of the non-time-series information is essential to forecast accuracy. Sanders & Ritzman (1992) also confirmed the importance of contextual information, as did Mathews & Diamantopolous (1989, 1990, 1992), who considered the case where initial statistical forecasts were subsequently adjusted on the basis of contextual information. The revision process significantly improved forecast accuracy.

A comparison of the accuracy of managers' and financial analysts' forecasts of company earnings per share also confirms the importance of contextual information. Brown et al. (1987), Hopwood & McKeown (1980) and Schnaars & Mohr (1988) demonstrate how judgemental forecasts were more accurate than those of the best available statistical models. Armstrong's review also confirms this conclusion (Armstrong, 1983).

Thus, studies point rather conclusively to the importance of a knowledge of non-time-series or contextual information. Webby & O'Connor (1996), in reviewing the studies comparing the performance of judgemental and statistical time-series forecasts, conclude that the more that the judgemental forecasts include contextual information, the greater will be the likely comparative accuracy of the judgemental process.

### 3.2.3 Information Acquisition and Utilization

Given the importance of contextual information to the accuracy of the judgemental forecasts, it is important to determine the capacity of people to utilize this information. In other words, are they capable of utilizing it efficiently? Even though this information may be contributing positively to accuracy, people may be inefficient in using it and incorporating it into their final forecasts. Andreassen (1991), in an unpublished study, compared the accuracy of judgemental extrapolation and judgemental causal forecasting. People assigned to the former group were asked to provide a forecast on the basis of the time-series information alone. People assigned to the causal forecasting group were provided with the diagnostic or causal information necessary to the task. Results indicate that judgemental extrapolation was significantly more accurate than causal forecasting. However, it appeared that people were merely using a very simple and efficient heuristic (the last actual value) in the extrapolation group, and this contributed significantly to forecast accuracy. Harvey, Bolger & McClelland (1994) asked people to use information about likely travel by criminals on the train network to predict future citizen (i.e. non-criminal!) movements. They found that forecasting on the basis of the criminal data alone was less accurate than pure extrapolation of the citizen time-series. However, the simple sinusoidal time-series pattern could quite easily be understood without the causal information. Thus, if the past is a good predictor of the future in the time series, or very simple heuristics based on time-series information are relatively good, there is probably little need for the causal information. However, if the above are not appropriate, causal information may be the key information that leads to high forecast accuracy.

Studies from cognitive psychology on the use of causal information convey a mixed picture. On the one hand, a number of studies (e.g. Schustak & Sternberg, 1981) have found that causal inference is sub-optimal and subject to many biases—such as the under-estimation of negative evidence and neglect of base rate information. There is also the evidence that people perceive illusory correlations (Chapman & Chapman, 1969; Einhorn & Hogarth, 1982). On the other hand, people seem to be sensitive to differences in the validity or reliability of the causal information (Brehmer, 1976), where the causal information with the highest reliability was utilized more fully than information of lower reliability. This result was also verified in applied (albeit laboratory) settings by Ashton (1981) and Casey & Selling (1986). In the former study, people were asked to infer the relationship between price and one of three causal variables (demand, cost and competition). In this case, people were able to infer and utilize information that reflected differences in the reliability of the information. In the latter study (Casey & Selling, 1986), bankruptcy predictions with high-reliability information were more accurate than with the low-reliability information.

The above studies have been concerned with the task where a final criterion was predicted from a single causal cue (of varying reliability). Naturally, studies have been also concerned with the ability to predict a criterion from multiple cues. Clearly, the discourse presented at the beginning of this chapter showed that a large number of pieces of information was taken into account in the process of setting the forecasts. In the light of the fact that people are sensitive to variations in cue reliability, but are almost always under-utilizing the information (see Connolly & Serre, 1984), it is not surprising that people have considerable trouble with multiple cues.

In terms of the acquisition of information (as opposed to the utilization of the information), a number of biases are also apparent. When purchasing or acquiring information, people tend to spend too much on information of low validity and too little on information of high validity (Connolly & Serre, 1984). People have also been found, when dealing with multiple cues, to be relatively insensitive to information of varying reliability (Snapper & Peterson, 1971). Furthermore, people seem to affected by the framing of the problem (Connolly & Gilani, 1982), minor changes in task context (Payne, 1982) and the amount of information available (Levine, Samet & Brahlek, 1975).

In summary, the need to consider contextual or causal information in forecasting has been demonstrated. The foregoing papers have shown that people are able to identify and make better use of high-reliability information, as compared to low-reliability information. But we have not yet covered the question as to the effectiveness of that use. That is, are people able to utilize the full value of the contextual information or is their use inefficient? Only a few studies have been focused on this issue. The remainder of this chapter reviews these studies from the forecasting domain, and is divided into two distinct sections. First, Section 3.3 reviews some laboratory studies which have directly examined the ability of people to use single and multiple cues effectively in addition to time-series information. Second, Section 3.4 describes a comprehensive field study of the forecasting practices in Australian organizations where contextual information is of paramount importance.

## 3.3 LABORATORY STUDIES

### 3.3.1 The Use of a Single Piece of Causal Information

Lim & O'Connor (1996) describe a laboratory-based study of the use of causal information in a time-series forecasting setting. In order to isolate the effects of causal information, they assigned people to one of four groups. The four groups were: *judgemental extrapolation*—where people were only presented with the time series; *judgemental adjustment*—where people were presented with both the time-series and a good statistical forecast (damped exponential forecasting); *causal adjustment*—where people were presented with a single piece of information that was causally related to the time series (also presented); and *mixed adjustment*—where people were presented with the time series, the statistical forecast and the causal cue. The time-series setting was one which had (arguably) a considerable amount of ecological or external validity—sales of ice cream at a nearby surfing beach in Sydney, Australia. Since sales of ice cream rise and fall with the temperature of the day, the time series was artificially generated from actual temperature data. Thus, knowledge of the temperature for the next day was the causal cue used to predict sales for the next day. People were asked to do this task repetitively for 30 periods (days). The actual value for the previous day was revealed to them as they started a new period. At each period, subjects were asked to provide an estimate based on the time series alone. They were then asked to make an adjustment after the new information (statistical forecast and/or temperature information) was revealed to them. Performance was measured in terms of the improvement in forecast accuracy (termed IMP) from the initial extrapolation to the final forecast.[1] Table 3.1 presents the mean improvement (IMP) for the four experimental groups.

Results (ANOVA) reveal that there was a significant improvement in accuracy where the statistical forecast was provided ($F = 6.1, p < 0.005$) and also where the causal information was supplied ($F = 16.1, p < 0.0005$). Thus, causal information was beneficial to forecast accuracy. Whilst there appears to be a difference in IMP between the

**Table 3.1** IMP across the four experimental groups. From Lim and O'Connor, 1996, with permission

|  | Information used | IMP |
|---|---|---|
| Judgemental extrapolation | Time series | −0.09 |
| Judgemental adjustment | Time series + statistical forecast | 0.46 |
| Causal adjustment | Time series + causal information | 1.12 |
| Mixed adjustment | Time series + statistical forecast + causal information | 1.25 |

judgemental adjustment group (who used the statistical forecast) and the causal adjustment group (who used the causal cue only), this was only significant at the $p = 0.086$ level. There was no difference in IMP between the causal and mixed adjustment groups.

The study also examined whether people utilized causal information of different reliability. Two levels of reliability were offered—one with a correlation of cue to criterion that was substantially less than the correlation of the statistical forecast and the criterion, and one where the correlation was substantially greater than that for the statistical forecast. Regression analysis was performed to determine what factors people were using in the derivation of their final forecasts. For the statistical adjustment, causal adjustment and mixed adjustment groups, the standardized regression weights for the relevant information are presented in Table 3.2.[2]

Results in Table 3.2 show that people placed an excessive reliance on the initial forecast in all conditions. In addition, the weight people placed on the causal information was rather weak, especially in the high causal condition. So, the conclusion from this study is that people showed that they could use the causal information and that it certainly improved forecast accuracy. However, they did not utilize effectively the information content from the cue.

Recall from the discourse presented at the start of the chapter that people were mostly focusing on the causal information in their discussion of appropriate forecast levels. The results from Lim & O'Connor (1996) suggest that use of causal information may indeed contribute to accuracy, but there are doubts as to whether people utilize it optimally. However, Lim & O'Connor (1996) only examined use of a single cue.

**Table 3.2** Standardized regression weights of actual ($\beta$) and optimal ($\beta^*$) information usage. From Lim and O'Connor, 1996, with permission

| | Causal information groups | | | | | |
|---|---|---|---|---|---|---|
| | No causal | | Low causal | | High causal | |
| | $\beta$ | $\beta^*$ | $\beta$ | $\beta^*$ | $\beta$ | $\beta^*$ |
| Initial forecast | 0.77 | 0.22 | 0.61 | 0.36 | 0.66 | 0.13 |
| Statistical forecast | 0.22 | 0.43 | 0.33 | 0.28 | 0.26 | 0.41 |
| Causal information | NA | NA | 0.17 | 0.27 | 0.24 | 0.73 |
| Adjusted $R^2$ | 0.81 | 0.32 | 0.74 | 0.40 | 0.83 | 0.82 |

### 3.3.2 The Use of Multiple Pieces of Information

Handzic (1997) examined the ability of people to use *multiple* pieces of contextual information, in a study design similar to that of Lim & O'Connor (1996). She provided people with a time series and three contextual cues that were causal determinants of the time series. The task environment was similar to that of Lim & O'Connor (1996), being sales of ice cream at a famous surfing beach in Sydney. The three cues presented were the forecast temperature for the next day, the number of visitors likely for the next day at the beach, and the ratio of sunshine hours to total daylight hours. The cues and the time series were constructed such that the correlation of each cue to the criterion was equal, and the correlation of the last actual value to the actual was relatively small. Like Lim & O'Connor (1996), people were required to forecast the likely sales of the ice creams for the next day, based on the information provided to them. Like Lim & O'Connor, the task was repeated for 30 trials. The order of presentation of the cues was randomized to prevent any extraneous presentation effects that may have influenced the results.

People were assigned to one of three groups according to the amount of information provided to them. Thus, the study was designed (in part) to investigate whether people could use increasing amounts of causal information in the task of forecasting. To determine which information was being used, the available cues were regressed against the forecast on a person-by-person basis. Thus, for example, where two cues were presented to a person, they were both regressed against the forecast for the 30 trials, and a cue was considered to be used if it entered the (stepwise) regression equation (using normal regression limits)[3]. In this way, we would know which cues were being used by each person. Table 3.3 presents the percentage of time people used the cues in accordance with the information provided to them.

Where people were provided with a single cue, Table 3.3 reveals that only 62.5% of people actually used it, the others (37.5%) preferring to rely solely on the time series pattern. Where people were provided with two cues, the majority of people tended to use only one of the cues, with the proportion of people using no causal cue dropping to a relatively low value. Where they were provided with three causal cues, nobody was found to be using all three pieces of information. The majority of people used two out of the three pieces of information, with about one-third using a single cue. But for those people who were provided with

**Table 3.3**  Percentage usage of provided information by information available

|  |  | Amount of information provided | | |
|---|---|---|---|---|
|  |  | One | Two | Three |
| Amount of information used | None | 37.5 | 12.5 | 8.3 |
|  | One | 62.5 | 54.2 | 29.2 |
|  | Two |  | 33.3 | 62.5 |
|  | Three |  |  | 0 |

either two or three cues, detailed analysis revealed that they were not using the information equally (as designed in the experiment). In almost all cases, the results of the regression revealed that, although people were found to be significantly using more than one cue, one of the cues was weighted much higher than the other. Thus, people were using two cues, but the information content of the second cue was not being utilized fully.

Thus, Handzic (1997) found that, whilst people were able to use up to two pieces of causal non-time-series information, they were effectively using only a single piece. Remember that the discourse extract presented at the start of the case emphasized the fact that there was quite a large amount of information that was considered by the meeting, ranging from the effects of advertising to the appointment of new distributors and raw material problems. The results of Handzic suggest that there is little likelihood that the forecasting meetings would be able to utilize all this information effectively. The point at which information overload occurs seems to be relatively low.

### 3.3.3  The Use of Soft Information in Judgemental Forecasting

The previous studies under review have focused on the use of causal information in forecasting a criterion or variable. An important characteristic of this type of information is that the relationship between the cue and the criterion could be expressed as a correlation. In other words, for every value of the criterion there was a corresponding value for the cue. In terms of the case discourse presented at the start of the chapter, it was an empirical test of the influence of temperature on sales.

Analysis of the types of information referred to in the case suggests that there is another type of information that was viewed as especially relevant to the process of sales forecasting. Apart from the temperature information, the nature of the remaining information was of a "one-off" or "special event" variety. The lack of blueberries in the raw material market, the incidence of a specialized advertising campaign, the appointment of a new distributor, etc. are types of occurrences that do not typically recur, yet they are causal. In most cases, one must make an assessment of the impact of each event without any prior information for guidance. For example, because a national advertising campaign had not been undertaken before, it was difficult to accurately determine its effect.

In the cognitive psychology field, this type of information is referred to as "broken leg" cues (Kleinmuntz, 1990). In the organizational behaviour literature, this type of information is referred to as "soft". In this latter field, Mintzberg (1973) presented evidence that managers prefer this type of information, and they accordingly spend relatively little time analysing "hard" numbers. A large number of studies have confirmed Mintzberg's findings (see Kurke & Aldrich, 1983). Perhaps, the focus of the discourse in the case of these one-off pieces of information presented in the case is another illustration of the desire for future-oriented soft information and a disregard for the hard numbers in the time series. Indeed, Johnson (1988) demonstrates that the ability to deal with these broken leg cues distinguishes an expert from a novice. One possible reason for this preference may be that the soft information mostly relates to the future, but the time series always dwells in the past. And we know that the past is not necessarily a good predictor of the future.

In the forecasting literature, Gorr (1986) showed in a case study that soft information was beneficial to the forecasting process in that it provided an insight into the behaviour of the series. In most cases, such information points to a discontinuity in the time series under consideration. In the absence of such information, a number of studies have shown that people do not forecast discontinuous series very well (O'Connor, Remus & Griggs, 1993, 1997). Yet surveys have shown that forecasters believe that this information is of vital importance (Collopy & Armstrong, 1992). In many cases, it is this soft information that provides the advanced indication that a discontinuity may have occurred.

One study has examined in controlled laboratory conditions the ability of people to incorporate this information into their forecasting process. Webby (1994) carefully devised a case study where a base time series was transformed by 12 different events that changed the shape of the base time series. The task of the forecaster was to make assessments of the events and to make forecasts based on their knowledge of the soft event information. Some of the events related to the past time series and some related to the forecast period. Examples of the events were: information on new technology employed; new distribution channels; price reductions; promotions; and product shortages. Thus, they were much like the events described in the case at the start of the chapter.

In Webby (1994) people were assigned to one of three information conditions: where no event information was provided (the control condition); where people were presented with four pieces of event information; and where people were presented with eight pieces of information. The research issues were to determine whether people could make reasonable assessments of the impact of the events, and to determine whether information load affected the ability of people to forecast. A further research issue was to examine the contribution of computer support of this assessment process. A prototype decision support system (GRIFFIN) was presented to half the subjects, with the other half required to do it manually. It was expected that the computer support would be particularly relevant for high information load conditions.

Table 3.4 presents the forecast accuracy (mean absolute percentage error, or MAPE) for the three information conditions and the computer support (GRIFFIN).

As expected, where more events were introduced into the forecasting task, MAPE deteriorated significantly. This occurred for both the manual condition and the GRIFFIN condition, but overall GRIFFIN subjects were much more accurate in their forecasts than the manual subjects. Thus, the complication of these events had an expected deterioration in forecast accuracy.

**Table 3.4** MAPE for manual and computer-supported groups across information load conditions

|                             | Manual | GRIFFIN |
|-----------------------------|--------|---------|
| Time series only            | 15.8   | 13.8    |
| Time series with four events| 25.7   | 19.4    |
| Time series with eight events| 32.4  | 23.4    |

When we relate this finding to the case material presented at the start of the chapter, we note that there are often a number of pieces of information that are being considered by the forecast meeting. We must expect that accuracy will deteriorate. But an interesting result from this study was the lack of an interaction effect between the provision of computer support (GRIFFIN) and the amount of information that people were required to deal with. One would have expected that GRIFFIN would have been especially beneficial at high information load conditions. The MAPE statistics in Table 3.4 do not provide evidence of this, and neither do the statistical tests $p > 0.45$).

Nevertheless, the first empirical study (to our knowledge) of the way in which people were able to cope with "event" information in addition to the time series showed that people have problems with multiple pieces of information and that computer support designed to facilitate such event assessments can be extremely beneficial.

In summary, the literature and laboratory studies reviewed suggest that non-time-series information is of vital importance in the process of forecasting. In nature, this information is necessarily causally related to the series and can be of two main types—quantitatively and causally related to the criterion, or soft and also causally related to the criterion. Whilst the former may be easy to examine and possibly learn, the latter (the soft information) may be more important in the forecasting process, and is the type of information that is often preferred by the forecasters. The laboratory studies show that people have some sensitivity to the causal cues, but numerous studies have found that they are grossly inefficient at using it.

The next section presents the details of a comprehensive field study of the use of contextual and causal and soft information in sales forecasting practice.

## 3.4  A FIELD STUDY

The previous section reviewed some laboratory studies which were designed to consider the impact of contextual and causal information on forecast accuracy. In general, the results were rather mixed. On the one hand, people appreciated the relevance of the causal information. But they were insensitive to its importance, and tended to focus on other information (e.g. their own initial forecast or that of a statistical method). Nevertheless, past studies of product forecasting (e.g. Edmundson,

Lawrence & O'Connor, 1988; Sanders & Ritzman, 1992) have shown that this type of information may have a great effect on forecast accuracy. In these studies, a case study of a single organization was made.

With the specific objective of increasing understanding of the importance of contextual information, Lawrence, O'Connor & Edmundson (1997) conducted a field survey of 13 large Australian national and international manufacturing-based organizations selling branded, frequently purchased consumer goods and infrequently purchased durable items. Representatives of sales forecasting management in each company were interviewed in person and the objectives of the study explained. Monthly actual sales for a selected range of products (identified by the company as important products for achieving good forecasting accuracy), generally covering a 13-month period, were obtained from the participating companies. In total there were around 4500 actual sales values and 24 000 forecasts in the database.

In order to determine the importance of the contextual information, a forecast based only on the time-series information was required to be used as a base for comparison with that of the company forecast. The longest run of history data collected was 43 months, but for most of the organizations there was only about 12 months' data. This length of data history precluded the calculation of seasonal factors. For some of the organizations seasonality was an important factor, and it was possible that this could be true for most of the organizations in the sample. Thus, quantitative forecasts derived ignoring seasonal factors could be poor forecasts (in the sense that if more data had been available, better forecasts could have been estimated) and this must be borne in mind when the results are considered.

Two quantitative forecasts were estimated: a naive and an exponential smoothing forecast. Both these techniques performed well in the M-competition (Makridakis et al., 1982). The exponential smoothing forecast was optimized on the first half of each data series and then the errors calculated over the full length of the series. Even though this overstates its accuracy, its performance was not overall greatly different from the naive forecast, and in a number of companies, its error was much worse than naive. This poor performance was possibly due to the effects of seasonality and the short time-span of data used to optimize the model. Because of these difficulties it was decided to use only the naive method for comparison with the company forecast results.

The forecast accuracy was measured using mean absolute percentage error (MAPE) and symmetric mean absolute percentage error (SMAPE) (Makridakis, 1993). The error for each time period was averaged, for each company, over the products to give an average accuracy for a company. These accuracies are reported in the results. Their statistical significance was calculated using paired $t$-tests, where the pairing was over the same product in the same period.

Table 3.5 presents the results for the comparison of the 1-month-ahead forecast accuracies. This table contains the MAPE and SMAPE scores for the naive and the company judgemental forecasts. The SMAPE measure avoids the asymmetry and extreme value problems of the MAPE measure, which are particularly evident when the actual drops suddenly to near zero, driving the MAPE to a very large number: in this regard, note Company 2, where the MAPE of 1087% (caused by some very low actual values) drops to a SMAPE of 71 %. Despite the differences in the measures, the two sets of results are in agreement as to whether the company or naive forecast is more accurate. In addition, the table indicates for which companies the naive forecast accuracy (using

**Table 3.5** One period ahead forecast error—comparison of company and naive forecasts

| Co. No. | MAPE | | Cases | SMAPE | | $t$-Test | Best |
|---|---|---|---|---|---|---|---|
| | Company | Naive | | Company | Naive | | |
| 1 | 22 | 18 | 104 | 17 | 18 | n.s. | |
| 2 | 1087 | 33 | 169 | 71 | 30 | ** | Naive |
| 3 | 31 | 46 | 153 | 19 | 31 | ** | Company |
| 4 | 104 | 172 | 239 | 57 | 77 | ** | Company |
| 5 | 23 | 24 | 294 | 20 | 23 | n.s. | |
| 6 | 71 | 45 | 376 | 36 | 36 | n.s. | |
| 7 | 43 | 51 | 284 | 51 | 32 | ** | Naive |
| 8 | 42 | 58 | 252 | 31 | 48 | ** | Company |
| 9 | 21 | 35 | 95 | 18 | 30 | ** | Company |
| 10 | 76 | 50 | 755 | 31 | 31 | n.s. | |
| 11 | 114 | 84 | 1552 | 37 | 37 | n.s. | |
| 12 | 27 | 23 | 149 | 23 | 23 | n.s | |
| 13 | 28 | 21 | 165 | 23 | 20 | n.s. | |

*Note*: ** Significant $p < 0.001$. n.s. = not significant.

the SMAPE measure in a paired *t*-test) is statistically significantly different from the company forecast accuracy (at the 0.001 level). The Table shows that for four out of the 13 companies, the 1-month-ahead judgemental company forecasts were significantly more accurate than the naive. However, for two companies the naive forecasts were significantly more accurate, and for seven of the comparisons, the difference in accuracy was insignificant. Thus, for only about one-third of the forecast comparisons was judgement significantly more accurate. However, there is no strong evidence that, in general, the companies should abandon judgement and embrace a naive forecast. But it would appear, on balance, that *the company judgemental forecasts were not generally more accurate than naive forecasts even when these forecasts were not seasonally adjusted, and, in addition, incorporated no contextual information.* Had seasonal adjustment of the naive forecast been performed, it would most likely have demonstrated much improved accuracy over the unseasonally adjusted naive forecast.

The results presented above indicate that the output of the sales budgeting process may not be as accurate as might be expected—especially given the past studies of Edmundson, Lawrence & O'Connor (1988) and Sanders & Ritzman (1992). Only for a minority of companies was the final company forecast more accurate than the naive forecast. Despite the fact that a seasonally adjusted naive forecast is known to be relatively accurate, we would have expected that, in view of the considerable company effort spent in the process and the extent of the contextual data gathered and used, that the final company forecast would be considerably more accurate than an *unseasonalized* naive.

Possible reasons for these results centre around two main issues—the use made and value of contextual information, and the use made of the historical information. In other words, it is possible that either the contextual information was of limited usefulness, and/or the use made of the historical information was inefficient and masked the impact of the contextual information.

### 3.4.1  Use of Contextual Information

It is important to consider the emphasis placed on the process of forecasting and budgeting by each of the companies. As the discourse extract presented at the start of the chapter illustrates, in all cases this process involved a monthly meeting of all interested parties. Whilst the characteristics of the meetings varied, in most cases they would last about 2–3 hours. In one case the product managers spent about 1 week in every 4 preparing forecasts full-time! These facts alone suggest that the companies consider it worthwhile to expend financial and temporal resources on the process. Could they be blind to the shortcomings of the process? What might be some of the reasons for the disappointing results of the forecasts that include a rich variety of contextual information?

Some possible reasons can be advanced for the apparent failure of the available contextual information to influence forecast accuracy:

(1) Could the contextual information for half the organizations be of no value for forecasting? If this were true, there would be no point in the companies gathering the data and discussing its likely influence on sales. The companies in the study certainly believe that contextual data is important. New marketing initiatives, promotion plans, actions of competitors, industry developments, manufacturing problems and other forms of contextual information dominated discussion in each of the forecasting meetings we attended. In fact, time-series data received relatively little attention. Furthermore, setting the levels of some of the contextual data parameters (e.g. reducing price or increasing promotion activity) afforded the companies some control of the sales of their products. It thus seems unlikely that contextual information does not play a key role in product level sales forecasting.

(2) Data overload may lead the contextual information to be either ignored or to be given the wrong weighting (e.g. it may be overemphasized). As the case study at the start of the chapter emphasizes, there were often a number of information cues to be processed in the company forecasting meetings. Furthermore, there were often a number of different interpretations of a single cue aired at the meeting, e.g. where different views were expressed as to the usefulness or expectations from upcoming advertising programs. Thus, there may be some truth in this explanation of the failure of the importance of the contextual information. We are, however, unable to determine whether this was a reasonable proposition, since our study was not designed to investigate such an issue.

(3) Recent random movements in the time series may be being misunderstood as signals, and so be confounding the interpretation and incorporation of contextual information. There is considerable

support for this proposition from past literature. Lawrence & O'Connor (1992), in modelling judgemental forecasting from time-series data alone, determined that people anchored on the last actual value in making their new forecast. Similarly, O'Connor, Remus & Griggs (1993) found that, in a dynamic feedback environment, people over-reacted to the feedback of the last actual value. Furthermore, Lawrence & O'Connor (1995) showed that people often over-adjust to the last actual value in setting their new forecasts. These studies, combined with those of cognitive psychology (Hogarth, 1987), suggest that people under-appreciated the influence of noise in the time-series forecasting process. Thus, it is possible that the task of incorporating new contextual information into the final forecast is upset by the tendency to over-inflate the influence of the past contextual information on the time series, and thus to over-react to the last actual value (the last month's actual).

### 3.4.2 Use of Past Historical Information

In another forecast task environment, a number of studies have analysed analysts' forecasts of quarterly and annual company earnings and found evidence that the forecasts did not utilize available (past) information efficiently (Ali, Klein & Rosenfeld, 1992; Mendenhall, 1991; Abarbanell & Bernard, 1992). Specifically, they found evidence of bias and serial correlation in forecast errors. The question arises as to whether inefficiency and bias characterizes monthly company sales forecasts, and whether they might be a cause of the poor accuracy of the final company forecasts. To investigate the issue of the efficiency and bias of the company forecasts, the forecast and the past error were regressed against the error of the current period. If the forecasts are efficient, we expected that there will be no serial correlation in the errors from period to period, i.e. that the regression coefficient for past error will be zero. In other words, people learn to accommodate the lessons from the past error in setting their new forecast. If there is no bias in the forecasts, we expect that the regression coefficient for the forecast will be zero, i.e. there is no relationship between the error and the forecast.

Results of this regression show that for the two companies where the naive forecasts were better than the company forecasts, the company forecasts displayed highly significant bias and highly significant inefficiency in the forecasts. For the seven cases where there was no difference in accuracy, five of them displayed highly significant bias and inefficiency. And for the four cases where the company forecasts excelled, three exhibited bias and one inefficiency. The Lawrence, O'Connor & Edmundson (1997) study also shows that if the bias and inefficiency of the forecasts was removed, the restated forecasts would be now more accurate than the naive forecasts. This suggests a significant contribution of contextual information after all. That is, the findings presented in Table 3.5 detailing the disappointing accuracy of the (context-laden) company forecasts can be explained in terms of the strong influence of bias and inefficiency that masks any contribution of the additional information.

## 3.5  CONCLUSIONS

This chapter has emphasized the role of contextual (i.e. non-time-series) information in the process of forecasting. Past studies have demonstrated that contextual information is of vital importance to forecast accuracy. The comprehensive field survey reviewed in this chapter has also confirmed the importance of contextual information, but has suggested that this may be masked by inefficient use of the past information and bias in the forecasts, whether deliberate or not. Given the importance of the contextual information, the first section reviews some empirical laboratory studies which suggested that the contextual information may be beneficial for the forecasting process, but it seems to be used quite inefficiently. People do not seem to be able to "milk" as much content out of the information as possible.

Further research should focus on the way in which people are able to use the correlational (causal) information together with the soft information. It should also focus on how good people are at making correct assessments of the soft information.

## NOTES

(1)  For the control condition (judgemental extrapolation), people merely made an initial forecast and then were given the opportunity to revise it.

(2)  The regression equation was different for each condition, but for the mixed adjustment group it was: $forecast_{revised} = \alpha + \beta^* forecast_{initial} + \gamma^* forecast_{statistical} + \delta^*$ causal information.

(3)  Thus, for this case, the regression model would be: $forecast = \alpha + \beta^*$ cue $1 + \gamma^*$ cue 2.

# REFERENCES

Abarbanell, J.S. & Bernard, V.L. (1992)  Tests of analysts' overreaction/underreaction to earnings information as an explanation for anomalous stock price behaviour. *Journal of Finance*, **47**, 1181–207.

Adelman, L. (1981)  The influence of formal, substantive, and contextual task properties on the relative effectiveness of different forms of feedback in multiple cue probability learning tasks. *Organizational Behavior and Human Decision Processes*, **27**, 423–42.

Ali, A., Klein, A. & Rosenfeld, J. (1992)  Analysts' use of information about permanent and transitory components in forecasting annual EPS. *The Accounting Review*, **67**, 183–98.

Andreassen, P.B. (1991)  Causal prediction versus extrapolation: effects of information source on judgmental forecasting accuracy (unpublished).

Armstrong, J.S. (1983)  Relative accuracy of judgemental and extrapolative methods in forecasting annual earnings. *Journal of Forecasting*, **2**, 437–47.

Ashton, R. (1981)  A descriptive study of information evaluation. *Journal of Accounting Research,* **19**(1), 42–61.

Brehmer, B. (1976)  Subject's ability to find the parameters of functional roles in probabilistic inference tasks. *Organizational Behavior and Human Decision Processes*, **17**, 388–97.

Brehmer, B. & Kuylenstierna, J. (1980)  Content and consistency in probabilistic inference tasks. *Organizational Behavior and Human Decision Processes*, **26**, 54–64.

Brown, L.D., Hagerman, P.A., Griffin, P.A. & Zmijewski, M.E. (1987)  Security analyst superiority relative to univariate time series models in forecasting quarterly earnings. *Journal of Accounting and Economics*, **9**, 61–87.

Carbone, R. & Makridakis, S. (1986)  Forecasting when pattern changes occur beyond the historical data. *Management Science*, **32**, 257–71.

Casey, C. & Selling, T. (1986)  The effect of task predictability and prior probability disclosure on judgement quality and confidence. *The Accounting Review*, **61**(2), 302–17.

Chapman, L.J. & Chapman, J.P. (1969)  Illusory correlation as an obstacle to the use of valid psychodiagnostic signs. *Journal of Abnormal Psychology*, **74**(3), 271–80.

Collopy, F. & Armstrong, J.S. (1992) Expert opinions about extrapolations and the mystery of the overlooked discontinuities. *International Journal of Forecasting*, **8**, 575–82.

Connolly, T. & Gilani, N. (1982) Information search in judgement tasks: a regression model and some preliminary findings. *Organizational Behavior and Human Decision Processes*, **30**, 330–50.

Connolly, T. & Serre, P. (1984) Information search in judgement tasks: the effects of unequal cue validity and cost. *Organizational Behavior and Human Decision Processes*, **34**, 387–401.

Edmundson, R.H., Lawrence, M.J. & O'Connor, M.J. (1988) The use of non time series information in sales forecasting: a case study. *Journal of Forecasting*, **7**, 201–11.

Einhorn, H. & Hogarth, R. (1982) Prediction, diagnosis and causal thinking in forecasting. *Journal of Forecasting*, **1**, 23–36.

Gorr, W.L. (1986) Special event data in shared databases. *MIS Quarterly*, **10**, September, 239–55.

Handzic, M. (1997) *The Utilization of Contextual Information in a Judgemental Decision Making Task*. Unpublished PhD thesis, University of New South Wales.

Harvey, N., Bolger, F. & McClelland, A. (1994) On the nature of expectations. *British Journal of Psychology*, **85**(2), 203–29.

Hogarth, R. (1987) *Judgement and Choice*, 2nd edn. Wiley, New York.

Hopwood, W.S. & McKeown, J.C. (1980) Evidence on surrogates for earnings expectations within a capital market context. *Journal of Accounting, Auditing and Finance*, **5**, 339–68.

Johnson, E. (1988) Expertise and decision under uncertainty: performance and process. In M.R. Glaser & M. Farr (eds), *The Nature of Expertise*, Erlbaum, Hillsdale, NY.

Kahneman, D. & Tversky, A. (1979) Prospect theory: an analysis of decisions under risk. *Econometrica*, **47**, 263–91.

Kleinmuntz, D. (1990) Why we still use our heads instead of formulas: toward an integrative approach. *Psychological Bulletin*, **107**(3), 296–310.

Koele, P. (1980) The influence of labelled stimuli on nonlinear multiple cue probability learning. *Organizational Behavior and Human Decision Processes*, **26**, 22–31.

Kurke, L. & Aldrich, H. (1983) Mintzberg was right! A replication and extension of The Nature of Managerial Work. *Management Science*, **32**(6), 683–95.

Lawrence, M.J., Edmundson, R.H. & O'Connor, M.J. (1985) An examination of the accuracy of judgemental extrapolation of time-series. *International Journal of Forecasting*, **1**, 25–35.

Lawrence, M.J. & O'Connor, M.J. (1992) Exploring judgemental forecasting. *International Journal of Forecasting*, **8**, 15–26.

Lawrence, M.J., & O'Connor, M.J. (1995) The anchoring and adjustment heuristic in time series forecasting. *Journal of Forecasting*, **14**, 443–51.

Lawrence, M.J., O'Connor, M.J. & Edmundson, R.H. (1997) A field of sales forecasting accuracy. Unpublished working paper, University of New South Wales.

Levine, J., Samet, M. & Brahlek, R. (1975) Information seeking with limitations on available information and resources. *Human Factors*, **17**(5), 502–13.

Lim, J.S. & O'Connor, M.J. (1996) Judgmental forecasting with causal and time series information. *International Journal of Forecasting*, **12**, 139–53.

Makridakis, S. (1993) Accuracy measures: theoretical and practical concerns. *International Journal of Forecasting*, **9**, 437–529.

Makridakis, S., Anderson, A., Carbone, R., Fildes, R., Hibon, M., Lewandowski, R., Newton, J., Parzen, E. & Winkler, R. (1982) The accuracy of extrapolation, time series, methods: results of a forecasting competition. *Journal of Forecasting*, **1**, 1–153.

Mathews, B.P. & Diamantopoulos, A. (1996) Judgemental revision of sales forecasts: a longitudinal extension. *Journal of Forecasting*, **8**, 129–40.

Mathews, B.P. & Diamantopolous, A. (1992) Judgemental revision of sales forecasts: the relative performance of judgementally revised versus non-revised forecasts. *Journal of Forecasting*, **11**, 569–76.

Matthews, B.P. & Diamantopolous, A. (1990) Judgemental revision of sales forecasts: effectiveness of forecast selection. *Journal of Forecasting*, **9**, 407–15.

Matthews, B.P. & Diamantopolous, A. (1989) Judgemental revision of sales forecasts: a longitudinal extension. *Journal of Forecasting*, **8**, 129–40.

Mendenhall, R.R. (1991) Evidence on the possible underweighting of earnings-related information. *Journal of Accounting Research*, **29**, 170–79.

Miller, P.M. (1971) Do labels mislead? A multiple cue study within the framework of Brunswik's probabilistic functionalism. *Organizational Behavior and Human Decision Processes*, **6**, 480–500.

Mintzberg, H. (1973) *The Nature of Managerial Work*. Harper & Row, New York.

O'Connor, M.J., Remus, W. & Griggs, K. (1997) Going up—going down: how good are people at forecasting trends and changes in trends? *Journal of Forecasting*, **16**, 165–76.

O'Connor, M.J., Remus, W. & Griggs, K. (1993) Judgemental forecasting in times of change. *International Journal of Forecasting*, **9**, 163–72.

Payne, J. (1982) Contingent decision behaviour. *Psychological Bulletin*, **92**, 382–402.

Sanders, N. & Ritzman, L. (1992) The need for contextual and technical knowledge in judgemental forecasting. *Journal of Behavioral Decision Making*, **5**, 39–52.

Schnaars, S.P. & Mohr, I. (1988)  The accuracy of *Business Week*'s industry outlook survey. *Interfaces*, **18**(5), 31–8.

Schustak, M.W. & Sternberg, R.J. (1981)  Evaluation of evidence in causal inference. *Journal of Experimental Psychology: General*, **110**(1), 101–20.

Snapper, K. & Peterson, C. (1971)  Information seeking and data diagnosticity. *Journal of Experimental Psychology*, **87**, 429–33.

Sneizek, J. (1986)  The role of variable labels in cue probability learning tasks. *Organizational Behavior and Human Decision Processes*, **38**, 141–61.

Webby, R. (1994).  Graphical Support for the Integration of Event Information into Time Series Forecasting: An Empirical Investigation. Unpublished PhD dissertation, University of New South Wales.

Webby, R. & O'Connor, M.J. (1996)  Judgmental versus statistical time series forecasting: a review of the literature. *International Journal of Forecasting*, **12**, 91–118.

Willemain, T. (1989)  Graphical adjustments of statistical forecasts. *International Journal of Forecasting*, **5**, 179–85.

# Chapter 4

# Enhancing Judgemental Sales Forecasting: The Role of Laboratory Research

Paul Goodwin
*University of the West of England, Bristol, UK*

## SUMMARY

There is evidence that judgement is widely used in sales forecasting. However, the task of producing judgemental sales forecasts can have a great variety of characteristics, with some tasks being inappropriately categorized as forecasting. Given that the application of judgement is often highly contingent on the nature of the task and its environment, how can research provide support for this variety of tasks? Assuming that the objective of researchers is to identify conditions which are most favourable to judgemental sales forecasting accuracy, this chapter contrasts the field and the psychological laboratory as environments for identifying these conditions. It suggests that, in sales forecasting, the commonly perceived contrast between the expert, highly motivated real world forecaster and the inexpert, poorly motivated laboratory subject may be untrue and that the laboratory has much to offer in providing support for, and enhancing, real-world forecasting.

*Forecasting with Judgment.* Edited by G. Wright and P. Goodwin.
© 1998 John Wiley & Sons Ltd.

## 4.1 INTRODUCTION

Recent reviews of the literature show that there has been a growing interest in judgemental forecasting by researchers over the last decade (Bunn & Wright, 1991; Goodwin & Wright, 1993; Webby & O'Connor, 1996). The main motivation for this interest appears to be the widespread use of human judgement in forecasts made by businesses and other organizations, particularly in sales forecasting (Dalrymple, 1987; Sanders & Manrodt, 1994). Research has therefore been directed to answering questions such as: how accurate are judgemental forecasts compared to statistical ones (e.g. Lawrence, 1983; Carbone & Gorr, 1985); what cognitive processes do people use when making judgemental forecasts (e.g. Andreassen & Kraus, 1990); what biases emanate from these cognitive processes (e.g. Lawrence & Makridakis, 1989; O'Connor, Remus & Griggs, 1993); and how can the accuracy of judgemental forecasts be improved (e.g. Edmundson, 1990)?

Given the assumption that the ultimate objective of researchers is to provide support for judgemental forecasting in practice, this chapter addresses some of the difficulties involved in providing that support in sales forecasting. The main problems appear to be the variety of tasks that, rightly or wrongly, are referred to as judgemental forecasting, the even greater variety of characteristics that each of these tasks can manifest and the sensitivity of judgemental forecasters to even minor changes in task and context. We start with a consideration of the forms that judgemental sales forecasting can take and then identify some tasks which are often inappropriately referred to as judgemental forecasting. Then we consider how researchers can provide support for sales forecasters by contrasting the roles of field and laboratory studies.

## 4.2 WHAT IS JUDGEMENTAL FORECASTING?

We first attempt some definitions of the forms that judgemental forecasts can take:

- *Forecast.* A forecast is the set of probabilities attached to a set of future events (Fischhoff, 1994). These events may be represented by nominal data (e.g. winners of a horse race), ordinal data (e.g. Beaufort wind forces), interval scale data (e.g. temperatures on a Celsius scale) or ratio scale data (e.g. next month's sales).

- *Distribution forecast.* Where the probabilities of the events are represented by a probability distribution, this will be referred to as a distribution forecast. In judgemental forecasting this will, of course, be a subjective probability distribution. For the purposes of this chapter it will also be assumed that such a forecast is an honest representation of the forecaster's beliefs about the future. In some instances the distribution forecast may be approximated by specifying probabilities for a small number of values. For example, triangular distributions are derived from estimates of minimum, most likely and maximum values, while in the PERT project management technique a beta distribution of an activity's duration is obtained from optimistic, pessimistic and most likely values. Alternatively, in some Bayesian forecasting methods a normal distribution is assumed, with a mean and standard deviation specified by the judgemental forecaster (Pole, West & Harrison, 1994).

- *Prediction interval.* This is an interval which has a stated probability of including the actual value. For example, we may estimate that there is a 95% probability that next month's sales will be between 2000 and 4000 units. (In statistical forecasting some writers distinguish prediction intervals from *confidence intervals*. They use the latter term to refer to an interval which has a stated probability of including the *expected value* of the probability distribution, rather than an individual actual value.)

- *Point forecast.* This is a measure of central tendency taken from the distribution forecast. If a parametric statistical method is used to derive the point forecast it will be the mean (or expected value) of the distribution. If the point forecast is estimated judgementally, without assessing the probability distribution, it may be unclear whether it represents the forecaster's estimate of the most likely value (the mode), the expected value, or the value which has a 50% probability of being exceeded (the median). It seems that most sales forecasts in practice are expressed as point forecasts. For example, in Dalrymple's (1987) survey, 77% of respondents either did not provide prediction intervals or did so only occasionally.

The task of producing forecasts in each of these different forms can have a wide variety of characteristics.

- *Who is making the forecasts?* Forecasts can be made by an individual or a group. Individual forecasters will vary in the extent to which they are familiar with the task of forecasting, the extent to which they are technically trained to perform this task (Sanders & Ritzman, 1992) and in the expertise they have relating to the variable to be forecast. The process by which a group of people arrive at a forecast may involve either mathematical or behavioural aggregation (Goodwin & Wright, 1997). Behavioural aggregation, itself, may be unstructured or structured using one of a variety of techniques, such as Delphi (see e.g. Rowe & Wright, 1996), Best Member (Sniezek, 1989) and Modified Consensus (Ang & O'Connor, 1991).

- *What information is available to the forecaster?* Forecasters may have access to time series information on the forecast variable, contextual information (e.g. information that a competitor is about to launch a promotion campaign) and the forecasts of a statistical method. For example, in forecasting the sales of a new product, only contextual information might be available, while other tasks may simply involve judgementally extrapolating the time series pattern. In some tasks forecasters may also receive feedback on the last actual value (outcome feedback), on their own performance or even on their strategy for making their forecasts (process feedback).

- *How is the information presented?* Details of the past time series and any variable related to it may be presented in the form of either tables or graphs or both (Harvey & Bolger, 1996). Presentation may be restricted to the last few values of the variable(s) or it may consist of the entire series history to date. Sometimes modifications of the original variable, such as first differences (Andreassen, 1990), are presented.

- *What are the characteristics of the time series for the forecast variable?* The time series of the forecast variable can usually be conceived as consisting of a combination of an underlying signal and noise. Underlying signals may vary in terms of their complexity (e.g. the signal may simply be a constant or it may involve both a trend and seasonal pattern) and stability, while, of course, the level of noise around the signal can vary both within and between different series.

- *What are the forecasters asked to do?* Forecasters may be asked to use judgement to produce an entire forecast, taking into account whatever information is available. Alternatively, the task may be decomposed into separate elements so that judgement is applied to these elements rather than the entire task (Edmundson, 1990; Wolfe

& Flores, 1990). Where a statistical forecast is provided, the task may consist of making judgemental adjustments to this forecast (e.g. Mathews & Diamantopoulos, 1990) or adjusting the components of the statistical forecasting model (Bunn, 1992). Both the lead time of the forecast and the time interval between making forecasts will vary between tasks. In some organizations, existing forecasts for a particular time period are revised as the period approaches. Forecasters may also be asked to submit their forecasts either using pencil and paper or by interacting with a computer system[1].

## 4.3  WHAT JUDGEMENTAL FORECASTING IS NOT

Consider the graph in Figure 4.1. This shows judgemental "forecasts" of the number of new UK customers recruited by an Internet service provider over a period of 26 weeks in 1994 (the data has been coded for

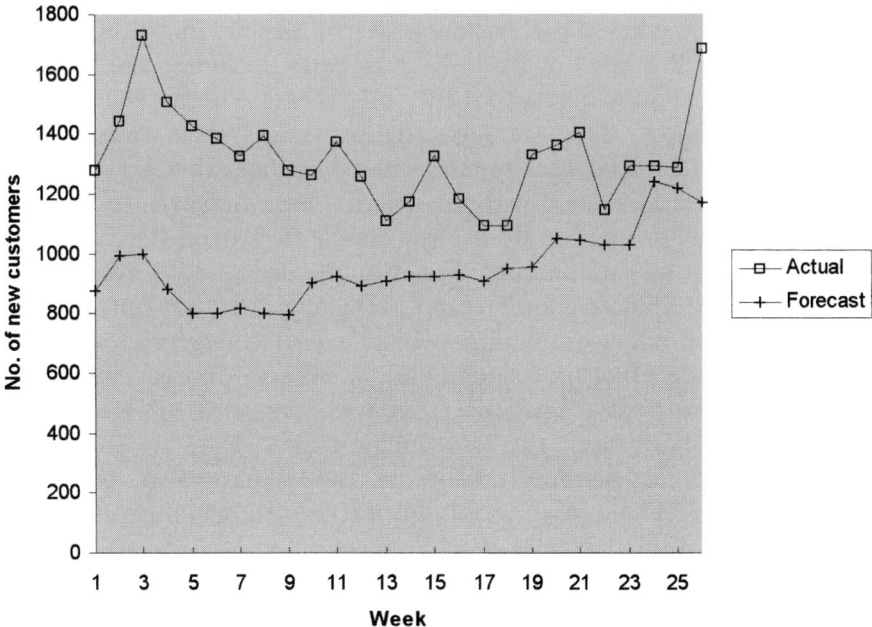

**Figure 4.1**  Forecasts and actuals for Internet service provider

confidentiality). The actual number of customers who were recruited each week is also shown. Clearly, the accuracy of the forecasts is extremely poor, simply fitting a ruler through the "actual number of customers" graph and extrapolating would lead to improved forecasts. One is tempted to speculate that this is an extreme example of flawed judgements; of judgemental forecasters using simplifying heuristics and, as a result, grossly underestimating customer recruitment. The reality is different. When questioned, the manager who supplied the data explained that the "forecasts" were produced by the marketing department, who earned political capital if the number of customers they recruited exceeded the "forecasts". He admitted that this had created much tension with the operations personnel who had been using the "forecasts" to plan workloads. Nevertheless, the tendency to "forecast low" had persisted (although the graph shows that the degree of underestimation gets less as time progresses).

The truth is that these so called "forecasts" were really *decisions*. They were values *chosen* by the marketing department with the aim of maximizing (or at least advancing) their political standing, presumably subject to the constraint that the "forecasts" had to maintain some semblance of credibility. This blurred notion of what constitutes a forecast may be common in businesses and other organizations. In an admittedly small sample of five UK companies (including the Internet provider) who allowed access to their "judgemental forecasts" as part of a research project, three were overtly presenting their decisions as forecasts. Confusion between forecasts and decisions can arise whenever the loss function associated with the decision is asymmetric, so that the "cost" of under-estimating by a given unit differs from the "cost" of over-estimating by that amount. For example, the sales "forecasts" of an industrial equipment manufacturer in the research study reflected the greater cost of under-estimating (which led to emergency over-time working and loss of customer goodwill), as opposed to over-estimating (which led to excessive inventory that was soon cleared) (Goodwin, 1996). As we have seen, the loss function may relate to qualitative attributes such as political advantage and it may also be multi-attributed: e.g. we may wish to minimize costs *and* maximize customer goodwill.

Normative methods for making decisions under uncertainty usually involve the separation of forecasting from the evaluation of possible outcomes (cf. Goodwin & Wright, 1997). For example, probabilities of particular levels of demand for a product will be assessed separately from the evaluation of the costs, both qualitative and quantitative, of failing to meet this demand. Indeed, because forecasting is only part of the task of decision making, then decision making is likely to be the more difficult task. This implies that people who, for example, simply look at the past time series pattern and derive a decision directly from it are likely to produce poorer decisions than those that would be suggested by a normative decision model (Goodwin, 1996, provides some evidence for this).

Even if asymmetric loss functions do not apply, as we shall see, other types of judgement are also put forward as, or confused with, forecasts (Fildes & Hastings, 1994). These include *targets* and *plans*. A target is either a value which we hope to achieve or what we say we hope to achieve in order to motivate appropriate personnel. A target may also be used as a standard with which future performance can be compared. "Planning is the process of setting goals and developing ways to achieve them" (Dominiak & Louderback, 1991). Thus, we may plan to have sales of 5000 units per month in 3 years' time and gear our production, marketing and distribution activities towards achieving this goal. This is clearly not the same as a forecast of 5000 units.

## 4.4 IMPLICATIONS FOR FORECASTING SUPPORT

Given the variety of tasks that constitute judgemental forecasting and the fact that several other tasks are often misrepresented as judgemental forecasts, how should researchers go about providing support for practical forecasters in the field? It is assumed that the ultimate objective of such support is congruous with Winkler & Murphy's (1973) statement that:

> The ultimate *practical* question with regard to studies of human behaviour in inferential and decision making situations is this. How does a highly motivated, experienced individual in an operational setting in his area of expertise, given appropriate feedback regarding past predictions and decisions, perform inferential and decision-making tasks, and can his performance be improved upon in any manner?

It may be useful to examine the role of forecasting support from the point of view of a consultant, called in to advise an organization on its sales forecasting, and facing questions such as: "Should we use judgement or a statistical model to forecast sales?", "What biases are likely to be associated with the use of judgement?", "Is it worth adopting strategies such as decomposition, graphical display and feedback provision?"

The first thing the consultant would need to establish is that the forecasts really are forecasts. If not, then the consultant may be able to advise on the forecasting component of the task and how it relates to the wider task. If the organization does require "genuine" forecasts, then an assessment would need to be made of the nature of the forecasting task and its environment, possibly using the characteristics outlined earlier. For example, who are the forecasters, how expert are they, what information is available to them, what exactly are they being asked to do, and so on? The consultant might then try to match these characteristics with those of research studies and use these as the basis for any advice given. For example, he might advise against the use of judgement for series exhibiting growth, since several research studies have suggested that judgemental forecasters tend to underestimate upward trends (e.g. Lawrence & Makridakis, 1989; Wagenaar & Sagaria, 1975). But how reliable is the consultant's advice likely to be?

One of the key concerns of researchers has been elaborated by Payne (1982) who has argued, albeit in the context of decision making:

> The finding that decision behaviour is sensitive to seemingly minor changes in task and context is one of the major results of years of decision research.

It seems that the consultant's matching of the client's problem to that explored in research studies might need to be very close indeed before any reliable advice can be given. Indeed, in their contingency model of judgemental forecasting, Beach, Barnes & Christensen-Szalanski (1986) have attempted to identify the key characteristics of a forecasting task that will determine how the task will be approached. These are given below:

(1) *The forecaster's knowledge of possible strategies for tackling the problem.* Beach, Barnes & Christensen-Szalanski identify two main types of strategy. *Aleatory strategies* characterize elements by their class membership, rather than their unique properties (e.g. given that you are member of a particular profession, you will have a 70% probability of living to an age of 80 or more). In contrast, *epistemic strategies* use information about the unique characteristics of the element in question (e.g. an estimate of the probability

of you seeing your 80th birthday will be based on your individual lifestyle, diet, medical history, heredity and so on).

(2) *The forecaster's selection of a strategy from his/her strategy repertory.* Beach, Barnes & Christensen-Szalanski provide evidence that different tasks, and different interpretations of tasks, evoke different strategies.

(3) *The forecaster's motivation for accuracy.* This, in turn, will depend upon the perceived benefits of accuracy, the extent to which a forecast, having been made, can be revised, whether the task is perceived to be within the forecaster's area of competence (if it is, one's reputation as an expert might suffer if the forecast is inaccurate), and the quality of information provided (incomplete, unreliable or incomprehensible information will tend to demotivate).

Beach, Barnes & Christensen-Szalanski (1986) go on to criticize much of the research literature in judgemental forecasting:

> ... consider that most experimental studies of judgemental forecasting are done with undergraduates who have little appreciation of the study's scientific or applied ramifications (benefits), who do not regard themselves as expert in the task (competence) and who are presented with problems divorced from the meaningful framework that usually accompanies whatever forecasting task they encounter (information).

All of this casts doubt on the generalizability, and hence the practical value, of much laboratory work. Indeed, it might suggest that researchers should place a greater emphasis on field research, rather than the laboratory. However, as we argue below, in judgemental sales forecasting the field may, in some circumstances, be a far from ideal environment for research and carefully designed laboratory studies can have a pivotal role in supporting real-world forecasting.

## 4.5 WHERE FIELD STUDIES CAN BE PROBLEMATICAL

The above arguments imply that there is a dichotomy between a real world and the laboratory. In the former, well-motivated experts regularly make forecasts, having had access to reliable information and feedback on past performance. In the latter, poorly motivated and inexperienced individuals with access to poor quality information make forecasts for which they have no expertise. However, while the above portrait of the expert forecaster may be true of areas like weather forecasting, there is evidence that the dichotomy may not apply to sales forecasting as practised in many businesses.

Studies of sales forecasting by Rothe (1978), Fildes & Hastings (1994) and Watson (1996) paint a picture of real-world forecasting which is very different from that alluded to above. While providing further evidence of the predominant use of judgement in forecasting, these studies suggest that sales forecasting is:

(1)  Rarely treated as a specialized professional function.
(2)  Often only a small part of the duties of the person making the forecasts (taking up an average of only 8.9% of this person's time in one of the studies).
(3)  Often carried out by people with minimal training in forecasting.
(4)  Rarely monitored for accuracy (poor record keeping was a feature of both recent studies).
(5)  Often done with no use of computers for forecasting or data storage and retrieval (45% of respondents in one of the studies made no use of computers).
(6)  Often undertaken by people on the periphery of organizations.
(7)  Often based on a paucity of information. In the Fildes & Hastings study, forecasters expressed a high level of dissatisfaction with information that was currently available to them (particularly lack of market research data), leading to a perceived over-reliance on sales history data alone.

The overall impression gained from these studies and others (e.g. Sanders & Manrodt, 1994) is one of demotivated and under-trained forecasters undertaking a task which is seen to have a low priority by colleagues and senior managers. This is reflected in poor information provision to forecasters and lack of feedback on past forecasting performance. Indeed, the heavy reliance on judgemental as opposed to statistical forecasting methods in most organizations is seen by the authors of the above studies as a symptom of the low status of forecasting.

Of course, there are other major problems with field studies. These include the lack of control that the researcher has over the conditions under which the forecasts are made and incomplete knowledge about these conditions. Control of the forecasting task and its environment enables researchers to isolate the effect of individual conditions and to test the efficacy of particular improvement strategies. When the cost of inaccurate forecasts is high, organizations are unlikely to be willing to provide facilities for the experimentation that researchers require. Anyway, most organizations operate in a dynamic environment and it will usually be impossible to replicate exactly any particular set of conditions or to control the order in which forecasters consider their information sources (Winkler & Murphy, 1973).

Worse still, the researcher may be unaware of the true nature and origin of a series of data presented as judgemental forecasts. We saw earlier that forecasting can be bound up with organizational politics. Because of this, loss functions may not be made explicit and the researcher may unwittingly be analysing targets or decisions rather than forecasts. Reports of biases in judgemental forecasts from field studies (e.g. Mathews & Diamantopoulos, 1986) should therefore be treated with caution. It is easy to show how a perfectly unbiased decision maker can appear to be a biased judgemental forecaster when methods like Theil's decomposition of the forecasts' mean squared error (Theil, 1971) and the Brunswik lens model (Brunswik, 1952) are used to identify biases. These problems of incomplete knowledge of the origin of the data supplied can be exacerbated when the personnel producing the forecasts are unknown or have changed, or where an intermediary has modified the forecasts.

Field studies can also suffer from short time series, particularly in industries like electronics, where technological developments mean short product life-cycles (Watson, 1996). This may lead to only small samples of forecasts being examined, which is worrying if the data contains high levels of noise. Moreover, because no normative model (e.g. knowledge of the true value of the time series signal) is likely to be available, the evaluation of the quality of forecasts will have to be based on outcomes and hence will be contaminated by noise.

Lastly, the specific nature of a given organization or industry may mean that reliable inferences about judgemental forecasting in general cannot be drawn from a particular study. The fact that field studies are often based on a single organization, or the few organizations that the researcher has managed to gain access to, also limit the extent to which one can be confident about drawing general conclusions from the results.

Set against these problems, the advantages of the laboratory are clear. Conditions can be carefully controlled and manipulated to allow hypotheses to be tested. For example, the use of artificial time series can allow the experimenter to assess the ability of judgemental forecasters to identify and extrapolate a known signal from a noisy series. This provides a more precise assessment of the quality of forecasts than comparisons of forecasts with outcomes. Moreover, the people producing the forecasts are known and the process by which they arrived at their forecasts can be carefully monitored. Perhaps most surprising, given the recent evidence of Fildes & Hastings (1994) and Watson (1996), the technical knowledge and motivation of subjects in many laboratory studies may actually exceed that of real forecasters in the field. Researchers using laboratory studies frequently report the high level of motivation found amongst their subjects (e.g. Lim & O'Connor, 1996) and in many studies the subjects have, unlike many real world forecasters, recently completed a formal course in forecasting methods.

Of course, we are not arguing that field studies have no role to play in judgemental forecasting research. On the contrary, their role is crucial in identifying the nature of practical forecasting tasks, how they are carried out and the effects of the environment they are carried out within. Indeed, in some circumstances it may be possible to overcome the problems we have discussed above. The intention is merely to highlight the potential problems of field work and to show the valuable role that laboratory studies can play in the light of these problems.

## 4.6 WHERE LABORATORY STUDIES ARE PROBLEMATICAL

Given that the intention of laboratory studies is to provide reliable support for judgemental forecasting in practical situations, one of the main concerns, when assessing the results of a given study, is the extent to which the results are contingent on the specific character and conditions of the experiment. If the experimental results would have differed if there had been minor changes to the framing of questions, the computer screen display or the emphasis of the experimenter's voice when issuing oral instructions, then the ability to generalize the result to practical situations is likely to be limited, to say the least. Even the seemingly innocent act of labelling a graph with a title like "Sales" to make a task "more realistic" may have a profound effect, because experimental subjects then develop expectations about the nature of the series (e.g. that growth in sales tends to be damped) (Goodwin & Wright, 1993; Sniezek, 1986).

Indeed, expectations drawn from experience of the complications of the real world may cause people to bring strategies which are inappropriate for the simpler experimental task and lead to a mismatch in the understanding of the nature of the task between the subject and experimenter. For example, Winkler & Murphy (1973) have examined the literature which suggests that people tend to be too conservative in revising prior probabilities when they receive new information. They suggest that the conservatism reported in laboratory experiments may result from subjects bringing to experiments their experiences of a changing real-world where successive items of information are often redundant. These experiences would not be relevant to experiments where the problem remained constant and the successive items of information provided were highly diagnostic.

Nevertheless, there is nothing inherent in a laboratory environment that means that many of Beach et al.'s concerns cannot be overcome. Indeed, it is an environment which may allow the study of judgemental forecasting in conditions closer to the ideal than the demotivating environment described by Fildes & Hastings (1994) and Watson (1996). Real forecasters can be recruited to produce forecasts of variables for which their expertise is relevant (e.g. Wilkie, Onkal & Pollack, 1996). Tasks can be clearly explained and clarity tested through piloting of studies. Motivation can be simulated, at least partly, by providing prizes for accurate forecasts (e.g. Lim & O'Connor, 1996; Goodwin, 1997). If appropriate, other features of real-world forecasting can also be built into laboratory studies. For example, the forecaster can be given some control over the variable to be forecast (Brown, 1988; Einhorn & Hogarth, 1982). Similarly, the time interval between successive forecasts can be weeks or months, rather than a few seconds, as in most laboratory studies. Laboratory studies are also often criticized for giving subjects pre-structured problems to solve. For example, the choice of forecasting method and the information to be used have already been chosen by the experimenter. Again, there is no reason why this problem-structuring phase of forecasting (see Chapter 5) cannot be explored in the laboratory.

What is most difficult to simulate is the organizational environment. Information available to the forecaster may be both hard and soft, available only sporadically (Lim & O'Connor, 1996; Goodwin & Fildes, 1997) and have varying degrees of reliability. In some contexts the real rewards and costs of forecast accuracy may also be far greater, and of a different character, than a monetary prize offered in a laboratory experiment. For example, the fact that a laboratory forecast will not actually be used in a real-world decision may reduce motivation (Murphy & Brown, 1985). In many organizations the forecasting environment may be highly political (64% of respondents agreed with the statement that "forecasts were frequently politically modified" in the Fildes & Hastings, 1994, study). However, it is debatable whether these political aspects should fall within the direct brief of the judgemental forecasting researcher since, as we indicated earlier, such modifications would transform the forecast into a decision.

## 4.7 DRAWING PRACTICAL INFERENCES FROM LABORATORY STUDIES

We next consider the process which our consultant would need to go through to be able to provide reliable practical advice from results obtained in a laboratory study. There will almost certainly be individual differences between subjects in the study, but these will usually be summarized by the mean or median when the results are reported. Ideally, the experimenter will have designed the study, so that the either the robustness of the result over a range of experimental conditions or the dependency of the result on particular conditions can be ascertained. Studies which try to draw unconditional conclusions from a very limited range of experimental treatments should be treated with caution. For example, some early studies reached conclusions such as "statistical forecasts are more accurate than judgemental forecasts", or the converse when the experimental conditions were highly specific (anyway, common sense would suggest that some conditions will favour judgemental forecasting and others statistical). The experimental conclusions will then need to survive the transition from the laboratory to the real-world problem. For example, the consultant will need to assume that the conclusion that people tend to under-estimate growth is not a tendency which is restricted to the peculiar conditions of the laboratory.

The probability of an exact match between the real-world problem and a given laboratory study is low. To be useful the experimental result will therefore need to apply to a separable part of the problem. If there is any interaction between the part of the task to which the experimental result applies and aspects which were beyond the experimental study, then the result will not be useful. For example, the consultant would need to assume that people tend to under-estimate growth irrespective of the fact that in the real task contextual information will also be available, and the forecaster has a high level of technical expertise and knowledge about the forecast variable. Even then, the prediction of a given forecaster's behaviour will not be exact. There are bound to be individual differences between real forecasters and other unknown factors that will determine their behaviour.

All of this suggests that useful results need to be robust and separable. They need to be robust enough to survive the transfer from the laboratory to the real world and applicable over a set of circumstances that can be taken to be independent of other aspects of the real problem.

## 4.8 IMPLICATIONS FOR RESEARCH

The studies by Rothe (1978), Fildes & Hastings (1994) and Watson (1996) suggest that improving judgemental sales forecasting in practice may have as much to do with organizational changes as with the development of judgement-aiding techniques. In lieu of these changes, the laboratory may offer the best environment for testing the efficacy of judgement-aiding techniques under conditions that most approximate those identified by Winkler & Murphy (1973). Recall that these are:

(1) Forecasters with high motivation.
(2) Forecasters with experience of the task of forecasting.
(3) Forecasters with expertise relating to the variable to be forecast.
(4) Forecasters in their operational setting.
(5) Forecasters receiving appropriate feedback.

First, we need to know more about the consequences for particular tasks of failing to achieve these ideals in the laboratory. For example, there is evidence that, beyond a minimal level, expertise does not bring greater accuracy in judgemental forecasting (Armstrong, 1985). If this is the case, then expert subjects do not need to be employed in laboratory experiments. Similarly, Sanders & Ritzman (1992) have suggested that technical knowledge may not be important in judgemental time series forecasting (their definition of technical knowledge embraces both knowledge of statistical forecasting methods and knowledge of the biases inherent in human judgement).

In general, the more artificial the laboratory experiment then the greater is the scope for creating controlled conditions. However, while such artificiality is useful it should not be used gratuitously. There seems little point in designing experiments which are ultimately of little relevance to the real world, such as data presentations designed to confuse the subject or the use of trick questions designed to support the experimenter's hypothesis. Similarly, asking people to make forecasts for lead times which would never apply in a real task will probably serve no useful purpose.

Having tested hypotheses in a highly artificial setting, we need to see the extent to which results survive increasing "realism" in the laboratory. This increasing "realism" would, where appropriate, involve transitions from:

(1) Artificial to real series.
(2) Unfamiliar forecasters to forecasters familiar with the task, e.g. by training subjects (Winkler & Murphy, 1973).
(3) Non-experts (in relation to the forecast variable) to experts.
(4) Little information available to rich information availability (including sporadic, reliable and unreliable information, hard and soft information, and feedback).
(5) Low forecaster motivation to high motivation.
(6) A neutral environment to an operational environment.
(7) Forecasts made in "laboratory time" to forecasts made in real time.
(8) Simple irreversible forecasts to rolling forecasts.
(9) Forecasts having no effect on the environment to forecasts which may be partly self-fulfilling or self-negating (see Goodwin & Wright, 1993).

At each step, we need to define the scope for which a given result is valid (for example, "method X only improved judgemental extrapolations *where* conditions *a*, *b* and *c* apply to the series"). Ideally, we need to establish the extent to which results are repeatable, and therefore not dependent on the highly specific conditions that applied to a given experiment. However, Armstrong (1996) has pointed out the lack of incentives for researchers to carry out replications and the bias against publishing such work.

Applying laboratory results in the real world involves risks, but these should be reduced the closer the laboratory study is to the conditions applying in the real-world problem. Clearly, the implementation of any improvement strategies which have been designed and tested in the laboratory need to be carefully monitored. Studies of forecast errors before and after implementation will be a key part of this monitoring but of course need to be interpreted with care, given the possible confounding effects of time (e.g. the implementation may have coincided with a change in the environment, making the forecasting task more difficult).

Explanations need to be sought for any results that fail to survive the transitions. Any attempt to apply them in the real world should be rejected unless the explanations suggest otherwise. Such explanations will come from an increased understanding of the cognitive processes adopted by judgemental forecasters, underpinned by theory (thereby avoiding the "dust-bowl empiricism" criticized by Lichtenstein, Fischoff & Phillips, 1981). If we understand how and why forecasters react to a given situation we are more likely to be able to generalize to other situations. Policy capturing (e.g. Bolger & Harvey, 1993) and verbal protocol techniques (Curley et al., 1995) have a role to play here.

## 4.9 CONCLUSIONS

Three environments can be postulated for judgemental sales forecasting. First there is the real world where forecasting is actually practised. There is evidence that this is an environment which often has great potential for improvement: where inadequately supported, poorly trained and demotivated personnel put forward forecasts (and other quantities wrongly labelled as forecasts) that are not monitored for accuracy. Then there is an ideal world where practical forecasts are made and all the conditions conducive to accurate forecasting are in place. Finally, there is the psychological laboratory: a world of controlled conditions that can only approximate those of the ideal real world.

Ultimately, the objective of judgemental forecasting research is to identify the conditions necessary for the ideal world. Since the real world offers limited scope for experimentation and control, and lacks many of the ideal world conditions, the laboratory may be the best environment for achieving this. It can interact with real-world studies by analysing the types of task that exist and explaining the consequences of deficiencies in the way these tasks are carried out. It can show how the real world can move closer to the ideal by allowing improvement strategies to be tested and the scope of improvements to be determined. In many cases, changes in attitudes to forecasting in organizations and changes in the way forecasting is organized are the keys to improving judgemental forecasting accuracy. However, discoveries originating in laboratory studies, and shown to be robust, may help to spur these changes. By demonstrating what forecasters can achieve under favourable conditions, the status of sales forecasting in organizations can only be enhanced.

## NOTE

(1)   The discussion of tasks here focuses on the use of judgement in making estimates of quantities which relate directly to the forecast variable. As other chapters in this book show (Harvey & Bolger, Chapter 5 and Armstrong & Collopy, Chapter 10), judgement is also used in other aspects of forecasting, such as the selection of a forecasting method or the identification of a suitable statistical model. For example, Collopy & Armstrong (1992) have developed a system of rule-based forecasting where the judgements of experts have been encapsulated in sets of rules which specify how a forecast should be derived when particular conditions apply.

## REFERENCES

Andreassen, P.B. (1990)   Judgmental extrapolation and market overreaction: on the use and disuse of news. *Journal of Behavioral Decision Making*, **3**, 153–74.

Andreassen, P.B. & Kraus, S.J. (1990)   Judgmental extrapolation and the salience of change. *Journal of Forecasting*, **9**, 347–72.

Ang, S. & O'Connor, M. (1991)   The effect of group interaction processes on performance in time series extrapolation. *International Journal of Forecasting*, **7**, 141–9.

Armstrong, J.S. (1985)   *Long Range Forecasting. From Crystal Ball to Computer*. Wiley, New York.

Armstrong, J.S. (1996)   The ombudsman: management folklore and management science–on portfolio planning, escalation bias, and such. *Interfaces*, **26**, 25–55.

Beach, L.R., Barnes, V.E. & Christensen-Szalanski, J.J.J. (1986)   Beyond heuristics and biases: a contingency model of judgmental forecasting. *Journal of Forecasting*, **5**, 143–57.

Bolger, F. & Harvey, N. (1993)   Context-sensitive heuristics in statistical reasoning. *Quarterly Journal of Experimental Psychology*, **46A**, 779–811.

Brown, L.D. (1988) Editorial. Comparing judgmental to extrapolative forecasts: it's time to ask why and when. *International Journal of Forecasting*, **4**, 171–3.

Brunswik, E. (1952) The conceptual framework of psychology. In *International Encyclopedia of Unified Science*, vol. 1, No. 10. University of Chicago Press, Chicago.

Bunn, D. (1992) Synthesis of expert judgment and statistical forecasting models for decision support. In G. Wright & F. Bolger (eds), *Expertise and Decision Support*, Plenum, New York.

Bunn, D. & Wright, G. (1991) Interaction of judgmental and statistical forecasting: issues and analysis. *Management Science*, **37**, 501–18.

Carbone, R. & Gorr, W.L. (1985) Accuracy of judgmental forecasting of time series. *Decision Sciences*, **16**, 153–60.

Collopy, F. & Armstrong, J.S. (1992) Rule-based forecasting: development and validation of an expert systems approach to combining time series extrapolations. *Management Science*, **38**, 1394–1414.

Curley, S.P., Browne, G.J., Smith, G.F. & Benson, P.G. (1995) Arguments in the practical reasoning underlying constructed probability responses. *Journal of Behavioral Decision Making*, **8**, 1–20.

Dalrymple, D.J. (1987) Sales forecasting practices, results from a United States survey. *International Journal of Forecasting*, **3**, 379–91.

Dominiak, G.F. & Louderback, J.G. (1991) *Managerial Accounting*, 6th edn, PWS-Kent, Boston.

Edmundson, R. (1990) Decomposition: a strategy for judgemental forecasting. *Journal of Forecasting*, **9**, 305–14.

Einhorn, H.J. & Hogarth, R. (1982) Prediction, diagnosis and causal thinking in forecasting. *Journal of Forecasting*, **1**, 23–36.

Fildes, R. & Hastings, R. (1994) The organisation and improvement of market forecasting. *Journal of the Operational Research Society*, **45**, 1–16.

Fischhoff, B. (1994) What forecasts (seem to) mean. *International Journal of Forecasting*, **10**, 387–403.

Goodwin, P. (1996) Statistical correction of judgmental point forecasts and decisions. *Omega: International Journal of Management Science*, **24**, 551–9.

Goodwin, P. (1997) Adjusting judgemental extrapolations using Theil's method and discounted weighted regression. *Journal of Forecasting*, **16**, 37–46.

Goodwin, P. & Fildes, R. (1997) Judgmental forecasting with a sporadic cue: does providing a statistical forecast improve accuracy? Working paper, Department of Mathematical Sciences, University of the West of England.

Goodwin, P. & Wright, G. (1993) Improving judgmental time series forecasting: a review of the guidance provided by research. *International Journal of Forecasting*, **9**, 147–61.

Goodwin, P. & Wright, G. (1997) *Decision Analysis for Management Judgment*, 2nd edn. Wiley, Chichester.

Harvey, N. & Bolger, F. (1996) Graphs versus tables: effects of data presentation format on judgemental forecasting. *International Journal of Forecasting*, **12**, 119–37.

Lawrence, M.J. (1983) An exploration of some practical issues in the use of quantitative forecasting models. *Journal of Forecasting*, **2**, 169–79.

Lawrence, M.J. & Makridakis, S. (1989) Factors affecting judgmental forecasts and confidence intervals. *Organizational Behavior and Human Decision Processes*, **42**, 172–87.

Lim, J.S. & O'Connor, M. (1996) Judgmental forecasting with time series and causal information. *International Journal of Forecasting*, **12**, 139–53.

Lichtenstein, S., Fischhoff, B. & Phillips, L.D. (1981) Calibration of probabilities: state of the art to 1980. In D. Kahneman, P. Slovic & A. Tversky (eds), *Judgment under Uncertainty: Heuristics and Biases*. Cambridge University Press, New York.

Mathews, B.P. & Diamantopoulos, A. (1986) Managerial intervention in forecasting. An empirical investigation of forecast manipulation. *International Journal of Research in Marketing*, **3**, 3–10.

Mathews, B.P. & Diamantopoulos, A. (1990) Judgemental revision of sales forecasts: effectiveness of forecast selection. *Journal of Forecasting*, **9**, 407–15.

Murphy, A.H. & Brown, B.G. (1985) A comparative evaluation of objective and subjective weather forecasts in the United States. In G. Wright (ed.), *Behavioral Decision Making*. Plenum, New York.

O'Connor, M., Remus, W. & Griggs, K. (1993) Judgemental forecasting in times of change. *International Journal of Forecasting*, **9**, 163–72.

Payne, J.W. (1982) Contingent decision behaviour. *Psychological Bulletin*, **92**, 382–402.

Pole, A., West, M. & Harrison, P.J. (1994) *Applied Bayesian Forecasting and Time Series Analysis*. Chapman and Hall, London.

Rothe, J.T. (1978) Effectiveness of sales forecasting methods. *Industrial Marketing Management*, **7**, 114–18.

Rowe, G. & Wright, G. (1996) The impact of task characteristics on the performance of structured group forecasting techniques. *International Journal of Forecasting*, **12**, 73–89.

Sanders, N.R. & Manrodt, K.B. (1994) Forecasting practices in US corporations: survey results. *Interfaces*, **24**, 92–100.

Sanders, N.R. & Ritzman, L.P. (1992) The need for contextual and technical knowledge in judgmental forecasting. *Journal of Behavioural Decision Making*, **5**, 39–52.

Sniezek, J.A. (1986) The role of variable labels in cue probability learning tasks. *Organizational Behaviour and Human Decision Processes*, **38**, 141–61.

Sniezek, J.A. (1989) An examination of group processes in judgmental forecasting. *International Journal of Forecasting*, **5**, 171–8.

Theil, H. (1971) *Applied Economic Forecasting*. North-Holland, Amsterdam.

Wagenaar, W.A. & Sagaria, S.D. (1975) Misperception of exponential growth. *Perception and Psychophysics*, **18**, 416–22.

Watson, M.C. (1996) Forecasting in the Scottish electronics industry. *International Journal of Forecasting*, **12**, 361–71.

Webby, R. & O'Connor, M. (1996) Judgmental and statistical time series forecasting: a review of the literature. *International Journal of Forecasting*, **12**, 91–118.

Wilkie, M.E., Onkal, D. & Pollack, A.C. (1996) Experts versus novices: an examination of time series extrapolative judgment in a currency forecasting context. Paper presented at Sixteenth International Symposium on Forecasting, Istanbul, June.

Winkler, R.L. & Murphy, A.H. (1973) Experiments in the laboratory and the real world. *Organizational Behaviour and Human Performance*, **10**, 252–70.

Wolfe, C. & Flores, B. (1990) Judgmental adjustment of earnings forecasts. *Journal of Forecasting*, **9**, 389–405.

# Chapter 5

# Heuristics and Biases in Judgemental Forecasting

Fergus Bolger* and Nigel Harvey**

*City University and **University College London, London, UK

## SUMMARY

Armstrong (1985) has proposed the following stages in the forecasting process: implementation (i.e. formulation of the forecasting problem); choice of method; application of method; comparison and combination of forecasts; adjustment of forecasts; and evaluation. Judgement, for instance of probabilities or of the values of important variables, must be exercised at each of these stages.

More than two decades of research in the psychology of judgement and decision making have shown that people often rely on heuristics to make unaided judgements and that this can lead to bias (see e.g. Kahneman, Slovic & Tversky, 1982). Some heuristics which are relevant to forecasting are representativeness, anchor-and-adjust and availability. In this chapter we will present evidence, from our own research and that of others, of the use of these heuristics, both within the application of judgement as the principal forecasting method and at other stages in the forecasting process.

*Forecasting with Judgment.* Edited by G. Wright and P. Goodwin.

## 5.1   INTRODUCTION

Armstrong (1985) has proposed the following stages in the forecasting process: implementation (i.e. formulation of the forecasting problem); choice of method; application of method; comparison and combination of forecasts; adjustment of forecasts and assessment of uncertainty; and evaluation. Examining these various stages in forecasting we can see that there are at least three different types of processes involved. Two of these kinds of process are the basic fare of decision scientists, viz. judgement processes and decision-making processes. Judgement processes entail the assessment of values—either quantitative or qualitative —for particular variables of interest. Judgement can either be a component of a larger task (e.g. estimating probabilities and utilities of outcomes of alternative actions as a precursor to making a choice between alternatives), or it can be an end in itself (e.g. predicting Japan's GNP next year). Decision making normally involves selecting between two or more options (although there are some decisions, e.g. where a new policy is adopted, which are difficult to classify in this way); this may involve judgement, as in the previous example, or may not, as in the case of habits, e.g. choosing the forecast method one normally uses.

The third kind of process—which we shall term *problem structuring* —entails recognizing the need for judgement or decision making or both, identifying relevant variables, and searching for information relevant to these variables (e.g. recognizing the need for forecasting, identifying relevant outcome indicators and predictors, and finding values for these variables). Problem structuring has received relatively little attention from cognitive psychologists and decision scientists, perhaps because it is less well defined than judgement or decision making (in fact problem structuring is a process which involves *both* judgement *and* decision making, and also perception). A more likely reason why problem structuring has been ignored is because the laboratory tasks favoured by decision researchers tend to be well-structured to begin with, thereby obviating the need for structuring. However, in the real world, tasks are not usually so friendly and considerable effort must be put into the structuring process. In view of this it is perhaps not surprising that most of the research relevant to problem structuring has been conducted by those interested in so-called *naturalistic decision making* (NDM, see e.g. Klein et al., 1993), which involves real-world decision making, often conducted by experts and often under stress (e.g. fire-fighters, pilots and military commanders).

Problem structuring can usefully be divided into three stages: *problem detection* or *recognition*; *problem diagnosis* or *description* (see Smith & Sage, 1991); and *information search and collection*. These stages map on to Armstrong's (1985) first forecasting stage, "formulation of problem". After problem structuring it is necessary to decide between different strategies for solving the problem. In the case of forecasting this means choosing between different forecasting methods. We propose that in decision making there are two basic processing routes (see also e.g. Chaiken, Liberman & Eagly, 1989; Loewenstein, 1996; Petty & Cacioppo, 1986; Wason & Evans, 1975): a *fast route*, where decisions are made primarily using judgemental strategies (e.g. judgemental extrapolation of time series or forecasting on the basis of recalling similar patterns); and a *slow route* where decisions are made in a more or less systematic manner (e.g. forecasts are made by first estimating parameters of a statistical model then by application of that model). By "more or less analytic" we mean that the strategies in the slow route lie on a continuum of analytic rigour. Where an adopted strategy lies on this continuum depends on a number of factors, including the amount of time available for solving the problem, the quality and quantity of the data available for problem solution and the motivation of the forecaster (see Payne, Bettman & Johnson, 1994). Irrespective of whether fast- or slow-route strategies are used, this decision-making stage corresponds to Armstrong's (1985) "application of method" forecasting stage. However, the next two of Armstrong's stages—"comparison and combination of forecasts", and "adjustment of forecasts and assessment of uncertainty"—we regard as being an integral part of whatever decision-making strategy (forecasting method) is being applied, and hence are sub-stages of the "application of method" stage. After decision making (forecasting) has taken place there may be an appraisal of the success of that decision (forecast); this appraisal is Armstrong' s final "evaluation" stage. We will use this model of the decision-making (forecasting) process to structure the rest of this review.

Normative economic theory states that all information relevant to a decision should be considered when making a forecast (the *rational expectations hypothesis*, see e.g. Attfield, Demery & Duck, 1991). Further, normative decision theory states that the probabilities and utilities of outcomes are assessed in an unbiased manner, and that choices are made by systematic evaluation of the options (i.e. *maximization of expected utility*, see von Neumann & Morgenstern, 1944). However, there is a considerable body of research showing that, in practice, people rarely make decisions normatively (see e.g. Kahneman, Slovic & Tversky, 1982; Payne, Bettman and Johnson, 1993). Rather, the generally accepted view is that—because of cognitive capacity limitations—people rely on *heuristics*. Heuristics are rules of thumb that people use to produce judgements and decisions that are usually satisfactory but rarely optimal (Simon, 1956). They are fallible and may produce judgements that are systematically biased. The characteristics of these biases and the circumstances in which they occur provide researchers into human judgement and decision making with clues to the nature of the heuristics that people use (Tversky & Kahneman, 1974).

Two heuristics that have been identified in this way are those of availability and representativeness. People using the availability heuristic employ ease of recall as an indicator of importance. For instance, recent data might be overweighted in a description of a forecasting problem, leading to errors if there are important low-frequency patterns in the data. People using the representativeness heuristic are employing a form of stereotyping in which similarity dominates other cues as a basis for judgement and decision making. For example, a particular sequence of events may be seen as more typical or representative of the set of possible sequences than another equally likely sequence. As a consequence, it is wrongly judged as more likely to occur.

People using heuristics are seen as acting *irrationally* relative to optimal normative procedures. This has been used as an argument for aiding judgement or combining it with statistical methods (see e.g. Bolger & Wright, 1992). However, we must emphasize that heuristics are often worth using in terms of the savings they give in cognitive effort, computation time or both. Further, there is evidence to suggest that *selection* of heuristics may be rational (i.e. people choose the optimal heuristic given the constraints of the situation, see Payne, Bettman & Johnson, 1993).

Forecasting is not excepted from this conclusion regarding the limits of human reasoning (Bunn & Wright, 1991; Goodwin & Wright, 1993). Several studies have found sub-optimalities relative to statistical techniques (e.g. Lawrence & Makridakis, 1989; Sanders & Ritzman, 1992; Timmers & Wagenaar, 1977; Wagenaar & Sagaria, 1975; Wagenaar & Timmers, 1978, 1979). Also, as we shall discuss shortly, the use of specific heuristics has been identified in forecasting as leading to particular biases (e.g. Andreassen, 1990; Andreassen & Kraus, 1990;

Bolger & Harvey, 1993; Harvey, Bolger & McClelland, 1994; Lawrence & O'Connor, 1992).

In the following sections we will consider what heuristics and biases may be present at each of the stages of decision making (forecasting) described above. Where possible we will describe research findings to support our conjectures about possible suboptimalities in forecasting. However, at present there are relatively few studies which are directly relevant to them.

## 5.2 HEURISTICS AND BIASES IN PROBLEM STRUCTURING

### 5.2.1 Detection

In Signal Detection Theory there are two kinds of errors of detection: *misses* and *false alarms* (see e.g. McNicol, 1972). We would anticipate that forecasting needs are frequently overlooked due to the limited information-processing capabilities of forecasters and managers. There is plenty of evidence from the literature on expert judgement that relevant information is sometimes overlooked by decision makers. For example, Ebbesen & Konecni (1975) found that in making sentencing decisions, court judges used only a very restricted subset of available dimensions. Further, Gaeth & Shanteau (1984) found that expert soil judges referred to materials—when categorizing samples—which are irrelevant to the discrimination they are trying to make. Similar findings with respect to limited information use and use of irrelevant cues come from studies of State Registered Nurses (Shanteau et al., 1981), audit managers (Bamber, 1983), personnel selectors (Nagy, 1981), pathologists (Einhorn, 1974), stockbrokers (Slovic, 1969), and clinical psychologists (Goldberg, 1970). In some of these cases there may be extenuating circumstances[1]; however, it seems likely that in many cases the professionals fail to take into account all the information they should, simply because, unassisted, they cannot keep all this information in mind.

The selective attention invoked by decision makers in order to overcome the problem of limited cognitive capacity may result in biases. For example, a number of studies have shown that when people are asked to diagnose the causes of some problem, such as why a car will not start, they neglect a number of potential causes and focus on just a couple of particularly salient or common causes; this is true of both experts and novices (e.g. Fischhoff, Slovic & Lichtenstein, 1978). Failure to unpack implicit components of a problem results in undue confidence in the proposed solution (cf. Koehler & Tversky, 1994). This problem may be alleviated by using labels that identify all main categories of causes. The effectiveness of this approach appears to derive from an increase in availability of individual causes within each of the labelled categories (Russo & Kolzow, 1994).

False alarms—seeing forecasting needs where there are none—are less problematic than misses in that they do not in themselves result in forecast error. However, they do mean that resources are wasted and perhaps diverted from more important problems. This may indirectly lead to error. False alarms may come about as the result of the forecaster being overly keen not to miss some important event. Such over-vigilance tends to occur when the negative consequences of a miss are high (or, at least, perceived to be high), such as for doctors, social workers and parole officers.

### 5.2.2 Diagnosis

Errors in diagnosis or description of the forecasting problem can come about for a number of reasons, the three main ones being: over-simplification of the problem, again as the result of limited cognitive capacity; improper description of problem features (e.g. relevant predictors, forecasting goals, etc.); miscategorization of the forecasting problem, or misattribution of the cause of the problem, due to inappropriate or poorly applied cognitive models.

Prospect Theory (Kahneman & Tversky, 1979) is a well-established model of decision making that can be regarded as a modification of Subjective Expected Utility (SEU) theory, designed to be more descriptive of actual behaviour than the original (Savage, 1954). In Prospect Theory there is an *editing* phase before choice, during which it is suggested that several simplification processes operate. For example, probabilities are rounded, very small values are eliminated, and similar positive and negative outcomes are cancelled out. Dominance Structuring theory (Montgomery & Svenson, 1983) is another model within which similar simplification processes are proposed (some of which occur *subsequent* to choice, as a means of justifying that choice). In principle, simplification can lead to bias. For example, rounding of large probabilities to certainty could mean that some potential outcomes are overweighted relative to other potential outcomes that have been assigned more moderate probabilities of occurrence. In a forecasting context, such overweighting might mean that a forecaster tends to focus only on forecasting those events which are most likely to occur. This is similar to the drunk who searches only for his lost keys underneath the streetlight—because this is easiest—even though it is more likely that he dropped them further up the street. However, there is relatively little empirical support as yet for pre-choice editing, so the existence of biases in judgement and decision making as a consequence of simplification processes is still conjecture.

Improper description of the decision (forecasting) problem can occur due to failures in detection, as described in the previous section, or as the result of failures in memory. In other words, some relevant piece of information may be overlooked or there may be a failure to retrieve appropriate information from memory. Retrieval can be subject to biases as well as random error. We discussed above how use of the availability heuristic may result in errors in diagnosing the forecasting problem when important low-frequency patterns are present in the data. However, certain factors can bias memory retrieval, and thereby impair the effectiveness of using the availability heuristic, in situations in which it would otherwise produce a reasonably satisfactory judgement. More specifically, the form of questions used to elicit information from people affects the availability of different answers. Anyone using informants in their efforts to formulate a forecasting problem needs to be aware of the potential complications arising from these effects.

Schuman & Scott (1987) asked people to characterize the most important aspect of a problem. When possible candidates were suggested, 60% of people chose one of them as their answer; when they were not explicitly suggested, only 2% of people selected one of these candidates. Even when candidate responses are not suggested, the wording of a question can have a large effect on the answers that people provide (Harris, 1973; Hippler & Schwarz, 1986; Rugg, 1941). For example, this work suggests that asking someone to estimate how long the life of a product will be will produce a higher value than asking them to estimate how short the life of a product will be. Furthermore, when informants are provided with continuous analogue (Likert) scales on which to make their responses, the range of values used for the scale has a marked effect on the answers given (Schwarz et al., 1985). One final complication is that the form of words used to question informants about some experience they have undergone influences the way they remember that same experience when questioned about it again at a later date (Loftus, 1980). A forecasting problem may therefore be described inaccurately due to a false comparison with a superficially similar previous problem.

The third type of failure of diagnosis comes about through faulty domain knowledge (or faulty application of correct domain knowledge). A number of biases have been found which are relevant to this third type of failure. For example, the way a problem is *framed* can distort the description of that problem and consequent decision making. The classic example of a framing bias in decision making is that substantially more people accept a certain outcome over an uncertain, but potentially much better, outcome when the choice is framed in terms of gains. However, when the choice is framed in terms of losses the opposite tendency is observed (Tversky & Kahneman, 1981). The framing effect may operate through people adopting different schemes (or sets of expectations) for the different frames. For example, forecasting problems framed as predicting the amount by which a previously set sales target will be missed, and as predicting the actual level of sales, are formally equivalent but may lead to estimates that do not correspond. This is because the sales target is available as a mental anchor that may affect the judgement in the former but not the latter frame (see Bolger & Harvey, 1995a).

Another way in which the wrong sort of knowledge might be brought to bear is due to aspirational or motivational influences, such as wishful thinking. For example, it has been found in a number of studies that desirable events are seen as having a greater probability of occurring than undesirable events which are matched in terms of their true probability of occurrence (e.g. Babad, 1987; Harvey, 1992; Milburn, 1978; Uhlaner & Grofman, 1986; Zakay, 1983). In these cases people are bringing different knowledge schemes (and hence expectations) to bear in the two cases in a similar manner to the one due to differences in the problem frame. It seems likely that judgemental forecasts are particularly prone to errors of wishful thinking, given the role that many forecasts have in the setting of goals for the commissioning organization (see e.g. Goodwin, 1995).

Of course, the wrong knowledge scheme can be brought to bear for a number of other reasons, but most of these will result in non-systematic error rather than bias. For instance, lack of expertise may result in a forecaster applying an inappropriate model of the market to an economic forecasting problem. Further, the forecasts of an expert may be subject to error due to incorrect assumptions in the model she/he is applying.

### 5.2.3 Information Search and Collection

There are two basic sorts of failure associated with information search and collection: failure to search for and acquire information which will improve the quality of the forecast; and failure to *stop* searching for information which is irrelevant to improving the quality of the forecast (or at least does not improve it sufficiently to justify the cost of search and collection). Failure to collect could be due to failure to detect in the first place or could be due to the use of an inappropriate *inquiry system* (Smith & Sage, 1991). Essentially, an inquiry system can be either *top-down*, *bottom-up* or some mixture of the two. A top-down inquiry system will mean a search for information relevant to the parameters in the forecasting model one is using. Hence, with sufficient time and resources, the information collection process will be as adequate as the model which guides it. A bottom-up inquiry system will mean that information will be driven by available (and probably salient) data, which may or may not be relevant to the forecast(s) to be made. An inquiry system based on a mixture of top-down and bottom-up processes is the most flexible because it permits models to be modified in the light of data; this is particularly useful if the world is changing (e.g. as is the case with dynamic systems such as the weather).

Within an inquiry system, different search strategies may be used and these will tend to vary in their approach and exhaustiveness. For example, a search may be *breadth-first*, where all alternatives are considered on one attribute before the next attribute is considered, or *depth-first*, where all attributes of one alternative are considered before the next alternative is considered. Different types of search may be stopped at any point before an exhaustive search of all alternatives and all attributes is completed. There is a fair amount of evidence to suggest that deviations from an exhaustive strategy depend upon an *effort/accuracy trade-off* (Payne, Bettman & Johnson, 1993). In other words, if people have enough cognitive resources and enough motivation to do an exhaustive search then they will do one, otherwise they will reach an acceptable compromise between amount of effort expended (the most effort being for an exhaustive search) and the resulting level of accuracy.

Payne et al.'s research suggests that people are generally quite good at making this trade-off, in other words, decision makers are *adaptive*. Factors which influence the cognitive resources available—and hence effort which can be expended—include: complexity (i.e. the number of alternatives and attributes); discriminability (of alternatives and attributes); and time available to solve the problem. The desired level of accuracy will depend upon costs of errors which can be economic, social or otherwise. Exhaustive search is not always the best strategy. For example, if there is a limited amount of time, it may be better to consider one attribute from each alternative rather than to consider each alternative in depth and then run out of time before considering some of the alternatives at all. Further, exhaustive search is not always the optimal strategy, even when there is ample time, ability and motivation. Usually there is some cost to information search and collection, such that the benefit to be obtained by collecting some pieces of information is less than the cost of collection. There are normative statistical procedures for stopping information collection (e.g. Keeney & Raiffa, 1976; Pratt, Raiffa & Schlaifer, 1995). We found (Bolger & Harvey, 1995b) that people collected information in a manner that was close to optimal for relatively simple problems, but used more heuristic strategies as task complexity increased (e.g. collecting information to help them discriminate just between the best two alternatives).

Thus, there are indications regarding the conditions under which information search and collection will be sub-optimal, but it is not yet possible to identify particular biases, since the specific nature of sub-optimalities depends upon features of both the forecasting task and the forecasting strategy used.

## 5.3 HEURISTICS AND BIASES IN CHOICE OF FORECAST STRATEGY

In the same way that there are a number of information-search strategies, there are also a number of different choice strategies and, as was the case for information search, effort/accuracy trade-offs appear to govern which choice strategy is put into operation (see Payne, Bettman & Johnson, 1993). Some examples of choice strategies include, in decreasing order of analytic rigour: *weighted additive* (all attributes of each alternative are weighted by their importance—or probability—

then the alternative with the highest average worth is selected); *equal weight* (as for the weighted additive, but no weighting of attributes by their relative importance or probability); *satisficing* (alternatives are considered in a set order and the first alternative for which all its attributes exceed a pre-determined threshold is selected); and *lexicographic* (the alternative which scores highest on the most important attribute is selected). One distinction that is often made is between *compensatory* and *non-compensatory* choice strategies (see e.g. Frisch & Clemen, 1994). A compensatory strategy is one where good values on some attributes offset bad values on others, such as is the case with the weighted-additive and equal-weight strategies. With a non-compensatory strategy, good values on some attributes cannot compensate for bad values on others. For example, a forecaster choosing a forecast method may screen out from further consideration any method which requires modelling beyond first-order autoregression in the series. The satisficing and lexicographic strategies outlined above are examples of non-compensatory strategies.

Non-compensatory strategies are heuristic strategies and use of them can lead to error and, possibly but not necessarily, to bias. In the above example, not attempting to model beyond first-order autoregressive processes will have little impact on the quality of forecasts in the majority of cases sampled randomly from the population of forecasting problems. In a minority of these cases there will be some random error. However, if the forecaster who uses this method-selection strategy happens to sample his/her problems from a domain where, for instance, all the series have strong positive first- *and* second-order autocorrelation, then the forecaster will systematically forecast too close to the immediately preceding point.

As we mentioned in the Introduction, a number of writers suggest that, in many instances, choice is not necessarily even made by non-compensatory decision-making strategies but may be made purely by judgemental or perceptual processes (i.e. what we refer to as the "fast route" rather than the "slow route"). The essence of fast-route processes is the retrieval of some previously formed response on the basis of recognition of, or judged similarity to, a particular sort of situation. A characteristic of fast-route strategies is that they are usually *non-consequential* (see e.g. Frisch & Clemen, 1994), which means that there is no explicit analysis of whether application of the strategy will fulfil the decision-maker's goals (although, in practice, goals will be fulfilled in as much as they were the last time that the same strategy was used and the current situation matches the former). Several examples of non-consequentialism have been found in decision making (e.g. Shafir & Tversky, 1992; Tversky & Shafir, 1992), in social behaviour (e.g. Baron, 1994) and in reasoning tasks (e.g. Evans, 1996). Non-consequentialism also presents the possibility of error and bias. For example, choosing a forecasting strategy out of habit will result in suboptimal forecasts if the chosen strategy is unsuitable for solving the current problem. Further, if a judgemental heuristic such as availability or representativeness is used to determine the appropriateness of a proposed forecast strategy to the current situation then, as we have already noted, biases in forecasts may occur.

## 5.4 HEURISTICS AND BIASES IN THE APPLICATION OF A FORECASTING STRATEGY

Once a forecasting need has been recognized, the problem described, pertinent data collected, and a forecasting strategy selected, it is necessary to apply that strategy and make the forecast(s). The extent to which errors and bias (attributable to the forecaster, not the method) enter at this stage depends on the degree to which judgement is involved in the chosen strategy. However, the most statistically rigorous method is likely to involve *some* judgement, even if it is only the interpretation of the output of a model. Armstrong's (1985) stages of comparison and combination of forecasts, adjustment of forecasts, and assessment of uncertainty are particularly likely to involve substantial amounts of judgement on the part of the forecaster, irrespective of the forecast method used.

The representativeness and availability heuristics are sources of bias during the application of the forecast strategy in the same way as they were at previous stages in the forecasting process, so we will not discuss them further here. A heuristic which we have not so far mentioned, but which has received the most attention from researchers in relation to forecasting, is known as *anchor-and-adjust*. The anchor-and-adjust heuristic is where some supplied or salient value is taken as an anchor and then the final judgement made by adjusting away from this anchor. Typically, this adjustment is insufficient. In Tversky & Kahneman's classic (1974) experiment, participants were given a number randomly chosen from between zero and 100 then asked to estimate the number of African countries in the United Nations. The arbitrary numbers had a strong effect on the estimates people gave, such that high estimates were associated with high anchors and low estimates with low anchors.

Studies of anchor-and-adjust heuristics in a forecasting context have focused on the situation where the forecasting method being applied is the judgemental extrapolation of time series. (It should be noted, however, that an anchor-and-adjust heuristic may also be used where judgement is *not* the main forecast method being used, e.g. during comparison, combination or evaluation of forecasts.) These studies have shown that when judgementally extrapolating time series, forecasters sometimes anchor on recent values of the series (or the long-term mean/trend line), then make their forecast by adjusting from this anchor. The amount of adjustment made by the judgemental forecasters does not generally take sufficient account of other relevant features of the series, such as trend and autocorrelation. Hence, the resulting forecasts are not as extreme as they should be; specifically, trends are damped and assessed autocorrelations are too positive (see e.g. Andreassen, 1990; Andreassen & Kraus, 1990; Bolger & Harvey, 1993; Harvey, 1988; Harvey, Bolger & McClelland, 1994; Lawrence & O'Connor, 1992).

Use of anchor-and-adjust heuristics does not account for all the variance in people's judgemental forecasts. Bolger & Harvey (1993) suggested that the residual random error may arise partly because people have some tendency to represent data noise as well as data pattern in their forecasts. In other words, they use the representativeness heuristic to make their forecast sequence look similar to the data series. There is some evidence for this. Harvey (1995) found that noise in a sequence of forecasts was proportional to the noise in the data series that was used as the basis for the forecasts. It is worth also noting a recent study by Czaczkes & Ganzach (1996), which found *both* anchor-and-adjust and the representativeness heuristics in competition in a prediction task; since the representativeness heuristic tends to make forecasts more extreme, use of this heuristic would tend to cancel out the tendency of the anchor-and-adjust heuristic to make forecasts less extreme, thus the end result would be accurate forecasts[2]. Unfortunately, the heuristics do not usually operate at the same time. The anchoring heuristic is triggered by a salient anchor (e.g. a previous prediction or a clear trend), whereas the representativeness heuristic is used when the distribution of predictors is known and the predictors and outcome are on the same scale.

The particular version of the anchor-and-adjust heuristic used can vary in a number of ways, with some versions of the heuristic being more appropriate to certain types of series than others. For example, a heuristic which uses the last value of the series as an anchor, but adjusts by adding to this anchor a proportion of the difference between the last *two* values of the series, is better for forecasting trended series than a heuristic which anchors on the long-term mean of the series and adjusts by a proportion of the deviation of that point from the long-term mean (given that the difference between the last and penultimate points used by the first heuristic is a fairly reliable estimate of the trend). We (Bolger & Harvey, 1993) found that, in general, forecasters chose a version of the anchor-and-adjust heuristic that was appropriate to the characteristics of the series they were trying to forecast. This finding is compatible with the notion introduced above, that people can adaptively select strategies in response to task characteristics (Payne, Bettman & Johnson, 1993).

The format in which data are presented may also influence choice or use of judgement heuristics. Four studies suggest that judgemental forecasts benefit from graphical presentation as opposed to presentation as a table of numbers (Angus-Leppan & Fatseas, 1986; Dickson, DeSanctis & McBride, 1986; Lawrence, 1983; Lawrence, Edmundson & O'Connor, 1985). However, we (Harvey & Bolger, 1996) found that graphical presentation seems to help reduce forecast error, mainly through assisting the estimation of trends (i.e. the bias towards underestimating trends mentioned above was less for graphs than tables). For untrended series, tabular presentation resulted in slightly lower forecast error than graphical presentation. This was because subjects' tendency to overforecast and the inconsistency in their forecasts are greater when series are presented graphically.

If a to-be-forecast series is presented graphically, then the scaling and labelling of the plot can bias judgement. Lawrence & O'Connor (1992) found that forecast error declined as scale increased, with forecasts at smaller scales being biased so that the forecasts on average exceeded the actual value. In the same study, Lawrence & O'Connor found, counter-intuitively, that the more data points that were presented in a graph, the higher the forecast error. Finally, regarding biasing effects of data presentation, there is some suggestion that the labelling of a series affects the extent of forecast error. Both Koele (1980) and Sniezek (1986) found that performance in cue probability learning tasks was worse in the absence of meaningful labels. However, the lack of meaningful labels appears merely to increase the random error in forecasts, whereas there is reason to suspect that meaningful labels might actually bias forecasts. For example, many studies of judgemental forecasting have labelled the stimulus series "sales" or "profits", both of which are desirable and thus may contribute to the over-forecasting often found in these studies.

A number of different biases have been found in the subjective assessment of probability. In fact, subjective probability judgement has been one of the areas most extensively researched by decision scientists (see Wright and Ayton, 1994, for a comprehensive treatment of theoretical issues and empirical findings). One reason for this attention is that probability is a central component of normative decision theories (e.g. SEU) and also of leading descriptive theories (e.g. Prospect Theory). Furthermore, subjective probabilities are important inputs to decision-aiding technologies, including decision analysis, risk analysis and Bayesian systems (see e.g. Morgan & Henrion, 1990). The majority of the research has been concerned with the accuracy of subjective probability judgements and the findings have been that the judgements are either too extreme (normally referred to as *"over-confident"*) or not extreme enough (usually referred to as *"conservative"*), depending upon the type of task and the method of assessing accuracy (for more details on both the accuracy of probability judgement and other aspects of probability assessment relating to forecasting, see the chapter by Peter Ayton in this volume).

Perhaps the most common approach to determining the accuracy of probability judgements is to look at the correspondence between judge-ments and true probabilities. In this method—known as *calibration*—people are required to make a number of assessments of the likelihood of occurrence of certain events. Then, for each level of expressed likelihood, accuracy is determined by comparing the observed outcome probability with the expressed probability. For example, a weather forecaster might be asked to state the probability of rain at noon the following day on 100 different occasions. In order for the forecaster to be completely accurate (*perfectly calibrated*) it must rain on 70% of the occasions that the forecaster stated a 70% certainty that it would rain (with similar perfect correspondences for every other level of expressed likelihood). In practice, the overwhelming finding of a large number of studies using a variety of tasks and participants is that people tend to give subjective probabilities that are more extreme than are justified by the corresponding objective probabilities. In other words, their confidence in the occurrence or non-occurrence of the events is too great, hence they are "over-confident"[3] (see Lichtenstein, Fischhoff and Phillips, 1982).

Several reasons for the over-confidence bias have been suggested (see McClelland and Bolger, 1994, for a review) including: bias in the test materials; the effects of random error (in learning cues or making a response); faulty mental models; and the use of heuristics such as anchor-and-adjust (e.g. failure to adjust response criteria sufficiently in the light of changes in task difficulty) and representativeness (e.g. people place too much weight on unreliable cues that are somehow salient, rather than reliable cues which are not). Further, over-confidence might be a common personality trait that usefully motivates us to do things which we might not do otherwise (e.g. no one would attempt to start a new business on a fully objective analysis of the success rates of new businesses). There is a large body of research to support this view, showing that people are *over-optimistic*, i.e. they expect good things to happen to them more often than to others, and bad things less often (see e.g. Weinstein, 1980). At present it seems unlikely that either bias in the test material, or random error, or both combined, can fully account for over-confidence, hence we assume that it is again the use of heuristics— perhaps in combination with other factors—that results in this pervasive bias.

The second way in which subjective probability judgement has been assessed is by comparing people's estimates against the normative standard of Bayes' theorem which (amongst other things) specifies how much probabilities should be revised upon the receipt of new evidence. Typically it has been found that people do not revise their judgements in the light of new data as much as they should according to Bayes' theorem, hence they are referred to as being "conservative" (e.g. Phillips & Edwards, 1966; Fischhoff & Beyth-Marom, 1983).

It may appear strange that people are both too extreme in their probability judgements and not extreme enough; however, it has been shown (e.g. Erev, Wallsten & Budescu, 1994) that these conflicting biases are actually just one bias, and the apparent contradiction is merely an artefact of the way accuracy of judgement is measured (which in turn depends upon the sort of task[4]). As a consequence of this, the same kinds of explanation can be used for conservatism as for over-confidence.

Before leaving sources of potential bias in probabilistic forecasting, it is worth mentioning one final and oft-cited heuristic known as the *base-rate fallacy* (Tversky & Kahneman, 1982), in which people fail to take fully into consideration the prior probabilities associated with particular events (or in many cases people assume that base rates are irrelevant altogether, hence the "fallacy"). The use of this heuristic can bias forecasts in two ways: directly, by leading forecasters not to integrate historical information appropriately into their forecasts; and indirectly, by leading forecasters to give undue weight to other, less reliable sources of evidence, such as representativeness. Finally, it should be noted that the base-rate fallacy has been observed in professionals for tasks where they claim expertise, as well as in novices for laboratory tasks (see e.g. Ayton, 1992, for a review).

## 5.5  HEURISTICS AND BIASES IN THE EVALUATION OF FORECASTS

It is important to base evaluation on records of forecasts that were made at the time they were produced. This is because memory for forecasts is subject to a well-documented distortion, the hindsight bias: people tend to remember their forecasts as closer to the actual outcome than, in fact, they were (Hawkins & Hastie, 1990). This phenomenon, originally described by Fischhoff & Beyth (1975), has been replicated for many different types of forecast (e.g., Arkes et al., 1981; Leary, 1982) and appears to be fairly robust. It does not disappear when people are informed of its existence and told to avoid it (Fischhoff, 1977) but it is reduced by instructing them to consider carefully how events could have turned out differently (Slovic & Fischhoff, 1977). The bias suggests that our previous knowledge states are not available to memory (Hawkins & Hastie, 1990).

The evaluation of forecasts can be regarded as hypothesis testing. Many studies have shown that people tend to exhibit a confirmation bias: they are more inclined to search for evidence that confirms their hypotheses than for evidence that refutes them (e.g., Klayman & Ha, 1987; Wason, 1960; Wason & Johnson-Laird, 1972). Consider, for example, the conditional forecast that sales will only exceed some level ($x$) in regions where more than a certain level of resources ($y$) has been committed to marketing campaigns. Evaluators would be exhibiting the confirmation bias by restricting their efforts to confirming that sales were indeed above $x$ when marketing resources had been greater than y. A more thorough evaluation would also check that sales were not above $x$ in regions where marketing resources were not more than $y$.

A third bias which might operate in the evaluation of forecasts is known as the *sunk-cost effect*: the increased tendency to persist in an activity in which some investment has already been made (see e.g. Arkes & Blumer, 1985). Objectively the investment already made should not influence the decision to continue. For example, most would agree that it would be irrational to go on a holiday that you know you will not enjoy (e.g. because you are feeling ill) just because you have paid for it; however, a number of studies have shown this is exactly the way people behave in many circumstances (*op. cit.*). The sunk-cost effect can have some serious effects if the lost causes being pursued as a result of this bias happen to be, for instance, continuation of expensive public-works programs. In the context of evaluating forecasts, the sunk-cost effect may play a role when forecasts are being made strategically (i.e. as policy-making tools). In such instances, it is important that forecasts are not justified in terms of "not wasting" previously expended resources.

## 5.6 CONCLUSIONS

We have reported a number of judgement and decision-making heuristics which may potentially result in biased forecasts. We have also showed how such heuristics might bias forecasts even if judgemental techniques are *not* the main method of forecasting; this is as a consequence of judgement being applied at various other important stages of the overall forecasting process. Despite this apparently gloomy picture we have painted, we believe that there are positive lessons which forecasters can learn from the psychological literature we have reviewed. As we have already indicated in a number of places, heuristics are usually well-adapted, hence biases should only be the consequence of their use in a minority of cases. Furthermore, the research literature is beginning to give indications of the conditions under which significant biases are likely to occur (and also the precise nature of these biases). However, further research needs to be conducted—particularly with respect to problem structuring—before we would be confident enough to be able to make strong practical recommendations. Also the majority of the research into heuristics and biases has not been conducted in a forecasting context, therefore an applied program of research such as this would seem to hold the most promise for the development of debiasing aids and decision support for forecasters.

## NOTES

(1)   The extenuating circumstances include: (a) using additional cues does little to improve performance in some domains (e.g. clinical diagnosis); (b) "irrelevant" cues are actually relevant in most situations, but the experimental task is atypical (i.e. lack of ecological validity, see e.g. Gigerenzer, Hoffrage & Kleinbolting, 1991); (c) there are subtle relationships between cues which are appreciated by the experts but not captured by the "gold standard" to which performance is compared (usually a linear model, see e.g. Camerer & Johnson, 1991 on the use of configural cues).

(2)   Czaczkes & Ganzach (1996) argue that normative forecasts tend to be regressive in the sense that the predicted value is less extreme than the predictor. Forecasts made using the anchor-and-adjust heuristic are similarly regressive (or even over-regressive) because the extent of the adjustment away from the anchor (predictor) is normally less than optimal. In contrast, forecasts made using the representativeness heuristic are non-regressive (i.e. too extreme); this is because they are based upon informal observations about the relationship between predictor and outcome which tend to lead to the overweighting of salient (or extreme) co-variations.

(3)   It is an over-simplification to say that over-confidence is always observed. First, the degree of over-confidence is dependent on task difficulty, so that more over-confidence is observed for more difficult tasks and under-confidence can be observed for very easy tasks (the *hard–easy effect*: see e.g. Suantak, Bolger & Ferrell, 1996). Second, good calibration can be observed in experienced judges, including weather forecasters (see Bolger & Wright, 1992, for a review).

(4)   In calibration tasks such as forecasting, uncertainty tends to be an internal property of the subject and thereby not independently measurable, whereas in Bayesian revision of probability tasks (e.g. drawing balls from urns in order to discriminate between different hypotheses about the composition of the urns) the uncertainty is an external property of the world which is easily quantifiable as a posterior probability. This difference means that traditionally objective probability has been studied as a function of subjective probability in the calibration case and subjective probability as a function of objective probability in the case of Bayesian revision. These opposing methods of analysing the data result in the apparently conflicting conclusions of "over-confidence" vs. "conservatism", respectively.

# REFERENCES

Andreassen, P.B. (1990)   Judgmental extrapolation and market overreaction: on the use and disuse of news. *Journal of Behavioral Decision Making*, **3**, 153–74.

Andreassen, P.B. & Kraus, S.J. (1990)   Judgmental extrapolation and the salience of change. *Journal of Forecasting*, **9**, 347–72.

Angus-Leppan, P. & Fatseas, V. (1986)   The forecasting accuracy of trainee accountants using judgmental and statistical techniques. *Accounting and Business Research*, **16**, 179–88.

Arkes, H.R. & Blumer, C. (1985)   The psychology of sunk cost. *Organizational Behavior and Human Performance*, **35**, 129–40.

Arkes, H.R., Wortman, R.L., Saville, P.D. & Harkness, A.R. (1981)   Hindsight bias among physicians weighing the likelihood of diagnoses. *Journal of Applied Psychology*, **66**, 252–4.

Armstrong, J.S. (1985)   *Long Range Forecasting: From Crystal Ball to Computer*. Wiley, New York.

Attfield, C.L.F., Demery, D. & Duck, N.W. (1991)   *Rational Expectations in Macroeconomics: An Introduction to Theory and Evidence*, 2nd edn. Basil Blackwell, Oxford.

Ayton, P. (1992)   On the competence and incompetence of experts. In G. Wright & F. Bolger (eds), *Expertise and Decision Support*. Plenum, New York.

Babad, E. (1987)   Wishful thinking and objectivity among sports fans. *Social Behaviour: An International Journal of Applied Social Psychology*, **4**, 231–40.

Bamber, E.M. (1983)   Expert judgment in the audit team: a source reliability approach. *Journal of Accounting Research*, **21**, 396–412.

Baron, J. (1994)   Non-consequentialist decisions. *Behavioral and Brain Sciences*, **17**, 1–42.

Bolger, F. & Harvey, N. (1993)   Context sensitive heuristics in statistical reasoning. *Quarterly Journal of Experimental Psychology*, **46A**, 779–811.

Bolger, F. & Harvey, N. (1995a)   Judging the probability that the next point in an observed time-series will be below, or above, a given value. *Journal of Forecasting*, **14**, 597–607.

Bolger, F. & Harvey, N. (1995b)   Predecisional information acquisition: non-compensatory screening or part of compensatory choice. Paper presented at SPUDM-15, Jerusalem, August.

Bolger, F. & Wright, G. (1992)   Reliability and validity in expert judgment. In G. Wright & F. Bolger (eds), *Expertise and Decision Support*. Plenum, New York.

Bunn, D. & Wright, G. (1991)   Interaction of judgmental and statistical forecasting methods: issues and analysis. *Management Science*, **17**, 501–18.

Camerer, C.P. & Johnson, E.J. (1991)  The process–performance paradox in expert judgement: how can experts know so much and predict so badly? In K.A. Ericsson & J. Smith (eds), *Toward A General Theory of Expertise*. Cambridge University Press, Cambridge.

Chaiken, S., Liberman, A. & Eagly, A.H. (1989)  Heuristic and systematic information processing within and beyond the persuasion context. In J.S. Uleman & J.A. Bargh (eds), *Unintended Thought*. Guilford Press, New York, pp. 212–52.

Czaczkes, B. & Ganzach, Y. (1996)  The natural selection of prediction heuristics: anchoring and adjustment versus representativeness. *Journal of Behavioral Decision Making*, **9**, 125–39.

Dickson, G.W., DeSanctis, G. & McBride, D.J. (1986)  Understanding the effectiveness of computer graphics for decision support: a cumulative experimental approach. *Communications of the ACM*, **29**, 40–47.

Ebbesen, E. & Konecni, V. (1975)  Decision making and information integration in the courts: the setting of bail. *Journal of Personality and Social Psychology*, **32**, 805–21.

Einhorn, H.J. (1974)  Expert judgment: some necessary conditions and an example. *Journal of Applied Psychology*, **59**, 562–71.

Erev, I., Wallsten, T.S. & Budescu, D.V. (1994) Simultaneous over- and underconfidence: the role of error in judgment processes. *Psychological Review*, **101**, 519–27.

Evans, J. St B.T. (1996)  Deciding before you think: relevance and reasoning in the selection task. *British Journal of Psychology*, **87**, 223–40.

Fischhoff, B. (1977)  Perceived informativeness of facts. *Journal of Experimental Psychology: Human Perception and Performance*, **3**, 349–58.

Fischhoff, B. & Beyth, R. (1975)  "I knew it would happen": remembered probabilities of once-future things. *Organizational Behaviour and Human Performance*, **13**, 1–16.

Fischhoff, B. & Beyth-Marom, R. (1983)  Hypothesis evaluation from a Bayesian perspective. *Psychological Review*, **90**, 239–60.

Fischhoff, B., Slovic, P., & Lichtenstein, S. (1978)  Fault trees: sensitivity of estimated failure probabilities to problem representation. *Journal of Experimental Psychology: Human Perception and Performance*, **4**, 330–44.

Frisch, D. & Clemen, R.T. (1994)  Beyond expected utility: rethinking behavioral decision research. *Psychological Bulletin*, **116**, 46–54.

Gaeth, G. & Shanteau, J. (1984)  Reducing the influence of irrelevant information on experienced decision makers. *Organizational Behavior and Human Performance*, **33**, 263–82.

Gigerenzer, G., Hoffrage, U. & Kleinbolting, H. (1991)  Probabilistic mental models: a Brunswikian theory of confidence. *Psychological Review*, **98**, 506–28.

Goodwin, P. (1995)  Asymmetric loss functions and biased forecasts: evidence from British companies. Paper presented at SPUDM-15, Jerusalem, August.

Goodwin, P. & Wright, G. (1993) Improving judgmental time series forecasting: a review of guidance provided by research. *International Journal of Forecasting*, **9**, 147–61.

Goldberg, L.R. (1970) Man versus model of man: a rationale, plus some evidence for a method of improving clinical inferences. *Psychological Bulletin*, **73**, 422–32.

Harris, R.J. (1973) Answering questions containing masked and unmasked adjectives and adverbs. *Journal of Experimental Psychology*, **97**, 399–401.

Harvey, N. (1988) Judgmental forecasting of univariate time series. *Journal of Behavioral Decision Making*, **1**, 95–110.

Harvey, N. (1992) Wishful thinking impairs belief-desire reasoning: A case of decoupling failure in adults? *Cognition*, **45**, 141–62.

Harvey, N. (1995) Why are judgments less consistent in less predictable task situations? *Organizational Behavior and Human Decision Processes*, **63**, 247–63.

Harvey, N. & Bolger, F. (1996) Graphs vs. tables: effects of data presentation format on judgmental forecasting. *International Journal of Forecasting*, **12**, 119–37.

Harvey, N., Bolger, F., & McClelland, A.G.R. (1994) On the nature of expectations. *British Journal of Psychology*, **85**, 203–29.

Hawkins, S.A. and Hastie, R. (1990) Hindsight: biased judgments of past events after outcomes are known. *Psychological Bulletin*, **107**, 311–27.

Hippler, H. & Schwarz, N. (1986) Not forbidding isn't allowing: the cognitive basis of the forbid–allow asymmetry. *Public Opinion Quarterly*, **50**, 87–96.

Kahneman, D. & Tversky, A. (1972) Subjective probability: a judgment of representativeness. *Cognitive Psychology*, **3**, 430–54.

Kahneman, D. & Tversky, A. (1979) Prospect theory: an analysis of decision under risk. *Econometrica*, **47**, 263–91.

Kahneman, D., Slovic, P. & Tversky, A. (eds) (1982) *Judgment Under Uncertainty: Heuristics and Biases*. Cambridge University Press, Cambridge.

Keeney, R.L. & Raiffa, H. (1976) *Decisions with multiple objectives: Preferences and Value Trade-offs*. Wiley, New York.

Klayman, J. & Ha, Y. (1987) Confirmation, disconfirmation and information in hypothesis testing. *Psychological Review*, **94**, 211–28.

Klein, G., Orasanu, J., Calderwood, R. & Zsambok, C. (1993) *Decision Making in Action: Models and Methods*. Ablex, Norwood, NJ.

Koehler, D.J. & Tversky, A. (1994) Support theory: a non-extensional representation of subjective probability. *Psychological Review*, **101**, 547–67.

Koele, P. (1980) The influence of labeled stimuli on non-linear multiple-cue probability learning. *Organizational Behavior and Human Performance*, **26**, 22–31.

Lawrence, M.J. (1983) An exploration of some practical issues in the use of quantitative forecasting models. *Journal of Forecasting*, **2**, 169–79.

Lawrence, M.J., Edmundson, R.H., & O'Connor, M. (1985) An examination of the accuracy of the judgmental extrapolation of time series. *International Journal of Forecasting*, **1**, 25–36.

Lawrence, M.J. & Makridakis, S. (1989) Factors affecting judgmental forecasts and confidence intervals. *Organizational Behavior and Human Decision Processes*, **42**, 172–87.

Lawrence, M.J. & O'Connor, M. (1992) Exploring judgmental forecasting. *International Journal of Forecasting*, **8**, 15–26.

Leary, M.R. (1982) Hindsight distortion and the 1980 presidential election. *Personality and Social Psychological Bulletin*, **8**, 257–63.

Lichtenstein, S., Fischhoff, B. & Phillips, L.D. (1982) Calibration of probabilities: the state of the art to 1980. In D. Kahneman, P. Slovic & A. Tversky (eds), *Judgment under Uncertainty: Heuristics and Biases*. Cambridge University Press, Cambridge.

Loftus, E. (1980) *Memory: Surprising Insights into How We Remember and Why We Forget*. Ardsley House, New York.

Loewenstein, G. (1996) Out of control: visceral influences on behavior. *Organizational Behavior and Human Decision Processes*, **65**, 272–92.

McClelland, A.G.R. & Bolger, F. (1994) The calibration of subjective probabilities: theories and models, 1980–94. In G. Wright & P. Ayton (eds), *Subjective Probability*. Wiley, Chichester.

McNicol, D. (1972) *A Primer of Signal Detection Theory*. Allen & Unwin, London.

Milburn, M.A. (1978) Sources of bias in the prediction of future events. *Organizational Behaviour and Human Performance*, **21**, 17–26.

Montgomery, H. & Svenson, O. (1983) A think aloud study of dominance structuring in decision processes. In R. Tietz (ed.), *Aspiration Levels in Bargaining and Economic Decision Making*. Springer Verlag, Berlin.

Morgan, M.G. & Henrion, M. (1990) *Uncertainty: A Guide to Dealing with Uncertainty in Quantitative Risk and Policy Analysis*. Cambridge University Press, Cambridge.

Nagy, G.F. (1981) How are Personnel Selection Decisions Made? An Analysis of Decision Strategies in a Simulated Personnel Selection Task. Unpublished Doctoral Dissertation, Kansas State University.

Payne, J.W., Bettman, J.R., & Johnson, E.J. (1993) *The Adaptive Decision Maker*. Cambridge University Press, Cambridge.

Petty, R.E. & Cacioppo, J.T. (1986). The elaboration likelihood model of persuasion. *Advances in Experimental Social Psychology*, **19**, 123–205.

Phillips, L.D. & Edwards, W. (1966) Conservatism in a simple probability inference task. *Journal of Experimental Psychology*, **72**, 346–54.

Pratt, J.W., Raiffa, H. & Schlaifer, R. (1995) *Introduction to Statistical Decision Theory.* MIT Press, Cambridge, MA.

Rugg, D. (1941) Experiments in wording questions: II. *Public Opinion Quarterly,* **5,** 91–2.

Russo, J.E. & Kolzow, K.Y. (1994) Where is the fault in fault trees? *Journal of Experimental Psychology: Human Perception and Performance,* **20,** 17–32.

Sanders, N.R. & Ritzman, L.P. (1992) The need for contextual and technical knowledge in judgmental forecasting. *Journal of Behavioral Decision Making,* **5,** 39–52.

Savage, L.J. (1954) *The Foundations of Statistics.* Wiley, New York.

Schuman, H. & Scott, J. (1987) Problems in the use of survey questions to measure public opinion. *Science,* **236,** 957–9.

Schwartz, N., Hippler, H., Deutsch, B. & Strack, S. (1985) Response scales: effects of category range on reported behaviour and comparative judgements. *Public Opinion Quarterly,* **49,** 388–95.

Shafir, E. & Tversky, A. (1992) Thinking through uncertainty: Nonconsequential reasoning and decision making. *Cognitive Psychology,* **29,** 449–74.

Shanteau, J., Grier, M., Johnson, J. & Berner, E. (1981) Improving decision making skills of nurses. In *ORSA–TIMS Proceedings.* ORSA–TIMS, Houston, TX.

Simon, H.A. (1956) Rational choice and the structure of the environment. *Psychological Review,* **63,** 129–38.

Slovic, P. (1969) Analyzing the expert judge: a descriptive study of a stockbroker's decision processes. *Journal of Applied Psychology,* **53,** 255–63.

Slovic, P. & Fischhoff, B. (1977) On the psychology of experimental surprises. *Journal of Experimental Psychology: Human Perception and Performance,* **3,** 544–51.

Smith, C.L. & Sage, A.P. (1991) A theory of situation assessment for decision support. *Information and Decision Technologies,* **17,** 91–124.

Sniezek, J.A. (1986) The role of labels in cue probability learning tasks. *Organizational Behavior and Human Decision Processes,* **38,** 141–61.

Suantak, L., Bolger, F. & Ferrell, W.R. (1996) The hard-easy effect in subjective probability calibration. *Organizational Behavior and Human Decision Processes,* **67,** 201–21.

Timmers, H. & Wagenaar, W.A. (1977) Inverse statistics and misperception of exponential growth. *Perception and Psychophysics,* **21,** 558–62.

Tversky, A. & Kahneman, D. (1974) Judgment under uncertainty: heuristics and biases. *Science,* **185,** 1124–31.

Tversky, A. & Kahneman, D. (1981) The framing of decisions and the psychology of choice. *Science,* **211,** 453–8.

Tversky, A. & Kahneman, D. (1982) Evidential impact of base rates. In D. Kahneman, P. Slovic & A. Tversky (eds), *Judgment under Uncertainty: Heuristics and Biases*. Cambridge University Press, Cambridge.

Tversky, A. & Shafir, E. (1992) The disjunction effect in choice under uncertainty. *Psychological Science*, **3**, 305–9.

Uhlaner, C.J. & Grofman, B. (1986) The race may be close but my horse is going to win: wish fulfilment in the 1980 Presidential election. *Journal of Political Behavior*, **8**, 101–29.

von Neumann, J. & Morgenstern, O. (1944). *Theory of Games and Economic Behaviour*. Wiley, New York.

Wagenaar, W.A. & Sagaria, S.D. (1975) Misperception of exponential growth. *Perception and Psychophysics*, **18**, 416–22.

Wagenaar, W.A. & Timmers, H. (1978) Extrapolation of exponential time series is not enhanced by having more data points. *Perception and Psychophysics*, **24**, 182–4.

Wagenaar, W.A. & Timmers, H. (1979) The pond and duckweed problem: three experiments on the misperception of exponential growth. *Acta Psychologica*, **43**, 239–51.

Wason, P. (1960) On the failure to eliminate hypotheses in a conceptual task. *Quarterly Journal of Experimental Psychology*, **12**, 129–40.

Wason, P.C. & Evans, J. St B.T. (1975) Dual processes in reasoning? *Cognition*, **3**, 141–54.

Wason, P. & Johnson-Laird, P.N. (1972) *Psychology of Reasoning: Structure and Content*. Harvard University Press, Cambridge, MA.

Weinstein, N.D. (1980) Unrealistic optimism about future life events. *Journal of Personality and Social Psychology*, **39**, 806–20.

Wright, G. & Ayton, P. (eds) (1994) *Subjective Probability*. Wiley, Chichester.

Zakay, D. (1983). The relationship between the probability assessor and the outcomes of an event as a determiner of subjective probability. *Acta Psychologica*, **53**, 271–80.

# Chapter 6

# Financial Forecasting with Judgment

Dilek Önkal-Atay

*Bilkent University, Ankara, Turkey*

## SUMMARY

Judgment plays a prominent role in financial forecasting. This chapter reviews previous work on judgmental forecasting of critical financial variables like earnings, exchange rates, stock prices and interest rates. Forecasting accuracy of judgmental point, categorical and probability forecasts are examined with a special focus on the effects of expertise, forecast horizon, task format and contextual information. It is concluded that future research into the needs of both providers and users of judgmental forecasts is crucial for the dissemination of financial knowledge and uncertainty. Within this framework, it is argued that the issues of information utilization, use of heuristics and resultant biases, combining of judgmental forecasts, and investigations of the effects of feedback and different elicitation formats on forecasting accuracy remain important directions for future financial forecasting research.

*Forecasting with Judgment.* Edited by G. Wright and P. Goodwin.
© 1998 John Wiley & Sons Ltd.

## 6.1 INTRODUCTION

Financial forecasting entails predicting future values of stock and commodity prices, exchange rates, earnings, interest rates, volatilities and other variables critical for making financial decisions. Such forecasts are made and used extensively by security analysts, management and lending institutions, as well as other players in financial markets.

The richness and complexity of financial domains require that the forecasters rely primarily on judgment in making their predictions (Armstrong, 1983; Batchelor & Dua, 1990). Depending on contextual factors, financial forecasts could be based solely on judgment, judgment could be used to adjust the forecasts given by quantitative techniques or, at the very least, judgment could be used in deciding which technique to employ, which model to select, and which information to include. Uncertainties prevailing in financial markets, the resultant widespread use and apparent decision consequences of forecasts make finance an ideal application domain for exploring the use of judgment in forecasting.

Finance theory has initially shown some skepticism as to the forecastability of financial variables, as expressed via the "efficient market hypothesis". This hypothesis suggests that, in an efficient market, a set of information is immediately and fully reflected in market prices (making prices unpredictable given that information set). The particular information set determines the form of efficiency. That is, a market would be weak-form efficient if prices reflected only past prices, and would be semi-strong-form efficient if prices also reflected all publicly available information (e.g. balance sheet, income statement information). In its strong form, this hypothesis regards the changes in asset prices as approximately random because of market efficiency, which means that prices would absorb and reflect all available information (including insider information) rapidly and accurately (Fama, 1970; Granger, 1992). Recent results and research interest in this area appear to signal a fading of this paradigm (De Bondt, 1992, 1993; Mills, 1996) in favor of the recognition of usefulness and indispensability of forecasts in financial domains. In fact, financial forecasts have been attracting research attention since the 1930s. Cowles (1933) reports one of the earliest attempts to evaluate the judgmental forecasts of financial experts. Studying stock recommendations provided by 16 financial services and 24 financial publications for the 1928–1932 period, Cowles (1933) sketches a dim picture of forecasting performance. This profile is reproduced in a follow-up study 10 years later (Cowles, 1944). Since then, a considerable body of research has accumulated on the accuracy of judgmental financial forecasts, with promising findings on forecast quality. Given the unequivocal importance of such empirical accuracy studies for forecasting practice (Fildes & Makridakis, 1995), this chapter aims to review the pertinent work in financial forecasting. In so doing, it attempts to delineate future research directions to explore further the role of judgment in this domain.

Judgmental predictions can assume the form of point forecasts (e.g. value of dollar/mark exchange rate), categorical forecasts (e.g. increase vs. no increase in stock price), or probabilistic forecasts (e.g. probability of an interest rate increase, probability of earnings falling by more than 3%). Judgmental forecasting studies using point/categorical predictions are summarized next, followed by studies requesting probabilistic predictions.

## 6.2 POINT AND CATEGORICAL FORECASTS

Within financial forecasting research, there has been a strong emphasis on judgmental point forecasts of earnings given by security analysts (see Brown, 1993, for an extensive review). This focus is mainly due to the significance of earnings forecasts in firm-valuation processes (Fried & Givoly, 1982), especially their role in providing information for future cash flows (Finger, 1994). Relatedly, it is suggested that earnings forecasts are immediately incorporated into the stock prices (Elton, Gruber & Gultekin, 1981), and that analysts' earnings forecasts are useful for stock recommendation decisions (Bandyopadhyay, Brown & Richardson, 1995). Guerard & Lawrence (1992) also demonstrate that the security analysts' forecasts "... add value to the portfolio construction process ... by enhancing portfolio returns" (p. 153). We next review the studies focusing on forecasts of earnings.

### 6.2.1 Earnings Forecasts

An important branch of earnings research involves comparisons of analysts' judgmental forecasts with the predictions given by time-series models. In a remarkably comprehensive study, Brown et al. (1987)

compared the relative accuracy of earnings forecasts reported by security analysts with those given by three univariate Box–Jenkins models for 233 firms over 20 quarters, and for 212 firms over four quarters. Security analyst forecasts proved to be more accurate than each of the time-series models for all forecast horizon and fiscal quarter combinations analyzed. Their findings were also robust to method of handling outliers, definition of forecast error, and the nature of tests (parametric vs. non-parametric) employed. Brown & Rozeff (1978), Fried & Givoly (1982), Armstrong (1983), Collins, Hopwood & McKeown (1984), O'Brien (1988), Hopwood & McKeown (1990) and Branson, Lorek & Pagach (1995) have similarly provided unanimous empirical support for the higher accuracy of security analysts' forecasts as compared with time-series models.

In an interesting extension of this research, Affleck-Graves, Davis & Mendenhall (1990) compared earnings forecasts of analysts with those of students and time-series models. They found that students possessing the same historical information as time-series models performed as accurately as the sophisticated models. Analysts who had access to a broader information set, on the other hand, outperformed both students and time-series models. These results were interpreted as suggesting that while the students could effectively utilize their limited information to render judgmental forecasts with an accuracy comparable to the models, the analysts' superior performance primarily stemmed from their information advantage.

Several studies investigated sources of analyst superiority in detail (Fried & Givoly, 1982; Brown et al., 1987; Brown, Richardson & Schwager, 1987; Kross, Ro & Schroeder, 1990). Brown (1993) summarizes this research and concludes by attributing the analysts' performance edge to their "... private information acquisition activities, which may enable them to better distinguish between permanent, transitory and price-irrelevant earnings shocks" (p. 301). This argument also complements the finding that analysts produce better forecasts of stock prices given their possession of firm-specific private information (Dimson & Marsh, 1984; Elton, Gruber & Grossman, 1986; Brown, Richardson & Trzcinka, 1991). In addition to their information advantage, research shows that analysts also have a timing advantage, i.e. they report their forecasts after model forecasts are issued (Fried & Givoly, 1982; Brown et al., 1987). Taken together, these findings confirm Foster's (1986) predication that higher accuracy of judgmental forecasts stems from analysts' ability to: (a) immediately adjust to structural changes in the forecasting environment; (b) consolidate information from diverse sources; and (c) continuously revise forecasts upon receipt of new information. Importance of these factors in ascertaining the superior accuracy of judgmental forecasts is also pronounced in research focusing on management forecasts of earnings.

Management forecasts differ from analyst forecasts in that they are provided by a limited number of firms and are mostly for one-year-ahead earnings only (Foster, 1986). It has been noted that management provides financial forecasts to rectify the deceptive expectations of analysts and other players in financial markets (Ajinkya & Gift, 1984; Barry & Jennings, 1992) but not all management forecasts are perceived as being equally credible (Jennings, 1987). In a detailed analysis of previous work on earnings forecasts, Armstrong (1983) compared judgmental forecasting performances of managers with analysts, finding a higher accuracy for management forecasts. One possible explanation was provided by management's conceivable impact on performance and potential influence on reported earnings. The other important determinant was believed to be management's access to more (and recent) information, especially internal information. These results again stress the comparative advantage of judgmental forecasts in providing flexibility to continuously accommodate the plethora of incoming information, leading to superior forecasting accuracy in information-rich domains like finance.

Even though the judgmental forecasts of earnings are found to be quite accurate, they naturally are not error-proof. Elton, Gruber & Gultekin (1984) investigated potential causes of analysts' forecast errors. They found that the errors could be attributed to the difficulties in forecasting relative performances of individual industries, in addition to the complexities in forecasting individual company performances (relative to industry averages). That is, the environmental uncertainties were important constituents of forecasting difficulty. In spite of the perceived difficulties, however, analysts' earnings forecasts were found to be overly optimistic (Fried & Givoly, 1982; O'Brien, 1988; Ali, Klein & Rosenfeld, 1992). It is claimed that the independent analysts overestimate earnings more than the company analysts (Basi, Carey & Twark, 1976) and analysts' forecasts are more optimistic when making negative stock recommendations (Francis & Philbrick, 1993). Interestingly, Brown (1996) argues that the optimism bias observed in previous studies has switched to one of pessimism in recent years. Brown contends that this shift may in turn be mirroring the changing institutional pressures from managers. Overall, these findings corroborate Schipper's (1991) work showing that motivational factors may induce intentional biases in forecasts.

Biases observed in analysts' forecasts may be viewed as signalling a potential for further improvements in performance (Wright, 1980). Combining of judgmental and statistical forecasts provides one such avenue. Conroy & Harris (1987), Guerard (1987), Guerard & Beidleman (1987), Newbold, Zumwalt & Kannan (1987), Lobo & Nair (1990, 1991), Lobo (1991) and Guerard, Stone & Hansen (1992) have developed such "combined" models to predict earnings, demonstrating improved forecasting accuracy as a result of pooling. It is argued that combining mitigates unreasonable assumptions, hence evading large errors (Armstrong, 1986). Forecast errors and biases may also be improved via focused training and feedback. As will be addressed later in the chapter, these issues have not received much research attention in the earnings literature.

In summary, voluminous research on earnings has shown superior accuracy of judgmental forecasts in this field, with potential improvements accruing from combinations with statistical forecasts. Judgmental forecasts of other financial variables have not enjoyed as much of a research exposure. We next turn to the limited number of studies involving point or categorical forecasts of currencies, interest rates and bankruptcies.

### 6.2.2 Currency, Interest Rate and Bankruptcy Predictions

Judgmental forecasts of currencies, interest rates and bankruptcies received scant research attention. With regard to currencies, the analytic hierarchy process (AHP) attracted interest as a potential judgmental forecasting technique (Wolfe & Flores, 1990; Saaty & Vargas, 1991), in spite of apparent concerns for its use in this context (Salo & Bunn, 1995; Belton & Goodwin, 1996) (for details of the AHP and the role of judgment in this framework, see Saaty, 1990). Blair et al. (1987) reported an example of using the AHP framework to produce forecasts of Japanese Yen/US dollar exchange rates that incorporate expert judgment. Similarly, Ulengin & Ulengin (1994) focused on the US dollar/Deutschmark exchange rate forecasts, finding that the accuracy of AHP forecasts driven by expert judgment are comparable to the forecasting accuracy of powerful statistical models.

Another line of research examined the accuracy of currency forecasts issued by banks (Pollock & Wilkie, 1996; Pollock, Wilkie & Pollock, 1996). Stressing that the issued forecasts are predominated by judgment, this work revealed differing levels of accuracy depending on the particular exchange rate under consideration (Pollock, Wilkie & Pollock, 1996). Discrepancies observed in forecasting accuracy were attributed to the differential volatilities of specific currencies, as well as to the forecasters' selective over-reaction to news events taking place in the relevant period (Pollock & Wilkie, 1996).

Research on interest rates investigated experts' and non-experts' judgmental forecasts. In particular, Kolb & Stekler (1996) analyzed individual analysts' forecasts for short- and long-term interest rates. It was concluded that: (a) although no significant differences were found among analysts for short-term rates, there were performance differences for the long term; (b) there was a general agreement among the analysts concerning the direction of movement of short- and long-term rates; and (c) few analysts' forecasts outperformed the naive no-change forecasts. Alternatively, Angus-Leppan & Fatseas (1986) examined undergraduate students' short-term interest rate forecasts. They noted that, for this group of inexperienced partici- pants, the knowledge of the series did not improve accuracy, and the judgmental forecasts performed little worse than the best-performing statistical model.

More encouraging results concerning forecasting accuracy of experts were obtained with bankruptcy predictions. In particular, Libby (1975) asked bank loan officers to make predictions of failure/non-failure for 60 firms. Given a limited number of accounting ratios, loan officers were requested to (a) predict whether each firm would fail or not, and (b) rate their confidence in their predictions on a three-point scale. Loan officers' predictions were found to be consistent and reliable; with an average of 74% correct predictions exceeding the expected average of 51% correct.

In sum, research on financial forecasting has provided mostly promising results on the accuracy of judgmental forecasts presented in point or categorical form. It is worth noting that, unlike earnings research, studies on judgmental forecasts of other financial variables have been quite limited. Hence, further work explicating diverse financial variables is required to draw firmer conclusions on financial experts' judgmental forecasting performances.

## 6.3   PROBABILISTIC FORECASTS

In addition to point and categorical predictions, judgmental forecasts can also be expressed via subjective probabilities. Such probabilistic forecasts serve to communicate the forecaster's degrees of belief in the occurrences of relevant future outcomes. Probabilistic judgments are viewed to be more informative than categorical or point forecasts, since they reveal the uncertainty inherent in the forecasting situation (Murphy & Winkler, 1992). Another advantage of judgmental probability forecasts is that they allow the users/decision-makers to make the relevant tradeoffs using their personal values (Raiffa, 1968; Yates et al., 1996). Probabilistic forecasts are also useful for detecting the relative strengths and weaknesses of judgment in forecasting, so that common tendencies like over-reaction, over-forecasting or over-confidence could be discerned (Wilkie & Pollock, 1996).

### 6.3.1   Forecast Horizon, Task Format and Expertise

Judgmental probability forecasting of financial variables has attracted considerable research attention. In one of the earlier studies, Bartos (1969) asked three security analysts to assess probability distributions for the closing prices of five securities for forecast horizons of 1, 3 and 6 months. Analysts were requested to perform this task once a month for a total of 6 months. Uniform distribution (representing a no-knowledge forecaster who assigns equal probabilities to all possible outcomes) was found to consistently outperform the analysts' distributions.

Stael von Holstein (1972) analyzed multiple-interval probabilistic forecasts given for the closing prices of 12 stocks with a forecast horizon of 2 weeks. A total of 72 participants (10 stock-market experts, 10 bankers, 11 statisticians, 13 business teachers, and 28 management students) provided these forecasts for each of the 10 sessions. Overall, statisticians and stock market experts performed best, followed by business students, business teachers and bankers. Only three participants were found to perform better than the uniform distribution.

Mediocre performance of forecasters (relative to the uniform distribution) found in both Bartos' (1969) and Stael von Holstein's (1972) work was viewed as being an artifact of properties of the tasks employed in these studies. In particular, Winkler (1972, 1973) argued that a precise definition of the variable being forecast (i.e. closing price) was required to avoid multiple interpretations that could lead to confusion on the part of the forecasters as to what they are actually predicting. In a similar vein, Stael von Holstein (1972) attributed the findings to the choice of forecast horizons, arguing that the forecasters could perform better if they made predictions for ecologically valid lead times (i.e. the forecast horizons they regularly use). These assertions were supported by Kabus (1976), who reported a study where seven banking executives made multiple-interval forecasts for interest rates (for their usual forecasting horizon of 3 months) and attached probabilities to their intervals. Executives' probability forecasts were found to be quite accurate, and their forecasted direction of change was always correct. Further support for the importance of forecast horizon in mediating the effects of expertise came from research on stock price predictions in emerging markets. Specifically, it has been found that the performance of experts (professional portfolio managers) deteriorated relative to semi-experts (other banking professionals) for longer forecast horizons less frequently used in emerging markets, even though the experts demonstrated a clear superiority for shorter (more ecologically valid) lead times (Muradoglu & Önkal, 1994).

Studies have also shown that predicting stock prices remains a difficult task, even when probabilities are used to convey the uncertainties confronting forecasters. In an exploratory study, Lichtenstein & Fischhoff (1977) asked students to make directional probabilistic forecasts for the closing prices of 12 stocks. In particular, the subjects were asked (a) to predict whether the stock price of 1 month later would be higher or lower than the current price, and (2) to assess a probability (between 0.5 and 1.0) that the predicted direction would indeed occur. Even though only 47% of predictions turned out to be correct, students were quite over-confident, reporting a mean probability of 0.65 for their fallible forecasts.

Comparable results were reported by Yates, McDaniel & Brown (1991). These authors asked undergraduate and graduate finance students (labeled as "novices" and "semi-experts", respectively) to make multiple-interval probabilistic forecasts for stock prices and earnings. Stock price forecasts were found to be inaccurate in general, with novices performing better than semi-experts. Similar findings were recorded for earnings forecasts, leading researchers to attribute most of the observed difficulties in forecasting to market efficiency. Extending Yates, McDaniel & Brown's (1991) work to an emerging and inefficient stock market setting, Önkal & Muradoglu (1994) analyzed probabilistic forecasts of only stock prices. Confirming previous work, students with previous trading experience (so-called "semi-experts") were found to perform worse than students with no experience in active trading (so-called "novices"). Persistence of such an "inverse-expertise effect" in an emerging market was explained by the over-confidence of semi-experts, as displayed by their recurrent use of extreme probabilities.

There were two principal limitations to Yates, McDaniel & Brown (1991) and Önkal & Muradoglu's (1994) work: (a) both studies used students (either graduate students or students who have previously made investment decisions) as semi-experts; and (b) both studies only employed multiple-interval task formats. Addressing both limitations, Önkal & Muradoglu (1996) investigated the effects of different task formats on the accuracy of probabilistic forecasts given by recognized experts (i.e. portfolio managers), semi-experts (other banking professionals) and novices (students). Results no longer projected a significant inverse-expertise effect on the accuracy of judgmental probability forecasts of stock prices when actual experts were used. Furthermore, findings confirmed Ronis & Yates' (1987) assertion that the choice of task format could have a direct impact on probability judgment accuracy.

### 6.3.2 Contextual Information

The amount of contextual information provided to the forecasters may constitute another important determinant of probabilistic forecasting performance. For example, it could be argued that limited information may direct attention to only the appropriate cues, hence improving performance. Pursuing this argument in an interesting extension of previous work, Whitecotton (1996) asked financial analysts, MBA and undergraduate students to make probabilistic forecasts for earnings. Historical data from actual firms were used; however, unlike previous research, firm names and actual time frames were not provided. For each of the 16 companies, subjects were given: (a) current period's earnings; (b) financial information (in terms of six ratios) for the previous 2 years; (c) average change in earnings over the previous four periods; and (d) expectations for next period's earnings based on the previous four-period trend. Participants were requested to assess the probability (between 0 and 1.0) that next period's earnings would be more than what is indicated by trend. Subjects in the decision-aid condition also received probabilities of future earnings exceeding trend expectations, with the qualifier that these aid probabilities would be correct for 12 of the 16 cases. Results showed a higher accuracy for analysts and MBA students in comparison to undergraduates, with decision aid improving accuracy for all groups. However, the analysts were found to be more biased than the other two student groups. This was ascribed to analysts' knowledge of "real-world" base rates, which were not depicted in this particular study (which fixed the base rate at 50%).

Whitecotton (1996) attributed the discrepancies between her findings on earnings forecasts and the inverse-expertise results of Yates, McDaniel & Brown (1991) to the differences in accessibility of information. In particular, subjects were constrained to using a "prepackaged" information set in the Whitecotton study, while the participants of the Yates, McDaniel & Brown study could utilize an unconstrained set of information. It was argued that the presentation of selectively screened information precluded the experts from using irrelevant and unpredictive cues that usually lead to poor accuracy and excess scatter in probabilities. Thus, it was maintained that experts could better exhibit their performance superiority if given a constrained information set. In light of our previous discussion on task format effects, it is worth noting that the differences in findings could also be attributed to the diverse task structures employed by researchers. In particular, Whitecotton asked the subjects to assess a probability (between 0 and 1.0) that next period's earnings would be more than what is indicated by trend. Yates, McDaniel & Brown, on the other hand, asked the participants to make forecasts by assigning probabilities to the given intervals specifying potential earnings changes. As discussed earlier, it may be argued that such fundamental differences in elicitation formats could easily yield differential results on accuracies of probability judgments given by participants with differing levels of expertise.

Concern with contextual information effects has also sparked research interest in constructed time series (O'Connor & Lawrence, 1989; Bolger & Harvey, 1993; Webby & O'Connor, 1996). Applications of this research stream to financial forecasting have mainly involved judgmental currency forecasts (Pollock & Wilkie, 1992, 1993; Wilkie & Pollock, 1994; Wilkie, Önkal & Pollock, 1996). Revealing no contextual information (i.e. the particular exchange rates to forecast and the time frame for the given series), this line of work attempted to explore currency professionals' time series extrapolative judgment within a probability forecasting framework. In particular, these studies examined the accuracy of probabilistic directional forecasts obtained by first asking the subjects to indicate whether the exchange rate would go up or not, followed by requesting a probability conveying the participant's degree of belief in the occurrence of the indicated direction. When confronted with this task structure, currency professionals were found to perform better than a random-walk forecaster (i.e. a forecaster who assigns a probability of 0.5 to an arbitrary direction each time), in spite of their over-confidence (Wilkie & Pollock, 1994). An extension of this work showed that experts' probabilistic forecasts were still superior to those of non-experts, even under conditions of equal access to merely time-series information (Wilkie, Önkal & Pollock, 1996).

In summary, research on probabilistic forecasting has primarily examined the effects of task structure, forecast horizon, contextual information and expertise with applications to forecasts of earnings, interest rates, stock prices and exchange rates. This research has also implied that financial forecasts may be heavily influenced by judgmental heuristics and biases, an issue we turn to next.

## 6.4 HEURISTICS, BIASES AND INFORMATION USE

It may be argued that judgmental heuristics and resultant biases prevail in financial forecasting, as they do in all domains involving judgment under uncertainty (Tversky & Kahneman, 1974). The competitive, time-pressured and stressful nature of financial settings may serve to facilitate the use of judgmental heuristics, leading to biases in forecasts. Furthermore, the high volatilities enabling large gains and losses in financial markets may make judgmental biases especially prevalent in these contexts (Wilkie, Tuohy & Pollock, 1993).

In an exploratory study of these issues, Johnson (1983) asked students taking an advanced accounting course to make probability forecasts for potential bankruptcy facing 12 companies. Subjects were presented with (a) base-rate probabilities giving the frequency of bankruptcies observed for the particular industry under consideration, and (b) a financial profile of each company, including total assets and four financial ratios. Probability forecasts were found to be insensitive to base rates when the financial profile of a company was viewed as being representative of either bankruptcy or no-bankruptcy. When the financial profile was not judged to be directly representative, base rates were not ignored.

However, even in cases where base rates were taken into consideration, company-specific financial data still carried the most weight in final judgments. Emphasizing the importance of base-rate information for evaluating default risks and making loan decisions, Johnson (1983) voiced the need for detailed examinations of experts' (e.g. commercial loan analysts') use of representativeness and other heuristics, along with their financial consequences. Similar concerns were raised by Affleck-Graves, Davis & Mendenhall (1990), who attributed biases in analysts' earnings forecasts to their use of judgmental heuristics.

Among judgmental biases, the hindsight bias (i.e. individuals' tendency to exaggerate what could have been expected in foresight) has received a special attention in financial forecasting. Fischhoff (1982) has maintained that even when all the forecasts and the actual outcomes are undeniably present, financial forecasters still may display a tendency to provide causal interpretations for the outcomes: "...market analysts have an explanation for every change in price, whether purposeful or not. Some explanations ... are inconsistent; others seem to deny the possibility of any random component ... One of my favorite contrasts is that when the market rises following good economic news, it is said to be responding to the news; if it falls, that is explained by saying that the good news had already been discounted" (p. 345). Persistence of hindsight bias in earnings forecasts is also demonstrated by Camerer, Loewenstein & Weber (1989), who found this bias to persevere even in the face of high monetary incentives.

As a potential remedy to the biases discussed above, Silverman (1992) suggested a critiquing system that aims to aid a forecaster in recognizing judgmental biases in addition to signalling errors due to missing knowledge. Listing reasons that support or contradict the reported forecasts is also proposed as a method for detecting biases. In particular, Moser (1989) asked investors to make judgmental forecasts for Apple Computer Inc.'s earnings increasing by at least 5% (or not increasing by at least 5%) over a 1-year forecast horizon. Investors were asked to report their probability forecasts after listing supporting or contradicting reasons, and it was found that the order made a difference. In particular, investors generating supporting reasons first assigned higher probabilities, while those generating contradicting reasons first assigned lower probabilities. Investors' forecasts were claimed to be influenced by "output interference", i.e. investors' initial thoughts inhibited later thoughts (Hoch, 1984). Results were similar for those investors, who were only given the company name, vs. the remaining investors, who were given financial statement information in addition to the company name. It was concluded that the difficult and uncertain nature of forecasting in investment settings may lead forecasters to rely heavily on available (albeit questionable) information and arguments. These findings may have significant implications for investment decision-making and financial markets. As argued by Moser (1989), if the only available information (or majority of information) is coming from disproportionate media exposure or sensational and exaggerated news items, then a critical potential for over-reaction may be conjectured to exist. Similarly, De Bondt & Thaler (1985, 1987, 1989, 1990) suggested that stock prices may be influenced by non-expert investors' over-reaction to unexpected news items. Rooted in the heuristics and biases literature, this "over-reaction hypothesis" emphasized decision makers' misperceptions of future prices.

Other researchers argued that the market reaction to many types of financial information (e.g. equity offerings, share repurchases, earnings announcements, mergers, etc.) can be characterized by under-reaction (Abarbanell & Bernard, 1992; Ikenberry, Lakonishok & Vermaelen, 1995; Maines & Hand, 1996). A potential explanation reconciling the suggested over- and under-reaction effects is provided via saliency of information. In particular, Andreassen (1990) suggested that new information like news reports affects judgmental forecasts via its relative salience, implying that perceptions and use of news items could account for the anomalies observed in financial markets.

Studying financial analysts' information utilization is imperative for enhancing our understanding of judgmental forecasting in this domain (Slovic, 1969, 1972). Accordingly, several studies investigated fore-casters' use of information in bankruptcy prediction and credit evaluation tasks within the context of linear modeling (Shepanski, 1983; Whitred & Zimmer, 1985), yielding preliminary support for experts' identification and use of extra-model information (Chalos, 1985; Casey & Selling, 1986). This finding receives full confirmation from earnings research, which argues that security analysts outperform statistical models since their forecasts contain non-time series informa-tion such as management forecasts (Brown, et al., 1987), other firms' earnings reports (Foster, 1981), ongoing strikes (Brown & Zmijewski, 1987), and other analysts' forecasts (Brown, Richardson & Schwager, 1987). An important consideration affecting the information utilization of analysts may involve perceived pressures of accuracy. In particular, Foster (1986) reports that security analysts: (a) use other analysts' forecast revisions as valuable information in constructing their judgmental forecasts; and (b) attach high penalties to deviating from consensus. Perceived pressures to conform to consensus forecasts may be triggering motivational biases that could lead to distorted (but "harmonized") forecasts. Combining forecasts may serve to relieve these pressures, enabling a more representative forecasting performance.

## 6.5  COMBINING FORECASTS

Combining of judgmental forecasts remains an important research arena (Mentzer & Cox, 1984; Dalrymple, 1987; Armstrong, 1989; Clemen, 1989; Stickel, 1993; Maines, 1996), its exigency accentuated by the prevalent use of combined forecasts as inputs to business planning models (Menezes & Bunn, 1993). The appeal of combining forecasts comes from the notion of basing forecasts on broadened information sets (Granger, 1989; Lobo & Nair, 1990), so that the combined forecasts offer better surrogates for market expectations of financial variables such as earnings, stock prices and interest rates. In fact, Lobo & Nair (1990) defend combined models by making an analogy to portfolio theory: "The method of combining forecasts to form a composite is efficient in the same way that combining securities in a portfolio to diversify unsystematic risk is efficient" (p. 447).

Several studies investigated comparative forecasting accuracy of combined judgmental forecasts. In earnings research, Jacquillat & Grandin (1994) analyzed analysts' forecasts for 150 French companies from 1986 to 1994. They found better performance with combined forecasts and suggested that future work needs to analyze the long-term performance of combined earnings forecasts in different markets with varying volatilities. Working with exchange rate forecasts, MacDonald & Marsh (1994) concluded that combining removes systematic biases in forecasts and should be studied over extended horizons. In a related study, Fan, Lau & Leung (1996) proposed methods for combining ordinal forecasts of stock market movement (i.e. bullish, bearish or sluggish states of the market). Using the highly volatile Hong Kong stock market, the authors showed that the combined forecasts of weekly market movement outperformed the individual forecasts. Relative accuracy of combined forecasts reported by previous work has led McNees (1992) to suggest that forecasters and users need to focus on the differences between individual forecasts and the combined forecast, so that they can learn from the reasons behind the observed discrepancies.

Combining probabilistic forecasts presents an important yet neglected research problem (see Genest & Zidek, 1986; Clemen, Murphy & Winkler, 1995). In a distinctive application to judgmental financial forecasting, Stael von Holstein (1972) demonstrated that combined probability forecasts via aggregation rules assigning higher weights to good performers worked better in forecasting stock prices.

Revising statistical forecasts with judgment constitutes an extension of research on combining forecasts that has also been mostly overlooked. In a notable exception, Wolfe & Flores (1990) showed that judgmental adjustments to statistical forecasts of earnings lead to improved accuracy. It may be argued that judgmental revisions are essential, given the frequent need to accommodate structural changes and adjust for the omitted variables (Bunn & Salo, 1996). Further research on this issue is clearly warranted, especially considering Fildes & Hastings' (1994) report on 84% of the interviewed forecasters stressing the importance of modifying forecasts with judgment.

## 6.6 CONCLUSION AND DIRECTIONS FOR FUTURE RESEARCH

Volatile characteristics of financial markets tailor a critical role for judgment in financial forecasting. In fact, Brown (1996) maintains that the investment community over-emphasizes forecasts by time-series models at the expense of analysts' forecasts, whereas it could construct refined trading rules by focusing on how the judgmental forecasts are formulated. Clearly, experience in balancing data and judgment is a fundamental asset in financial markets, and the primary advantage of using judgmental forecasts lies in the incorporation of such experience (McHugh & Sparkes, 1993; Bunn, 1994; Winklhofer, Diamantopoulos & Witt, 1996).

Studies reviewed in this chapter have addressed different aspects of judgmental forecasting research within the realm of financial applications. While the variations in findings may be reflective of the different characteristics of financial variables being predicted and the particular task structures utilized, it can be deduced that firmer conclusions necessitate more comparative studies and detailed investigations of judgmental forecasting performance under varying market conditions (e.g. bull vs. bear markets) and in different (emerging vs. developed) financial markets. To be effective, such research would have to involve studying professional experts in their customary financial settings (Bolger & Wright, 1993, 1994; Wright et al., 1994).

Gaining an in-depth understanding of the cognitive processes that experts use in judgmental forecasting is essential for designing effective forecast support systems for financial decision-makers (Goodwin & Wright, 1993; Zmijewski, 1993). Relatedly, studying the cues used in judgmental financial forecasting constitutes a fertile area for future work. In constructing their forecasts, financial analysts typically utilize a wide range of qualitative and quantitative information sources (such as reports, discussions, macro-economic forecasts, etc.), with implicit or explicit weights assigned to these sources varying on the basis of changing situational factors (Firth, 1975; Foster, 1986). Capturing financial experts' skills in recognizing and flexibly using significant information constitutes a research goal vital to the development of support systems in this domain (Goodwin & Wright, 1991).

In an insightful study, De Bondt (1993) notes that, while most individuals appear to predict prices by extrapolating from past trends, forecasts of experts (assumed to portray rational investors) are radically different. He maintains that potential differences in knowledge structures or beliefs of investors stemming mainly from experience could account for the observed forecasting differences. Probabilistic forecasts provide a means for exploring this issue further. In particular, it is argued that the construction of a judgmental probability forecast requires the formation of a belief (i.e. belief-assessment phase), followed by the assessment of a probability qualifying the belief (i.e. probability-assessment phase) (Smith, Benson & Curley, 1991; Curley & Benson, 1994; Benson, Curley & Smith, 1995; Curley et al., 1995). It follows that the "goodness" of forecasts is a consequence of forecaster's performance in both stages. Within this framework, efforts to improve judgmental probability forecasts in the financial domain would necessarily involve further research into the belief-assessment phase, in addition to research on procedures for improving the final probability assessments. Such research would enhance our understanding of the processes used by financial experts in constructing forecasts, as well as the prevailing roles of reasoning and judgment in these processes.

Another promising research agenda involves studying the effects of feedback on financial forecasting performance. Feedback is critical for ensuring learnability and enhancing expertise in any domain (Bolger &

Wright, 1994), its impact highlighted especially in domains as inherently difficult as financial forecasting. Focusing on stock prices, Önkal & Muradoglu (1995) show that feedback is effective in improving probabilistic forecasts, with performance feedback leading to better accuracy than outcome (knowledge-of-results) feedback. Relatedly, Benson & Önkal (1992) argue that performance feedback affects the probability usage of forecasters, reflecting improved assessment of uncertainties embedded in the forecasting environment. Feedback representation and effectiveness of different types of feedback still remain important topics (Goodwin & Wright, 1994; Ganzach, 1994; Harvey & Bolger, 1996; Webby & O'Connor, 1996) that need to be addressed in the direction of specific factors like the judgment domain (Rowe & Wright, 1996). In particular, financial markets present dynamic forecasting environments where the forecast may influence the behavior of the market, and where the importance of cues may vary with time. Studying the impact of feedback in such volatile environments may prove especially vital for enhancing forecast support (Goodwin & Wright, 1993).

Communication between the providers and the users of financial forecasts remains a critical topic deserving research attention (Fischhoff, 1994). The investment community relies on experts' forecasts (Brown et al., 1987), making their communication a strategic issue. Users' understanding of the forecasts (as intended vs. not intended to be understood by the providers) has significant decision consequences. As noted by Bunn & Wright (1991), communicability of forecasts may in fact be more consequential than accuracy, due to its implications. The communication issue also implies that the needs of users should be considered when preparing and presenting forecasts. For example, users may find probabilistic forecasts more informative and more useful than simple point forecasts, since probabilities are viewed as reflecting indications of forecaster's confidence and uncertainty (Murphy & Winkler, 1992; Önkal & Dirimtekin, 1996). That is, the probabilities may aid the users in their interpretation of issued forecasts. As argued by Fischhoff (1994), "unless forecasters say how confident they are in forecasts, recipients are left to guess" (p. 393). Accordingly, there is a specific need for future research on the communication of judgmental probability forecasts to users/decision-makers (Abramson & Clemen, 1995).

It is also interesting that, when judgmental forecasts are given in probabilistic form, users' focus in evaluating these forecasts may be quite different from the accuracy dimensions emphasized by researchers (Yates et al., 1996). To have practical value, forecasts must adhere to users' expectations and evaluation criteria. Relatedly, Batchelor & Dua (1992) suggest that the consensus-seeking vs. variety-seeking behavior of forecasters (i.e. their tendency to give forecasts close to vs. far away from other analysts' forecasts) may be affected by users' expectations or preferences. For example, users may ignore forecasts that deviate too much from the consensus, but at the same time, dismiss forecasts too close to the consensus for not being informative. In a similar vein, McNees (1992) argues that the users employ the dispersion of individual point forecasts as an index of market uncertainty, so that the pressures to converge towards consensus could have significant implications for the use (and credibility) of these forecasts.

Use of interval forecasts may be effective in overcoming such perceived pressures, since they do not require commitment to one specific value (i.e. point forecast). It is interesting to note that interval forecasts have largely been ignored in financial forecasting research. Given that financial managers are found to prefer interval forecasts to point predictions for explicitly communicating uncertainty (Baginski, Conrad & Hassell, 1993; Pownall, Wasley & Waymire, 1993), use of interval predictions presents an intriguing research dimension waiting to be explored.

Scenario planning could also provide a promising alternative in communicating uncertainties about future values of financial variables. Scenario-based procedures for decomposing judgmental probability forecasts have already been proposed (Salo & Bunn, 1995). Further research is required to determine whether scenario planning could play an important role in judgmental forecasting of financial futures (Jungermann & Thuring, 1987; van der Heijden, 1994; Wright, 1996).

In conclusion, it is clear that apparently conflicting or ambiguous signals will continue to dominate financial markets (Renshaw, 1993), accentuating the role of judgment in these domains. It is also inevitable that financial players' expectations and judgmental forecasts will influence the platforms underlying futures, options and other crucial financial markets. Future research into the specific needs of financial agents (as both providers and users of judgmental forecasts) remains critical for disseminating financial knowledge and uncertainty, hence contributing towards effective decision making in these settings.

# REFERENCES

Abarbanell, J. & Bernard, V.L. (1992) Tests of analysts' overreaction/ underreaction to earnings information as an explanation for anomalous stock price behavior. *Journal of Finance*, **47**, 1181–1208.

Abramson, B. & Clemen, R. (1995) Probability forecasting. *International Journal of Forecasting*, **11**, 1–4.

Affleck-Graves, J., Davis, L.R. & Mendenhall, R.R. (1990) Forecasts of earnings per share: possible sources of analyst superiority and bias. *Contemporary Accounting Research*, **6**, 501–17.

Ajinkya, B. & Gift, M. (1984) Corporate managers' earnings forecasts and symmetrical adjustments of market expectations. *Journal of Accounting Research*, **22**, 425–44.

Ali, A., Klein, A. & Rosenfeld, J. (1992) Analysts' use of information about permanent and transitory earnings components in forecasting annual EPS. *The Accounting Review*, **67**, 183–98.

Andreassen, P.B. (1990) Judgmental extrapolation and market overreaction: on the use and disuse of news. *Journal of Behavioral Decision Making*, **3**, 153–74.

Angus-Leppan, P. & Fatseas, V. (1986) The forecasting accuracy of trainee accountants using judgmental and statistical techniques. *Accounting and Business Research*, **16**, 179–88.

Armstrong, J.S. (1983) Relative accuracy of judgemental and extrapolative methods in forecasting annual earnings. *Journal of Forecasting*, **2**, 437–47.

Armstrong, J.S. (1986) The ombudsman: research on forecasting: a quarter-century review, 1960–1984. *Interfaces*, **16**, 89–109.

Armstrong, J.S. (1989) Combining forecasts: the end of the beginning or the beginning of the end. *International Journal of Forecasting*, **5**, 584–8.

Baginski, S.P., Conrad, E.J. & Hassell, J.M. (1993) The effects of management forecast precision on equity pricing and on the assessment of earnings uncertainty. *The Accounting Review*, **68**, 913–27.

Bandyopadhyay, S.P., Brown, L.D. & Richardson, G.D. (1995) Analysts' use of earnings forecasts in predicting stock returns: forecast horizon effects. *International Journal of Forecasting*, **11**, 429–45.

Barry, C.B. & Jennings, R.H. (1992) Management earnings forecasts and security prices. In J.B. Guerard & M.N. Gultekin (eds), *Handbook of Security Analyst Forecasting and Asset Allocation*. JAI Press, Greenwich, CT, pp. 51–66.

Bartos, J.A. (1969) The Assessment of Probability Distributions for Future Security Prices. Unpublished PhD Thesis, Indiana University, Graduate School of Business.

Basi, B.A., Carey, K.J. & Twark, R.D. (1976)   A comparison of the accuracy of corporate and security analysts' forecasts of earnings. *The Accounting Review*, **51**, 244–54.

Batchelor, R. & Dua, P. (1990)   Forecaster ideology, forecasting technique, and the accuracy of economic forecasts. *International Journal of Forecasting*, **6**, 3–10.

Batchelor, R. & Dua, P. (1992)   Conservatism and consensus-seeking among economic forecasters. *Journal of Forecasting*, **11**, 169–81.

Belton, V. & Goodwin, P. (1996)   Remarks on the application of the analytic hierarchy process to judgmental forecasting. *International Journal of Forecasting*, **12**, 155–61.

Benson, P.G., Curley, S.P. & Smith, G.F. (1995)   Belief assessment: an underdeveloped phase of probability elicitation. *Management Science*, **41**, 1639–53.

Benson, P.G. & Önkal, D. (1992)   The effects of feedback on the performance of probability forecasters. *International Journal of Forecasting*, **8**, 559–73.

Blair, A.R., Nachtmann, R., Olson, J.E. & Saaty, T.L. (1987)   Forecasting foreign exchange rates: an expert judgment approach. *Socio-Economic Planning Sciences*, **21**, 363–9.

Bolger, F. & Harvey, N. (1993)   Context-sensitive heuristics in statistical reasoning. *Quarterly Journal of Experimental Psychology*, **46A**, 779–811.

Bolger, F. & Wright, G. (1993)   Coherence and calibration in expert probability judgement. *OMEGA*, **21**, 629–44.

Bolger, F. & Wright, G. (1994)   Assessing the quality of expert judgement: issues and analysis. *Decision Support Systems*, **11**, 1–24.

Branson, B.C., Lorek, K.S. & Pagach, D.P. (1995)   Evidence on the superiority of analysts' quarterly earnings forecasts for small capitalization firms. *Decision Sciences*, **26**, 243–63.

Brown, L.D. (1993)   Earnings forecasting research: its implications for capital markets research. *International Journal of Forecasting*, **9**, 295–320.

Brown, L.D. (1996)   Analyst forecasting errors and their implications for security analysis: an alternative perspective. *Financial Analysts' Journal*, Jan–Feb, 40–47.

Brown, L.D., Hagerman, R.L., Griffin, P.A. & Zmijewski, M.E. (1987)   Security analyst superiority relative to univariate time-series models in forecasting quarterly earnings. *Journal of Accounting and Economics*, **9**, 61–87.

Brown, L.D., Richardson, G.D. & Schwager, S.J. (1987)   An information interpretation of financial analyst superiority in forecasting earnings. *Journal of Accounting Research*, **25**, 49–67.

Brown, L.D., Richardson, G.D. & Trzcinka, C.A. (1991)   Strong-form efficiency on the Toronto Stock Exchange: an examination of analyst price forecasts. *Contemporary Accounting Research*, **7**, 323–46.

Brown, L.D. & Rozeff, M.S. (1978)   The superiority of analysts' forecasts as measures of expectations: evidence from earnings. *The Journal of Finance*, **33**, 1–16.

Brown, L.D. & Zmijewski, M.E. (1987)   The effect of labor strikes on security analysts' forecast superiority and on the association between risk-adjusted stock returns and unexpected earnings. *Contemporary Accounting Research*, **4**, 61–75.

Bunn, D.W. (1994)   Forecasting with judgmental, AI and computationally-intensive technologies. Research review paper presented at the EURO XIII/OR 36 Meeting, Glasgow, July.

Bunn, D.W. & Salo, A.A. (1996)   Adjustment of forecasts with model consistent expectations. *International Journal of Forecasting*, **12**, 163–70.

Bunn, D.W. & Wright, G. (1991)   Interaction of judgmental and statistical forecasting methods: issues and analysis. *Management Science*, **37**(5), 501–18.

Camerer, C., Loewenstein, G. & Weber, M. (1989)   The curse of knowledge in economic settings: an experimental analysis. *Journal of Political Economy*, **97**, 1232–55.

Casey, C. & Selling, T.I. (1986)   The effect of task predictability and prior probability disclosure on judgment quality and confidence. *The Accounting Review*, **61**, 302–17.

Chalos, P. (1985)   The superior performance of loan review committee. *Journal of Commercial Bank Lending*, **68**, 60–66.

Clemen, R.T. (1989)   Combining forecasts: a review and annotated bibliography. *International Journal of Forecasting*, **5**, 559–83.

Clemen, R.T., Murphy, A.H. & Winkler, R.L. (1995)   Screening probability forecasts: contrasts between choosing and combining. *International Journal of Forecasting*, **11**, 133–46.

Collins, W.A., Hopwood, W. & McKeown, J.C. (1984)   The predictability of interim earnings over alternative quarters. *Journal of Accounting Research*, Autumn, 467–79.

Conroy, R. & Harris, R. (1987)   Consensus forecasts of corporate earnings: analysts' forecasts and time series methods. *Management Science*, **33**(6), 725–38.

Cowles, A. (1933)   Can stock market forecasters forecast? *Econometrica*, **1**, 309–24.

Cowles, A. (1944)   Stock market forecasting. *Econometrica*, **12**, 206–14.

Curley, S.P. & Benson, P.G. (1994)   Applying a cognitive perspective to probability construction. In P. Ayton & G. Wright (eds), *Subjective Probability*. Wiley, Chichester, pp. 185–209.

Curley, S.P., Browne, G.J., Smith, G.F. & Benson, P.G. (1995)   Arguments in the practical reasoning underlying constructive probability responses. *Journal of Behavioral Decision Making*, **8**, 1–20.

Dalrymple, D.J. (1987) Sales forecasting practices. *International Journal of Forecasting*, **3**, 379–91.

De Bondt, W.F.M. (1992) What are investment advisors paid for? The Shefrin–Statman and competing views. In J.B. Guerard & M.N. Gultekin (eds), *Handbook of Security Analyst Forecasting and Asset Allocation*. JAI Press, Greenwich, CT, pp. 121–37.

De Bondt, W.F.M. (1993) Betting on trends: intuitive forecasts of financial risk and return. *International Journal of Forecasting*, **9**, 355–71.

De Bondt, W.F.M. & Thaler, R.H. (1985) Does the stock market overreact? *Journal of Finance*, **40**, 793–805.

De Bondt, W.F.M. & Thaler, R.H. (1987) Further evidence on investor overreaction and stock market seasonality. *Journal of Finance*, **42**, 557–81.

De Bondt, W.F.M. & Thaler, R.H. (1989) A mean-reverting walk down Wall Street. *Journal of Economic Perspectives*, **3**, 189–202.

De Bondt, W.F.M. & Thaler, R.H. (1990) Do security analysts overreact. *American Economic Review*, **80**, 52–7.

Dimson, E. & Marsh, P. (1984) An analysis of brokers' and analysts' unpublished forecasts of UK stock returns. *Journal of Finance*, **39**, 1257–92.

Elton, E.J., Gruber, M.J. & Grossman, S. (1986) Discrete expectational data and portfolio performance. *Journal of Finance*, **3**, 699–712.

Elton, E.J., Gruber, M.J. & Gultekin, M.N. (1981) Expectations and share prices. *Management Science*, **27**, 975–87.

Elton, E.J., Gruber, M.J. & Gultekin, M.N. (1984) Professional expectations: accuracy and diagnosis of errors. *Journal of Financial and Quantitative Analysis*, December, 351–63.

Fama, E.F. (1970) Efficient capital markets: a review of theory and empirical work. *Journal of Finance*, **25**, 383–417.

Fan, D.K., Lau, K.-N. & Leung, P.-L. (1996) Combining ordinal forecasts with an application in a financial market. *Journal of Forecasting*, **15**, 37–48.

Fildes, R. & Hastings, R. (1994) The organization and improvement of market forecasting. *Journal of the Operational Research Society*, **45**, 1–16.

Fildes, R. & Makridakis, S. (1995) The impact of empirical accuracy studies on time series analysis and forecasting. *International Statistical Review*, **63**, 289–308.

Finger, C. (1994) The ability of earnings to predict future earnings and cash flow. *Journal of Accounting Research*, **32**, 210–23.

Firth, M. (1975) The forecasting of company profits. *The Accountants Review*, **26**, 35–44.

Fischhoff, B. (1982) For those condemned to study the past: heuristics and biases in hindsight. In D. Kahneman, P. Slovic & A. Tversky (eds), *Judgment under Uncertainty: Heuristics and Biases*. Cambridge University Press, Cambridge, pp. 335–51.

Fischhoff, B. (1994)   What forecasts (seem to) mean. *International Journal of Forecasting*, **10**, 387–403.

Foster, G. (1981)   Intra-industry information transfers associated with earnings releases. *Journal of Accounting and Economics*, **3**, 201–32.

Foster, G. (1986)   *Financial Statement Analysis*, 2nd edn. Prentice-Hall, Englewood Cliffs, NJ.

Francis, J. & Philbrick, D. (1993)   Analysts' decisions as products of a multi-task environment. *Journal of Accounting Research*, **31**, 216–30.

Fried, D. & Givoly, D. (1982)   Financial analysts' forecasts of earnings: a better surrogate for market expectations. *Journal of Accounting and Economics*, **4**, 85–107.

Ganzach, Y. (1994)   Feedback representation and prediction strategies. *Organizational Behavior and Human Decision Processes*, **59**, 391–409.

Genest, C. & Zidek, J.V. (1986)   Combining probability distributions: a critique and an annotated bibliography. *Statistical Science*, **1**, 114–48.

Goodwin, P. & Wright, G. (1991)   *Decision Analysis for Management Judgment*. Wiley, Chichester.

Goodwin, P. & Wright, G. (1993)   Improving judgmental time series forecasting: a review of the guidance provided by research. *International Journal of Forecasting*, **9**, 147–61.

Goodwin, P. & Wright, G. (1994)   Heuristics, biases and improvement strategies in judgmental time series. *Omega*, **22**, 553–68.

Granger, C.W.J. (1989)   Combining forecasts—twenty years later. *Journal of Forecasting*, **8**, 167–73.

Granger, C.W.J. (1992)   Forecasting stock market prices: lessons for forecasters. *International Journal of Forecasting*, **8**, 3–13.

Guerard, J.B. (1987)   Linear constraints, robust-weighting and efficient composite modelling. *Journal of Forecasting*, **6**(3), 193–9.

Guerard, J.B. & Beidleman, C.R. (1987)   Composite earnings forecasting efficiency. *Interfaces*, **17**(5), 103–13.

Guerard, J.B. & Lawrence, K.D. (1992)   The effectiveness of security analysts' forecasts: a note. In J.B. Guerard & M.N. Gultekin (eds), *Handbook of Security Analyst Forecasting and Asset Allocation*. JAI Press, Greenwich, CT, pp. 153–61.

Guerard, J.B., Stone, B.K. & Hansen, G. (1992)   Composite forecasting of annual corporate earnings: implications for portfolio managers. In J.B. Guerard & M.N. Gultekin (eds), *Handbook of Security Analyst Forecasting and Asset Allocation*. JAI Press, Greenwich, CT, pp. 79–97.

Harvey, N. & Bolger, F. (1996)   Graphs versus tables: effects of data presentation format on judgemental forecasting. *International Journal of Forecasting*, **12**, 119–37.

Hoch, S.J. (1984)   Availability and interference in predictive judgment. *Journal of Experimental Psychology: Learning, Memory and Cognition*, October, 649–62.

Hopwood, W.S. & McKeown, J.C. (1990) Evidence on surrogates for earnings expectations within a capital market context. *Journal of Accounting, Auditing and Finance*, **5**, 339–68.

Ikenberry, D., Lakonishok, J. & Vermaelen, T. (1995) Market under-reaction to open market share repurchases. *Journal of Financial Economics*, **39**, 181–208.

Jacquillat, B. & Grandin, P. (1994) Performance measurement of analysts' forecasts. *Journal of Portfolio Management*, **21**, 94–102.

Jennings, R. (1987) Unsystematic security price movements, management earnings forecasts and revisions in consensus analyst earnings forecasts. *Journal of Accounting Research*, **25**, 90–110.

Johnson, W.B. (1983) "Representativeness" in judgmental predictions of corporate bankruptcy. *The Accounting Review*, **LVIII**, 78–97.

Jungermann, H. & Thuring, M. (1987) The use of mental models for generating scenarios. In G. Wright & P. Ayton (eds), *Judgmental Forecasting*. Wiley, Chichester, pp. 245–66.

Kabus, I. (1976) You can bank on uncertainty. *Harvard Business Review*, May–June, 95–105.

Kolb, R.A. & Stekler, H.O. (1996) How well do analysts forecast interest rates. *Journal of Forecasting*, **15**, 385–94.

Kross, W., Ro, B. & Schroeder, D. (1990) Earnings expectations: the analysts' information advantage. *The Accounting Review*, **65**, 461–76.

Libby, R. (1975) Accounting ratios and the prediction of failure: some behavioral evidence. *Journal of Accounting Research*, Spring, 150–61.

Lichtenstein, S. & Fischhoff, B. (1977) Do those who know more also know more about how much they know? *Organizational Behavior and Human Performance*, **20**, 159–83.

Lobo, G.J. (1991) Alternative methods of combining security analysts' and statistical forecasts of annual corporate earnings. *International Journal of Forecasting*, **7**, 57–63.

Lobo, G.J. & Nair, R.D. (1990) Combining judgmental and statistical forecasts: an application to earnings forecasts. *Decision Sciences*, **21**, 446–60.

Lobo, G.J. & Nair, R.D. (1991) Analysts' utilization of historical earnings information. *Managerial and Decision Economics*, **12**, 383–93.

MacDonald, R. & Marsh, I.W. (1994) Combining exchange rate forecasts: what is the optimal consensus measure. *Journal of Forecasting*, **13**, 313–32.

Maines, L.A. (1996) An experimental examination of subjective forecast combination. *International Journal of Forecasting*, **12**, 223–33.

Maines, L.A. & Hand, J.R.M. (1996) Individuals' perceptions and mis-perceptions of time series properties of quarterly earnings. *The Accounting Review*, **71**, 317–36.

McHugh, A.K. & Sparkes, J.R. (1983) The forecasting dilemma. *Management Accounting*, **61**, 30–34.

McNees, S.K. (1992) The uses and abuses of "consensus" forecasts. *Journal of Forecasting*, **11**, 703–10.

Menezes, L. & Bunn, D.W. (1993) Diagnostic tracking and model specification in combined forecasts of UK inflation. *Journal of Forecasting*, **12**, 559–72.

Mentzer, J.T. & Cox, J.E. (1984) Familiarity, application, and performance of sales forecasting techniques. *Journal of Forecasting*, **3**, 27–36.

Mills, T.C. (1996) Non-linear forecasting of financial time series: an overview and some new models. *Journal of Forecasting*, **15**, 127–35.

Moser, D.V. (1989) The effects of output interference, availability, and accounting information on investors' predictive judgments. *The Accounting Review*, **64**, 433–48.

Muradoğlu, G. & Önkal, D. (1994) An exploratory analysis of the portfolio managers' probabilistic forecasts of stock prices. *Journal of Forecasting*, **13**, 565–78.

Murphy, A.H. & Winkler, R.L. (1992) Diagnostic verification of probability forecasts. *International Journal of Forecasting*, **7**, 435–55.

Newbold, P., Zumwalt, J.K. & Kannan, S. (1987) Combining forecasts to improve earnings per share prediction. *International Journal of Forecasting*, **3**, 229–38.

O'Brien, P. (1988) Analysts' forecasts as earnings expectations. *Journal of Accounting and Economics*, **10**, 53–83.

O'Connor, M. & Lawrence, M. (1989) An examination of the accuracy of judgmental confidence intervals in time series forecasting. *Journal of Forecasting*, **8**, 141–55.

Önkal, D. & Dirimtekin, S. (1996) Effects of contextual information and feedback on judgmental forecasts of stock prices. Paper presented at the Sixteenth International Symposium on Forecasting, Istanbul, Turkey, June.

Önkal, D. & Muradoğlu, G. (1994) Evaluating probabilistic forecasts of stock prices in a developing stock market. *European Journal of Operational Research*, **74**, 350–58.

Önkal, D. & Muradoğlu, G. (1995) Effects of feedback on probabilistic forecasts of stock prices. *International Journal of Forecasting*, **11**, 307–19.

Önkal, D. & Muradoğlu, G. (1996) Effects of task format on probabilistic forecasting of stock prices. *International Journal of Forecasting*, **12**, 9–24.

Pollock, A.C. & Wilkie, M.E. (1992) Currency forecasting: human judgment or models. *VBA-Journal*, **3** (September), 21–9.

Pollock, A.C. & Wilkie, M.E. (1993) Directional judgemental financial forecasting: trends and random walks. In R. Flavell (ed.), *Modelling Reality and Personal Modelling*, Physica-Verlag, Heidelberg, pp. 253–71.

Pollock, A.C. & Wilkie, M.E. (1996) The quality of bank forecasts: the dollar–pound exchange rate, 1990–1993. *European Journal of Operational Research*, **91**, 306–14.

Pollock, A.C., Wilkie, M.E. & Pollock, J.F. (1996) A framework for examining the quality of bank forecasts: the yen-DM, 1990–1993. Paper presented at the Sixteenth International Symposium on Forecasting, Istanbul, Turkey, June.

Pownall, G., Wasley, C. & Waymire, G. (1993) The stock price effects of alternative types of management earnings forecasts. *The Accounting Review*, **68**, 896–912.

Raiffa, H. (1968) *Decision Analysis*. Addison-Wesley, Reading, MA.

Renshaw, E. (1993) Modeling the stock market for forecasting purposes. *Journal of Portfolio Management*, **20**, 76–81.

Ronis, D.L. & Yates, J.F. (1987) Components of probability judgment accuracy: individual consistency and effects of subject matter and assessment method. *Organizational Behavior and Human Decision Processes*, **40**, 193–218.

Rowe, G. & Wright, G. (1996) The impact of task characteristics on the performance of structured group forecasting techniques. *International Journal of Forecasting*, **12**, 73–89.

Saaty, T.L. (1990) *Multicriteria Decision Making: The Analytic Hierarchy Process*. RWS Publications, Pittsburgh, PA.

Saaty, T.L. & Vargas, L.G. (1991) *Prediction, Projection and Forecasting*. Kluwer Academic, Norwell, MA.

Salo, A.A. & Bunn, D.W. (1995) Decomposition in the assessment of judgmental probability forecasts. *Technological Forecasting and Social Change*, **49**, 13–25.

Schipper, K. (1991) Commentary on analysts' forecasts. *Accounting Horizons*, **5**, 105–21.

Shepanski, A. (1983) Tests of theories of information processing behavior in credit judgment. *The Accounting Review*, **58**, 581–99.

Silverman, B.G. (1992) Judgment error and expert critics in forecasting tasks. *Decision Sciences*, **23**(5), 1199–1219.

Slovic, P. (1969) Analysing the expert judge: a descriptive study of a stockbroker's decision processes. *Journal of Applied Psychology*, **53**, 255–63.

Slovic, P. (1972) Psychological study of human judgment: implications for investment decision making. *Journal of Finance*, **27**, 779–99.

Smith, G.G., Benson, P.G. & Curley, S.P. (1991) Belief, knowledge, and uncertainty: a cognitive perspective on subjective probability. *Organizational Behavior and Human Decision Processes*, **48**, 291–321.

Stael von Holstein, C.-A.S. (1972) Probabilistic forecasting: an experiment related to the stock market. *Organizational Behavior and Human Performance*, **8**, 139–58.

Stickel, S.E. (1993) Accuracy improvements from a consensus of updated individual analyst earnings forecasts. *International Journal of Forecasting*, **9**, 345–53.

Tversky, A. & Kahneman, D. (1974) Judgment under uncertainty: heuristics and biases. *Science*, **185**, 1124–31.

Ulengin, F. & Ulengin, B. (1994) Forecasting foreign exchange rates: a comparative evaluation of AHP. *OMEGA*, **22**, 505–19.

van der Heijden, K. (1994) Probabilistic planning and scenario planning. In P. Ayton & G. Wright (eds), *Subjective Probability*. Wiley, Chichester, pp. 549–72.

Webby, R. & O'Connor, M. (1996) Judgemental and statistical time series forecasting: a review of the literature. *International Journal of Forecasting*, **12**, 91–118.

Whitecotton, S.M. (1996) The effects of experience and a decision aid on the slope, scatter, and bias of earnings forecasts. *Organizational Behavior and Human Decision Processes*, **66**, 111–21.

Whitred, G. & Zimmer, I. (1985) The implications of distress prediction models for corporate lending. *Accounting and Finance*, **25**, 1–13.

Wilkie, M.E., Önkal, D. & Pollock, A.C. (1996) An examination of time series extrapolative judgment in a currency forecasting context. Paper presented at the Sixteenth International Symposium on Forecasting, Istanbul, Turkey, June.

Wilkie, M.E. & Pollock, A.C. (1994) Directional currency forecasting: an investigation into probability judgement accuracy. In L. Peccati & M. Viren (eds), *Financial Modelling*. Physica-Verlag, Heidelberg, pp. 354–64.

Wilkie, M.E. & Pollock, A.C. (1996) An application of probability judgement accuracy measures to currency forecasting. *International Journal of Forecasting*, **12**, 25–40.

Wilkie, M.E., Tuohy, A.P. & Pollock, A.C. (1993) Examining heuristics and biases in judgemental currency forecasting. *VBA-Journal*, **2** (June), 12–17.

Winkler, R.L. (1972) The assessment of probability distributions for future security prices. In J.L. Bicksler (ed.), *Methodology in Finance-Investments*. D.C. Heath, Lexington, MA.

Winkler, R.L. (1973) Bayesian models for forecasting future security prices. *Journal of Financial and Quantitative Analysis*, **8**, 387–405.

Winklhofer, H., Diamantopoulos, A. & Witt, S.F. (1996) Forecasting practice: a review of the empirical literature and an agenda for future research. *International Journal of Forecasting*, **12**, 193–221.

Wolfe, C. & Flores, B. (1990) Judgmental adjustment of earnings forecasts. *Journal of Forecasting*, **9**, 389–405.

Wright, G. (1996) Scenario planning: pros and cons. Paper presented at the Sixteenth International Symposium on Forecasting, Istanbul, Turkey, June.

Wright, G., Rowe, G., Bolger, F. & Gammack, J. (1994) Coherence, calibration, and expertise in judgmental probability forecasting. *Organizational Behavior and Human Decision Processes*, **57**, 1–25.

Wright, W.F. (1980) Cognitive information processing biases: implications for producers and users of financial information. *Decision Sciences*, **April**, 284–98.

Yates, J.F., McDaniel, L.S. & Brown, E.S. (1991) Probabilistic forecasts of stock prices and earnings: the hazards of nascent expertise. *Organizational Behavior and Human Decision Processes*, **49**, 60–79.

Yates, J.F., Price, P.C., Lee, J.-W. & Ramirez, J. (1996) Good probabilistic forecasters: the "consumer's" perspective. *International Journal of Forecasting*, **12**, 41–56.

Zmijewski, M.E. (1993) Comments on "Earnings forecasting research: its implications for capital markets research" by L. Brown. *International Journal of Forecasting*, **9**, 337–42.

# Chapter 7

# Reasoning with Category Knowledge in Probability Forecasting: Typicality and Perceived Variability Effects

Glenn J. Browne* and Shawn P. Curley**

*Texas Tech University, Lubbock, Texas, and
**University of Minnesota, Minneapolis, USA

## SUMMARY

Judgment in forecasting is claimed to emanate from an underlying reasoning process of constructing arguments. To understand the reasoning upon which judgments are based, a theoretically-grounded typology of arguments is presented that organizes argument types according to the knowledge that is used to warrant movement from evidence to claim. The chapter then focuses on arguments that are based on the direct application of category knowledge. Of particular interest are the distributional characteristics of people's category knowledge, which have impacts on the way that reasoning is performed. To explore these impacts, the chapter develops a theoretical understanding of the roles of typicality and variability in probability assessment. Perceptions

*Forecasting with Judgment.* Edited by G. Wright and P. Goodwin.
© 1998 John Wiley & Sons Ltd.

of variability—within and between categories—have been generally neglected by researchers. Such perceptions are expected to have impacts on the selection and use of evidence for probability forecasting and decision making, and these expected impacts are expressed in a series of propositions.

## 7.1 INTRODUCTION

Judgmental forecasting operates in a wide variety of managerial and other professional settings. Because of the variation that is inherent to all processes, forecasts and the decisions to which they apply entail uncertainty. A standard practice in decision analysis (the practice and techniques of aiding decision making) is to incorporate uncertainty formally through a metric, typically using probabilities. Even in more informal decision making, people deliberate risks and uncertainties in arriving at decisions. Thus, probability assessment has arisen as a major topic in the study of judgmental forecasting and of decision making more generally. However, although the use of probability assessment for forecasting requires the ability to apply category knowledge in arriving at such judgments (Browne, Curley & Benson, 1997a), the role of reasoning using category knowledge has not been explored in forecasting contexts. This chapter aims to further our understanding in this area by developing a theoretical account of category knowledge as applied to probability assessment.

The initial basis for such a theory is a cognitive explanation of the processes involved in probability assessment (Smith, Benson & Curley, 1991). A skeleton illustration of that explanation is shown in Figure 7.1. Constructing a probability involves several cognitive processes in conjunction. The generation of evidence is typically dominated by perceptual and memory processes. Forming beliefs about future events of interest is central to probability assessment, and is dominated by a process of reasoning in which arguments are constructed. The subsequent evaluation of evidence and arguments is dominated by judgmental processes, i.e. by activities in which stimuli are characterized along some scale or dimension. To the extent that a belief cannot be established with certainty, the belief is qualified, e.g. with a probability. Hence, the crux of the theory summarized by Figure 7.1 is that probabilities arise from limitations of arguments developed through reasoning.

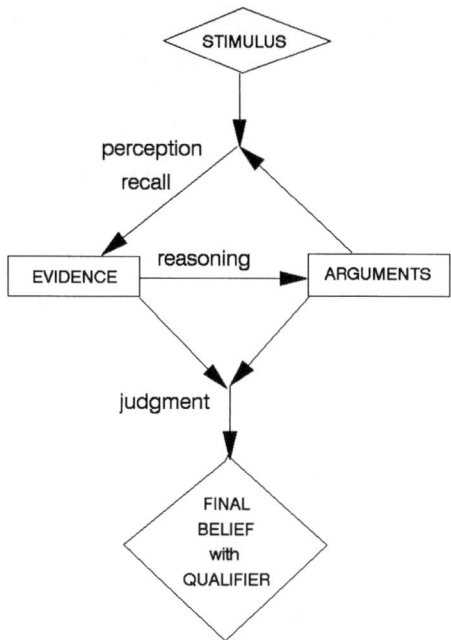

**Figure 7.1** Probability (qualifier) assessment as resulting from multiple cognitive processes

By "reasoning" we mean practical reasoning (Toulmin, 1958), rather than the formal structures of deduction. In reasoning for probability assessment, people form numerous arguments to establish conclusions in the same way that they argue with others to establish claims (Billig, 1987; Golden, Berquist & Coleman, 1983, Chapter 21). Practical reasoning is an exercise in argument construction, the building of data–warrant–claim connections that move the arguer from proposition to proposition. Figure 7.2 shows an example of an argument, demonstrating the components of argument according to the theory of Toulmin (1958). The warrant bridges the gap between data (i.e. evidence) and claim by providing a rationale for why the two should be connected (see also Brockriede & Ehninger, 1960). In addition to these essential components of data, warrant and claim, there are three optional characteristics of an argument. Backing can be used to support the warrant that is pivotal in justifying the movement between propositions. Backing reflects a type of argument chaining used to strengthen the reasoning. Rebuttals provide conditions under which the argument's claim may not hold, or serve as a means of limiting or countering arguments. A qualifier is an explicit acknowledgment of the inconclusiveness of the argument, and may be qualitative or quantitative. Probabilities are a quantitative form of qualifier.

To link propositions through the use of warrants, individuals rely upon their world knowledge. There are a number of forms of knowledge that are potentially available. People may have causal knowledge, testimony from more or less credible authorities, similarity connections, or rules and principles (formal or informal) upon which to draw. An important type of world knowledge that people use in practical reasoning is category knowledge (Curley et al., 1995). The example in Figure 7.2 demonstrates the use of category knowledge to form an argument from a proposition about instances to a proposition about the general category from which the instances were drawn. This is one of several types of arguments that derive from category knowledge.

Studying category knowledge from a cognitive perspective has only recently begun to be explored in decision research. The majority of cognitive research on categorization has addressed categorization itself as the task. Examples of such tasks include: to which category does B belong ($A_1$ or $A_2$)?; what are the properties associated with categories (do birds fly?); to what extent do instances share these properties (do penguins fly?); and how are such category–property connections

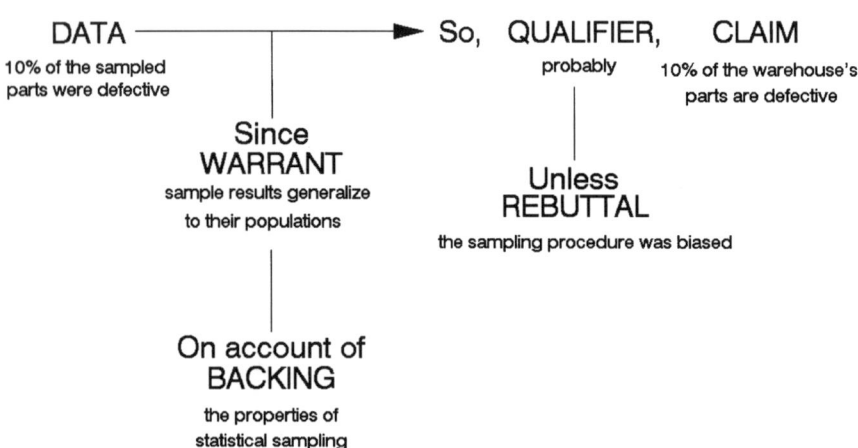

**Figure 7.2** Argument structure (Toulmin, 1958), with example

represented? Although of interest in their own right, there is no obvious, direct connection that is drawn between these tasks of category identification and object classification, on the one hand, and forecasting and decision making, on the other.

Although category knowledge may serve different functions in forecasting, of particular interest is its use in argument construction through reasoning. As is apparent from Figure 7.1, arguments can contribute to forecasting through both evidence evaluation and evidence selection. In evaluating evidence, people use category knowledge to create arguments for the purpose of forming beliefs about possible future realities. In evidence selection, people consider the arguments they have developed or that they might develop as guides for searching and bringing forth additional evidence of potential use (cf. Browne, Curley & Benson, 1997b).

The goal of this chapter is to explore the relevance, features and implications of the structure of category knowledge to further our understanding of probabilistic forecasting. The next two sections lay groundwork for studying the use of category knowledge in reasoning within probability assessment. The first of the sections covers basic information about category knowledge as it applies to reasoning. The subsequent section introduces a distributional approach to forecasters' uses of category knowledge. Once this groundwork is laid, the following sections apply the conceptualization to the use of individual arguments, and then to reasoning with multiple categories.

## 7.2 REASONING WITH CATEGORY KNOWLEDGE

The use of categorization as a means of organizing knowledge has several important benefits, including cognitive efficiency and the generation of relevant information to support inferences. These benefits are particularly important in the use of such knowledge for reasoning in forecasting situations. In forecasting, category knowledge may be used to construct a number of arguments for and/or against the future events in question (Smith, Benson & Curley, 1991). This does not mean that the person is necessarily performing a categorization task; rather, relevant category knowledge, often in combination with other knowledge, is used to construct various arguments having a bearing on the target proposition.

Several models of categorization have been proposed by researchers. Barsalou (1992, Chapter 2) usefully divided these into three types of models: exemplar, prototype and classical. Exemplar models represent a category as a collection of specific, concrete examples. Prototype models contain a single, idealized category representation; this representation is a collection of typical properties that, as a whole, may not even exist in reality. Classical models define categories in terms of abstracted rules of membership, e.g. defining the category "bachelor" in terms of the properties "unmarried" and "male". Evidence suggests that people's categories seem to employ a combination of these three models.

From the research motivated by these models, several principles of categorization have strong empirical support and are abstracted by Barsalou. Another useful summary of principles from categorization task research, within the context of probability assessment, is provided by Henderson & Peterson (1992). Among the principles that have been demonstrated and that apply directly to reasoning are:

- People's knowledge of elements is organized into groups or categories.
- Categories can contain exemplars, prototypical elements and defining properties.
- Categories can contain very specific knowledge about exemplars.
- Categories connect to a loose organization of shared properties.
- The properties associated with a category are not weighted equally.
- Elements have membership in multiple categories.
- Categorization is context-dependent.
- Categories are hierarchical. There are levels of abstraction.

Hierarchical relationships represent elements, categories and sub-categories, organized in terms of superset-to-subset relationships with associated features (Collins & Michalski, 1989). Hierarchies may capture "instance/type of" relationships (e.g. cat–mammal–animal), in which the links denote entities that share a similarity of features or characteristics that group them under a common superordinate. Alternatively, the links may capture "component/part of" relationships (e.g. paw–leg–body part), implying a partitioning into sub-systems or sub-elements.

In addition to vertical connections, hierarchical elements can also be connected as descriptors, e.g. a link between "body part" and "cat" can capture the knowledge that cats have legs and paws (sub-elements of "body parts"). In this link, "body part" is a *descriptor* of the node "cat", and "leg" and "paw" are possible *values* of this descriptor function. An illustration of the simplified hierarchical structure in generic form is shown in Figure 7.3.

Finally, there are two other principles noted by Barsalou and by Henderson & Peterson that deserve special emphasis for the application of category knowledge to probability assessment:

(1) *Categorization is spontaneous* (however, the use of category knowledge in reasoning is not). Categorization as a task, e.g. in concept identification and perception, is a spontaneous process. However, when using category knowledge for the construction of arguments, the knowledge is applied consciously. Category knowledge is available and used to reason in an active, conscious, deliberative fashion. This is a major difference between categorization as commonly studied as a task and the use of category knowledge in reasoning. An important implication for reasoning in probability assessment is that category selection is a choice of the forecaster. Presumably, people select categories and features to construct the strongest possible arguments. Since multiple categories are available at differing levels of hierarchical abstraction, the role of, and effects on, this choice are of research interest and will be discussed in a later section of the chapter.

(2) *Elements have graded membership in categories.* This concept of graded membership is related to the notion that, through experience in the world, people develop fuzzy classifications of categories that have something akin to distributional properties (Attneave, 1957; Fried & Holyoak, 1984; Glass & Holyoak, 1986).

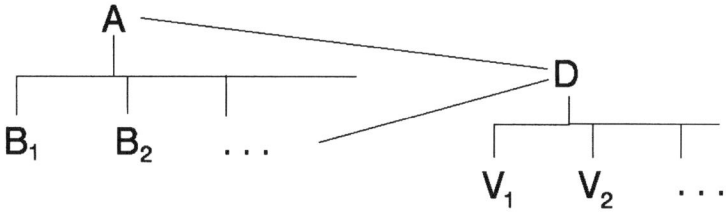

**Figure 7.3**  A generic illustration showing category $A$ with subcategories $B_i$, and a descriptor category $D$ with values $V_j$ connected to $A$ and the $B_i$. From Curley et al., 1995, with permission of John Wiley & Sons Ltd.

This distributional description of categorization is the subject of the next section.

## 7.3   A DISTRIBUTIONAL CHARACTERIZATION OF CATEGORIZATION

As noted above, prototypes and exemplars are established constructs for representing the centrality of a category, and such notions of central tendency have been studied extensively in psychology (e.g., Fried and Holyoak, 1984). Another distributional property relevant to the use of category knowledge is some sense of the variability of the category. However, perceptions of variability have been less studied.

This relative attention paid to centrality compared to variability has also occurred in the study of probability assessment. For example, typicality is a centrality concept and is related to use of the representativeness heuristic (Kahneman and Tversky, 1972; Smith and Medin, 1981). To demonstrate, consider one manifestation of the representativeness heuristic: when the probability that an individual has a particular property is judged by how representative the individual is of the target property. Tversky and Kahneman (1982) demonstrated how use of the heuristic can lead individuals to commit the conjunction fallacy using examples like that of the "Linda Problem". That problem was based on the following description:

> Linda is 31 years old, single, outspoken, and very bright. She majored in philosophy. As a student, she was deeply concerned with issues of discrimination and social justice, and also participated in anti-nuclear demonstrations (p. 92).

After reading the description, subjects ranked the likelihood of various statements. A modal response, demonstrating the conjunction fallacy, was to judge a conjunction such as "Linda is a feminist and a bank teller" to be more probable than "Linda is a bank teller". The more detailed proposition was judged by the experimenters as being more "typical" of a feminist. This typicality presumably led subjects to violate a basic rule of probability, namely, that a subset cannot be more likely than its superset.

Subsequently, Shafir, Smith & Osherson (1990) defined a "typicality effect" as "subjects' estimates of the probability that instance I belongs to category C is an increasing function of the typicality of I in C"

(p. 229). Shafir, Smith & Osherson gave descriptions of people to subjects, together with "typical" and "atypical" constituent and conjunctive categories. They then asked subjects for the probability that a person was a member of these various categories. They found support for the typicality effect. In particular, strong positive correlations were found between a "conjunction effect" (subjects' judged *typicality* of an instance belonging to a conjunctive category rather than a constituent category) and a "conjunction fallacy" (subjects' judged *probability* of the instance belonging to the conjunctive category rather than the constituent category), indicating that typicality was mediating subjects' likelihood judgments.

Thus, the impact of the first distributional property of centrality has been supported in probability assessment as it relates to reasoning with category knowledge. We can use the same experimental design to argue the impact of perceived variability. Consider ranking the following propositions after receiving the description of Linda:

— Linda is a bank teller.
— Linda is an accountant.

Our own initial investigations, using 68 undergraduates as subjects, indicated that the two propositions are perceived as equally typical for Linda (that is, both are judged quite atypical), but that "bank tellers" is perceived as a much more variable (i.e. heterogeneous) category than the category of "accountants". This perceived variability is expected to determine which of the occupations is judged as more likely to describe Linda. As preliminary support, a different group of 45 undergraduate subjects assigned a higher mean likelihood judgment to the heterogeneous category when the categories were atypical (and so in the above example selected bank teller as more likely). In contrast, a higher mean likelihood judgment was provided for a homogeneous category when the categories were judged typical of the person described. Hence, the following general proposition is advanced:

*Proposition 1*: Likelihood judgments are mediated not only by perceived typicality (centrality) but also by the second distributional property of perceived variability of categories.

Although perceived variability is an important feature of reasoning with categories, its role and influence in decision making and probability forecasting have not been extensively studied. Perceptions of variability influence perceived argument strength, and thereby influence the selection of arguments during forecasting. One focus of the remainder of this chapter, then, is to develop specific propositions about how perceived variability is hypothesized to influence reasoning in probability assessment. To begin this task, we now turn to a discussion of individual arguments using category knowledge and how they are influenced by perceived variability.

## 7.4 INDIVIDUAL ARGUMENTS

An individual argument can be classified according to its content and form. The content of the argument captures what the argument is about. Content is task-specific, so such an analysis is particular to the tasks used. In contrast, argument form can be separated from context. The form of arguments can be organized as an argument typology (Table 7.1)[1]. This typology classifies arguments in terms of the warrants that allow movement from data to claim, from one proposition to another. The typology extends one presented by Benson, Curley & Smith (1995; Curley & Benson, 1994), which had its origins in a scheme originated by Brockriede & Ehninger

**Table 7.1** A taxonomy of argument types organized by their underlying relationships (adapted from Benson, Curley, and Smith, 1995; Curley and Benson, 1994)

| Relationship | Argument type | Description | Example |
|---|---|---|---|
| Cause | Causal | Non-intentional causal link between data and claim | The product will be profitable because those responsible are very competent |
| | Motivational in cause | Intentions of human agents used as a cause of some result | The product will be successful because the CEO is determined for it to succeed |
| | Motivational in effect | Concludes that some human intention exists | The CEO is determined to succeed because his job is dependent on success |

**Table 7.1**  (*continued*)

| Relationship | Argument type | Description | Example |
|---|---|---|---|
| Co-variation | Sign | Co-variational, but no directly causal, relationship between data and claim | Japan has developed a high GNP because it has a developed high-tech industry |
| Categories | Generalization | Induction from a sample to its population | Roughly 10% of the parts in the warehouse are defective because 10% of the sampled parts were defective |
| | Individuation | Concluding from the general population to a specific individual | All employees want job security. Thus, Chuck, being an employee, wants job security |
| | Categorization | Establishes member- ship in a category from the presence of certain features | Chuck is an employee because he has a 75% time appointment with our firm |
| | Hierarchical exclusion | A necessity appeal among instances that are mutually exclusive | The product will not have a demand in department or hardware stores, so its demand must come from service stations and auto- parts stores |
| | Hierarchical combination | The conjunction of an exhaustive set of instances implies their superset | The market is covered because we are selling in grocery and convenience stores, discount chains and drug stores |

*continued*

**Table 7.1** (*continued*)

| Relationship | Argument type | Description | Example |
|---|---|---|---|
| Similarity | Parallel case | Concludes based on a similarity between instances | It will take 25 minutes to drive to the airport because that is what it took last time |
| | Analogy | Concludes based on a similarity of relationship with something outside of the current domain of interest | Our corporate strategy is like a stool; therefore, we need all three components to be successful |
| Testimony | Authority | Appeal to an external source with potentially relevant knowledge | The economy will rebound because the leading economists have so predicted |
| Rule | Principle | Appeal to a principle of behavior | We will not lay off our employees because it would be unethical to do so |
| | Theory | Appeal to a non-causal theory of operation | I expect this sample to represent the population by virtue of the Law of Large Numbers |

(1960). The current typology ties argument structure to the psychology of assessment by connecting the argument types to the relationships in people's knowledge bases that support movements from one proposition to another. The relationships are based on knowledge of cause, co-variation, categories, similarity, testimony and rules.

Category knowledge is incorporated directly in this typology as one of the knowledge bases from which arguments are derived. In one study, across a variety of assessment tasks, approximately 20% of the arguments that subjects produced were based on such knowledge (Curley et al., 1995). In addition, such knowledge supports other arguments indirectly.

For example, as noted above, research has demonstrated that individuals' categories contain very specific knowledge about exemplars. Such knowledge supports arguments from similarity. As another example, the loose organization of shared properties within and among categories supports arguments from co-variation.

For present purposes, however, we focus on arguments that use category knowledge directly and relate the argument types to the distributional properties of typicality and perceived variability. Figure 7.4 shows graphic representations of three argument types that draw conclusions from hierarchical category structures (using the notation of the generic structure shown in Figure 7.3): generalization, individuation and categorization (Curley et al., 1994). Dotted lines indicate presumptions of the argument, single solid lines indicate evidence, and double solid lines indicate the conclusion of the argument.

STRUCTURE                    ILLUSTRATION

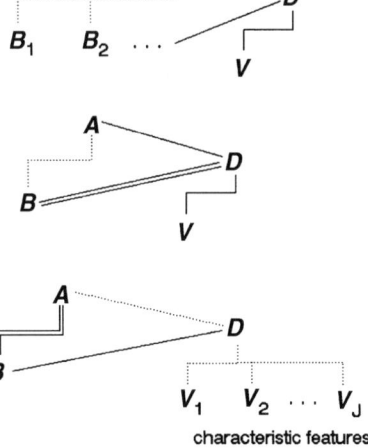

**(a) Generalization**

    Presume: $B_1$, $B_2$, ... are subsets of A.

    Evidence: $B_1$ has V; $B_2$ has V; ...

    Conclusion: A has V

**(b) Individuation**

    Presume: B is a subordinate of A.

    Evidence: A has V.

    Conclusion: B has V.

**(c) Categorization**

    Presume: Values $V_1$, ..., $V_J$ ($J \geq 1$) form

        a set of characteristic features of A.

    Evidence: B has $\{V_1, ..., V_J\}$.

    Conclusion: B is a subordinate of A.

**Figure 7.4** Three hierarchical argument types, the form of each argument, and an illustration of each argument. In the argument illustrations, dotted lines signify presumptions of the arguments, single solid lines signify the evidence, and double solid lines signify the conclusions of the arguments

## 7.4.1   Generalization

One argument structure derived from category knowledge is the inductive argument of *generalization*. In generalization, people reason from particular instances to a more general category based on their knowledge of such categories as stored in a hierarchical knowledge base. The observation of one or more instances ($B_1$, $B_2$ ...) sharing value $V$ is used to infer that the more general category $A$ has value $V$. This argument is typically applied to "instance/type of" hierarchies and has the structure shown in Figure 7.4a. For example, seeing numerous cats ($B_i$) with whiskers ($V$), I infer that all cats ($A$) have whiskers ($V$).

The generalization argument is influenced by perceived variability more than by typicality. In fact, it is not apparent that there is a consistent independent effect of typicality upon generalization. The readiness to generalize depends on the combination of any prior expectations about variability and of the variability present in the instances observed as evidence. Indeed, to the extent that there is homogeneity, *all* instances are typical. *Atypicality* sends a strong signal about possible variability.

The effect of perceived homogeneity on the evaluation of evidence in the generalization argument is captured in the following proposition:

> *Proposition 2*:   In evaluating evidence, people's readiness to generalize increases with the perceived homogeneity of the category for which instances are observed.

Thagard & Nisbett (1982) were among the first to marshal support for the notion that variability has an impact on generalizing from sample information to a larger class of events. Subsequently, Nisbett et al. (1983) demonstrated that subjects were sensitive to perceived variability in evaluating sample evidence for generalization. For example, for the color of a fictional bird found on a lost island (a feature which seems unlikely to vary from instance to instance of that species), subjects were willing to generalize to the broader class of all instances of the bird after observing only one instance, and the generalization did not change with increased sample sizes. However, when presented with one member of a tribe of people on the island who was obese (a more heterogeneous feature), subjects' willingness to generalize obesity to the larger class of the entire tribe decreased and sensitivity to sample size increased. Thus, this study demonstrated how perceived variability can have an impact on evidence evaluation, and provides support for Proposition 2.

It should also be noted that perceptions of variability are dynamic with accumulating evidence. That is, as new evidence is received, people will update their beliefs about the variability of a category. Thus, even for the obesity characteristic in Nisbett et al.'s study, subjects were eventually willing to generalize after receiving enough unanimous, maximally homogenous sample information. Ultimately, the consistency of the accumulating evidence altered the subjects' perceptions of the variability of obesity among the island's inhabitants, and allowed a strong generalization argument.

A second proposition regarding the generalization argument concerns the gathering of evidence:

*Proposition 3*:   In gathering evidence for generalization, people's need for more information decreases with the perceived homogeneity of the category for which instances are observed.

As a readily intuitive example of Proposition 3, consider the following:

(1)   Is Crystal Pepsi® soft drink good tasting?
(2)   Are soft drinks in general good tasting?

How many cans of soft drink will consumers sample before making each of these determinations?

In this problem, we expect that most people would sample one can in the first instance and some number of cans greater than one in the second. This is because there is a perception of greater variability in taste among instances of soft drinks in general than among instances of a particular soft drink brand. In fact, this perception would probably be employed to conduct sampling in the second instance. A person would sample brands, not several instances of one brand, presuming an absence of variability among instances within brands. We hypothesize that in generalization tasks, people will require more information for heterogeneous categories before taking action. This is because generalizing across entities with numerous differences is more difficult than generalizing instances with few differences, requiring greater information search.

### 7.4.2   Individuation

A second type of argument arising from category knowledge is the *individuation*[2] argument. Individuation is the complement of generalization, and is also typically applied within "instance/type of" hierarchies. In individuation, people reason from a general category to a conclusion about the particular instances within that category. Hence, in individuation, what holds for the general category is claimed to hold for an individual instance, as shown by the structure in Figure 7.4b. For example, cats ($A$) have whiskers ($V$); therefore, Felix ($B$), being a cat ($A$), has whiskers ($V$).

Unlike generalization, perceptions of typicality should have an impact on the evaluation of evidence for individuation.

> *Proposition 4*: In evaluating evidence, people more readily individuate to typical instances than to atypical instances of a category.

This proposition follows in a straightforward fashion from studies of graded membership. Statements about the category are hypothesized to apply more strongly to instances as their degree of membership increases. Stronger arguments imply greater certainty for the arguer, and greater resistance to the argument's refutation.

In terms of perceived variability, the following proposition for individuation parallels Proposition 2 for the generalization argument:

> *Proposition 5*: In evaluating evidence, people's readiness to individuate increases with the perceived homogeneity of the category.

As variability increases, the strength of an argument to one of the diverse individual instances weakens. There are fewer centralized, general features that prevail across the diverse instances to which the argument is being applied. Hence, there is more likely to be an instance that shares relatively fewer of the category's features, implying a weaker individuation argument that is more susceptible to refutation.

Unlike generalization, perceived variability is not expected to have an impact on evidence gathering for individuation. In generalization, the evidence consists of individual instances that can be accumulated to a greater or lesser extent. In individuation, the evidence consists of information about a single superset category under consideration. Since the particular superset is already identified as a presumption of the individuation argument, there is no point in gathering evidence to apply to the determination of which category to employ (that determination is the locus of the next argument type discussed—categorization).

### 7.4.3 Categorization

The *categorization* argument concludes what the first two arguments presume, and so is also typically used within "instance/type of" hierarchies. Categorization is a sufficiency argument, applying when the presence of features is sufficient to conclude that an entity belongs to a superordinate category. The argument has the structure shown in Figure 7.4c. For example, cats ($B$) are warm-blooded vertebrates that suckle their young with mammary glands ($V_j$); therefore, cats ($B$) are mammals ($A$). Cats satisfy sufficiency criteria for being categorized as mammals. In its strictest form this argument relates to the classical models, in which categorization is based on necessary and sufficient rules of category membership. However, in practical reasoning and under graded category membership, the argument can be applied more loosely and with some uncertainty.

> *Proposition 6*: In evaluating evidence, people more readily categorize typical instances of a category than atypical instances.

This proposition is well supported from categorization research (e.g. Barsalou, 1985; Homa, 1984). Indeed, the effect is prime motivation for the derivation of prototype models of categorization (Barsalou, 1992, Chapter 2). Categorization can be usefully viewed as the search for a category providing maximal graded membership.

For perceived variability, the effect of categorization upon evidence evaluation interacts with typicality. We will discuss this interactive effect as Proposition 12 in the context of categorizing with multiple available categories. For evidence gathering, however, we expect the following to hold:

> *Proposition 7*: In gathering evidence for categorization, people's need for information increases as the perceived homogeneity of the category increases.

For example, suppose a person is considering whether to argue that an animal is in the category of cats. He may perceive that there is little variability in the cat category. Therefore, to achieve argument strength, he will need to establish a large number of specific criteria, such as having a rounded head, short muzzle, sensitive whiskers, pointed ears, tongue with papillae, hind feet with four toes, and retractable claws. An animal with some but not all of these features (e.g. a civet) can be categorized as something else; this alternative possible category weakens the attempted categorization argument to "cats".

Alternatively, suppose a person is considering whether to argue that an animal is in the category of birds. Since she perceives that there is a lot of variability in the category of birds, she can argue inclusion in the category with relatively fewer features being present. So, since an ostrich is a warm-blooded vertebrate that has feathers and lays eggs, it can be included in the bird category even though it does not contain other prototypical features of a bird (e.g. ability to fly). The bird category's greater variability leads to a lower need for information to make a strong argument, and in this case makes refutation of the categorization argument more difficult.

In sum, across the three argument types that have been presented, a more consistent pattern of behavior is expected regarding the evaluation of evidence compared to evidence gathering. In evaluating evidence, consistency (homogeneity) in observed instances tends to imply relative certainty, and inconsistency (heterogeneity) tends to imply relative uncertainty. Thus, for both the generalization and individuation arguments, increased perceived variability decreases argument strength. However, perceived variability is expected to have quite different effects upon information acquisition for the three different argument types. Homogeneity leads to less information gathering for generalization, has no effect on information gathering for individuation, and leads to more information gathering for categorization.

## 7.5 ARGUING FROM MULTIPLE CATEGORIES

Propositions 2–7 apply to the basic structures in Figure 7.4. A fuller consideration of the use of categories in reasoning requires the recognition that arguments are constructed using a knowledge base containing multiple categories. The categories overlap, and individual elements have graded membership in categories at different levels of abstraction. This leads to a discussion of using knowledge of multiple categories in reasoning, the topic of this section. In particular, the forecaster in this situation is faced with a task of selecting a category from among those available with which to operate. We begin our analysis of this process by grounding category selection in the notion of selecting a target population, as discussed in existing probability assessment research. We then tie the issue of category selection to the argument types of generalization, individuation and categorization, developing specific propositions from this theoretical analysis.

### 7.5.1 Category Selection and Target Populations

When multiple categories are available to support reasoning, category selection becomes a relevant issue in forecasting. The task of selecting a category is similar to the selection of a target population, e.g. as arises in analyzing the quality of probability assessments in terms of their external correspondence. The external correspondence of probability judgments is the degree to which the assessments correspond with some external criterion, e.g. whether a target event ultimately occurs (Yates, 1982). Typically, the external correspondence of probability judgments is evaluated using scoring rules, applied over a series of assessments. In essence, quality is evaluated with a frequentistic criterion of perfor-mance using a suitable population of assessments that are assumed to be comparable. However, since the set of stimulus items may be arbitrary, the assumption of comparability is often questionable.

A similar issue arises in considering the use of categories. With multiple categories available, the selection of a target population by the assessor is typically discretionary. It is this point that Gigerenzer, Hoffrage & Kleinbölting (1991) argued in their critique of findings of over-confidence based on scoring rule analyses. Specifically, they asserted that over-confidence effects can be understood by viewing subjects as basing judgments on different reference groups, depending on the task. Sniezek & Buckley (1991) made a comparable argument in observing how assessments for individual items differed qualitatively from global assessments for groups of items. The point is that different problems or frames bring to mind differing target populations about which an assessment may be made. Differing task demands can lead to the use of different reference categories and to apparently inconsistent judgments.

Hence, in situations with multiple categories of potential relevance, the selection of category and the coding of instances has been shown to be an ambiguous step in assessment. The remainder of this section addresses this issue. We begin by expanding the distributional frame-work to accommodate the multiple category setting. An example using Simpson's paradox forms the basis of the discussion. We then apply the expanded framework to the issue of category selection, observing how the individual arguments from the previous section (Figure 7.4) operate with multiple, interconnected categories.

### 7.5.2 Simpson's Paradox and Selecting Among Multiple Categories

A methodology used by Schaller (1992) provides an experimental design for investigating the use of knowledge from multiple categories. A brief description of that study is therefore warranted.

The subject's task in Schaller's initial study was to select either of two players, Player 1 or Player 2, as a partner in an upcoming racquetball tournament. Subjects were given information about the players' performances in two different racquetball leagues, League X and League O. In particular, subjects were shown the first and second 2 × 2 tables in Table 7.2a. They were not shown the aggregate table at the right of Table 7.2a or the correlation coefficients. The task was one of discriminating between the two players. In this example, Player 1 has a higher winning percentage in each league, but Player 2 has the better overall percentage. Schaller suggested that subjects should use the league information to differentiate between the players, and prefer Player 1. However, the modal response of subjects in his study was to aggregate the evidence and choose Player 2.

Two points are worth noting about the example in Table 7.2a. First, Simpson's paradox, upon which the example is based, is valid. The basic idea, attributed to Simpson (1951), is that the aggregation of two contingency tables may lead to an overall relationship that is different than what is present within both of the two underlying tables, and so may be inappropriate. That is, aggregating subclasses and choosing a

**Table 7.2** Simpson's paradox in three different applications

|  | League X | | League O | | Aggregate | |
|---|---|---|---|---|---|---|
|  | Win | Loss | Win | Loss | Win | Loss |
| (a) With a small sample |  |  |  |  |  |  |
| Player 1 | 2 | 6 | 2 | 0 | 4 | 6 |
| Player 2 | 0 | 2 | 6 | 2 | 6 | 4 |
|  | $r = 0.25$ | | $r = 0.25$ | | $r = -0.20$ | |
| (b) The effect on a small sample of adding one more observation |  |  |  |  |  |  |
| Player 1 | 2 | 6 | 2 | 0 | 4 | 6 |
| Player 2 | 1 | 2 | 6 | 2 | 7 | 4 |
|  | $r = -0.08$ | | $r = 0.25$ | | $r = -0.24$ | |
| (c) With a large sample |  |  |  |  |  |  |
| Player 1 | 20 | 60 | 20 | 0 | 40 | 60 |
| Player 2 | 0 | 20 | 60 | 20 | 60 | 40 |
|  | $r = 0.25$ | | $r = 0.25$ | | $r = -0.20$ | |

higher level categorization may be inappropriate if there is reliable variability between the subclasses. In the racquetball situation, if there is a relationship between performance and league, then aggregating across leagues may be misleading and should be avoided.

Second, it is not clear that Simpson's paradox is operative in Table 7.2a, despite Schaller's suggestion that it is. The key issue relative to aggregation is whether there is significant between-leagues variability. If there is, then the paradox holds; however, if there is not, then there is no paradox and aggregation is appropriate. Using appropriate statistical analysis, the conditional independence of league on win/loss record given the player cannot be strongly rejected (Pearson $\chi^2(2) = 4.72$, $\delta = 1$, $p = 0.09$).[3] However, this analysis, even with the $\delta$ correction factor, is not reliable because of the small cell sizes in the table. The actual $p$ value is undoubtedly higher.

An illustrative portrayal of the low reliability for the between-leagues variation is the effect of a slight change in the evidence. In particular, suppose one game is added to Player 2's record in Table 7.2a, making the League X record one win and two losses. The effect of this one additional game is shown by Table 7.2b. Adding the game has little impact on the aggregate evidence; the correlation changes only slightly and Player 2 is still favored. However, the additional data point has a large impact on the results within League X. Player 2, not Player 1, now has the superior performance. Thus, the subclass data are very unstable and unreliable. Consequently, it is not at all unreasonable that subjects should aggregate, and they did.

Table 7.2c shows the second of the two data sets used by Schaller. Here the cell sizes are sufficient to perform a reliable statistical test. Statistically, the league variable is conditionally dependent on win/loss record given the player (Pearson $\chi^2(2) = 75.00$, $p < 0.001$). In this case, subjects' modal response was to not aggregate and to select Player 1. Thus, subjects arguably responded appropriately in both experimental conditions.

Tying the study to our theory of assessment, two interconnected categories are in operation in this experimental task. There are two instances within a higher category of "leagues". There are two instances within a higher category of "players". Thus, the decision of whether to aggregate hinges on two questions. First, is there a difference in performance between leagues? In this case, relative performance serves as an indicator of league quality. Even the data in Table 7.2a tend to support such a difference (collapsing across players and analyzing the resulting $2 \times 2$ table yields $\chi^2(1) = 7.2$, $p = 0.0073$). Second, is there evidence of a consistent difference between players within each league? As noted above, the data in Table 7.2a do not support such a difference, but the data in Table 7.2c do support a difference.

Thus, for the data in Table 7.2c, both questions can be reliably answered in the affirmative. Schaller's subjects behaved appropriately by not aggregating and using the lower level of abstraction—data within leagues. However, for the data in Table 7.2a, it is reasonable to assume that assessors would view the amount of variability between players as low relative to their expectations of the variability that exists among players in general. So, even if the subjects had perceived a difference in difficulty between leagues (and it is not certain from the study whether they did), they would not have perceived a meaningful difference between the players within each league. Subjects behaved as though they aggregated and used the higher level of abstraction, not differentiating between leagues.

More generally, this example suggests that the use of multiple categories introduces an additional distributional element beyond centrality and perceived variability within the categories, i.e. the perceived separation *between* categories also takes on significance. The hypothesized effects of this additional component upon category selection are discussed in the next sections within the context of each of the argument types discussed earlier (Figure 7.4): generalization, individuation and categorization.

### 7.5.3  Category Selection in Generalization

Recall that for the generalization and individuation arguments a person argues within a given hierarchy of categories, either from a lower level to a higher level (generalization) or from a higher level to a lower level (individuation). However, as in Schaller's racquetball task, a person can often choose among different positions within a single multiple-level hierarchy. Thus, for example, one can look at a player's performance in individual games, can aggregate to performance within leagues, or can aggregate to performance in general, irrespective of league. A key question for the subject in the racquetball task is whether to generalize performance in individual games to performance within leagues or to generalize to the higher level of overall performance.

The general principles by which people are expected to make this decision involve comparisons of distributional properties at the target levels. The individual is expected to use the level that he perceives to be most meaningful, i.e. that will promote greatest argument strength. This level is one with high homogeneity within the category and with high separation from other categories at the same level. At the subcategory level, as the perceived separation between subcategories increases, the individual is expected to use the sub-categories rather than to aggregate to the more general super-category. At the super-category level, as the perceived variability within a super-category increases, the individual is expected to decompose to multiple sub-categories with less heterogeneity.

As an example, consider a product class such as aspirin. If there is little perceived variability in the product class of aspirin, as is true for some consumers, then the evaluation of which product to buy is likely to hinge on extra-product factors, such as price. However, if variability is perceived, then the aspirin category may be decomposed into sub-categories. A consumer who perceives high variability among aspirins chooses, e.g. from "buffered aspirins" or from packages of "Bayer®️ aspirins". These sub-categories have meaning to the extent that there is perceived heterogeneity between sub-classes and homogeneity within each sub-class, relative to the super-class of "aspirins". Consider the following exchange between two people:

*Brenna:* I can't take aspirin. It upsets my stomach.
*Kate:* Have you tried buffered aspirin?
*Brenna:* Oh, nonsense! Aspirin is aspirin.

Kate thinks Brenna's reasoning is weak because she perceives heterogeneity in the super-category of aspirins and separation among underlying sub-categories, e.g. buffered aspirins. In turn, Brenna thinks Kate's reasoning is weak because she perceives homogeneity in the super-category of aspirins and consequently sees any attempt at separation into sub-categories as meaningless.

This idea can be applied to a generalization argument, as in the following example:

Barb and Jane are 23 year-old females residing in Minnesota. Jane is considering televisions for purchase. Barb has just purchased a television of Brand A. To what category do you wish to aggregate the information about Barb's purchase before presenting the evidence to Jane? You want to present the information to Jane in the most informative manner to allow Jane to forecast her satisfaction with different brands of television sets as well as possible. To aid her forecasting, you can present satisfaction ratings from one or more groups of owners of the products that include Barb. All the information is equally and highly reliable. Rank the sources of information from the most preferred (1) to the least preferred (9) source of information.

__ (a)  Adults residing in the USA.
__ (b)  Female adults residing in the USA.
__ (c)  Adults residing in the USA, 20–24 years of age.
__ (d)  Adults residing in Minnesota.
__ (e)  Female adults residing in the USA, 20–24 years of age.
__ (f)  Female adults residing in Minnesota.
__ (g)  Adults residing in Minnesota, 20–24 years of age.
__ (h)  Female adults residing in Minnesota, 20–24 years of age.
__ (i)  The ratings of Barb, a female residing in Minnesota, 23 years of age.

The respondent has a choice of levels for use in applying a generalization argument. The evidence classes in this example differ in the extent of aggregation. Item (a) is the broadest category. Items (b)–(d) sub-classify on one characteristic: gender, age and state, respectively. Items (e)–(g) classify using two characteristics. Item (h) uses all three characteristics. Finally, item (i) is the narrowest reference class, exemplifying *individuating* information, since it contains only one individual. Some past research has suggested that people show a preference for individuating information, tending to treat problems as unique (e.g. Kahneman & Lovallo, 1993).

In this setting, the assessor has available a super-category (adults in the USA) with some perceived variability over the target characteristic (television preference). The assessor is expected to generalize to the broadest class for which argument strength can be maintained. That is, the most meaningful level should correspond to the broadest low-variability reference class:

*Proposition 8*:  Individuals will generalize to the broadest category for which there is sufficient perceived homogeneity on the descriptor values of relevance to the task.

As perceived variability in the super-category increases, more specific classes should be chosen, because the subject will recognize that the broader classes are not reliable indicators (because of the variability in the class). As perceived variability decreases, broader reference classes should be selected, since they will be reliable indicators (because of the low variability in the class). This leads to the expectation that assessors will prefer the broadest low-variability reference class that is available.

Also, since categorization is context-dependent, the level of generalization will vary with the task.

### 7.5.4  Category Selection in Individuation

The example posed above arguably involves aspects of both generalization and individuation (generalizing from Barb, then individuating to Jane). The example focused more on the former argument, selecting the best category to use in making a generalization. In the following, the focus is on the latter argument of individuation.

Using the descriptions from the previous example, instead of asking how one would present information to Jane, one can take Jane's perspective of considering televisions for purchase. From which category would Jane want information?

> Jane is a 23 year-old female residing in Minnesota. You are attempting to forecast her satisfaction with different brands of television sets that she is considering for purchase. To aid your forecasting, you can present satisfaction ratings from one or more groups of owners of the products. All the information is equally and highly reliable. Rank the sources of information from the most preferred (1) to the least preferred (9) source of information.

Items paralleling those in the previous example (Items a–i) would be available, offering different levels of abstraction to the subject.

As in generalization, the use of categories in the converse argument of individuation is expected to have a crossover point, suggesting the following:

> *Proposition 9*:  People will individuate from the broadest category for which there is sufficient perceived homogeneity on the descriptor values of relevance to the task.

Initial investigations, using a total of 152 undergraduate subjects, suggest support for this proposition. Subjects generally preferred the narrower categories offered to them, e.g. the highest mean preference was for Item (h). However, the individuating information was not most preferred (Item i). Instead, it was always among the least preferred in two separate studies. Consistent with our main thesis, this suggests a preference crossover point between our narrowest category (Item h) and the individuating information (Item i).

A subsequent question arises as to the comparability of individuation and generalization: Should we expect subjects to individuate from the same category level to which they are willing to generalize? Our prior expectation is to expect the contrary result:

> *Proposition 10*: Individuals will be less willing to generalize to broader categories than they are willing to individuate from broader categories.

Highlighting specific instances, e.g. the purchase of Barb, is expected to highlight individual differences and perceived variability. This increases the perceived heterogeneity and inhibits generalization to the broader category. The expectation is consistent with Quattrone & Jones's (1980) finding of greater perceived variability of features within social groups to which individuals belong (highly familiar and variable in-groups) compared to social groups to which they do not belong (less familiar and variable out-groups). Similarly, Thagard & Nisbett (1982) observed that subjects assessed greater evidential impact for more detailed stimuli. Identifying instances is expected to increase perceived variability by enhancing the richness of cues that are available in the situation, i.e. increasing the number of descriptors attached to the instances. This enhancement of perceived variability is hypothesized to be less likely with individuation, in which the argument proceeds from the more generalized category, than with generalization, in which the argument proceeds from the more detailed instances.

### 7.5.5  Categorization with Multiple Categories

Unlike generalization and individuation, categorization need not be constrained within a single hierarchy. In practice, however, we expect that individuals will generally take this perspective. For example, it would be unusual for a forecaster to pose the question: "Is this proposed new company a software development firm or is it in Baltimore?" Although the forecaster may be interested in each of these categorizations (e.g. there may exist archival success data for startup firms in each category), he is still unlikely to see these as alternatives from which one must be selected in exclusion of the other.

To show how categorization with multiple categories occurs within a controlled setting, we consider a study reported by Kahneman & Tversky (1973). In that study, after being told that a sample of five will be drawn from a population of 70 lawyers and 30 engineers, subjects responded to descriptions of members of the sample, as in the following (p. 241):

> Jack is a 45 year-old man. He is married and has four children. He is generally conservative, careful, and ambitious. He shows no interest in political and social issues and spends most of his free time on his many hobbies which include home carpentry, sailing, and mathematical puzzles.
>
> The probability that Jack is one of the 30 engineers in the sample of 100 is ___%.

Other subjects responded to the same description after being told that the population consisted of 70 engineers and 30 lawyers. The modal response in the experiment, with either base rate (i.e. proportions of lawyers/engineers), was to respond in a manner consistent with ignoring the base-rate evidence and judging the similarity of the description of Jack to the target events, lawyer and engineer.

This behavior can be understood as an application of reasoning using category knowledge (Curley & Benson, 1994). The subject in the experiment is faced with three reference classes: engineers, lawyers, and the class of 100 people from which the sample was drawn. Two hierarchies are involved. Engineer and lawyer are subclasses of an occupation category; in this task, the subclasses are understood to be mutually exclusive (although they need not be in general). Jack and the other characters in the experimental stimuli are instances of the population created by the experimenters. The finding was that subjects evaluated the instance (Jack) relative to the two categories from their internal knowledge base—engineers and lawyers. They discounted the base-rate evidence in the reference class of 100 people that the experimenters created. Discounting this evidence could arise from either or both of the following explanations: (a) subjects may regard the experimenter-created hierarchy as artificial, and thus of less conse-quence then their own concrete knowledge as captured in the occupations hierarchy (this effect would parallel the preference for concrete vs. abstract information in inference, as supported by Thagard & Nisbett, 1982); (b) subjects may resist the complication of having to consider a second hierarchy, preferring the simpler, more straightfor-ward approach of making the categorization argument using the single occupations hierarchy.

From within the single occupations supercategory, subjects respond by reasoning as to whether Jack is an instance of the category of engineer or of the category of lawyer using stored knowledge about engineers and lawyers. As noted earlier, such reasoning in the multiple category task is influenced not only by the variability within each of the two categories, but also by the separation between the categories. To understand the impact of the between-category separation, consider altering the categories. For example, instead of using lawyers and engineers, we might use electrical engineers vs. chemical engineers, or corporate lawyers vs. tax lawyers. This would be expected to decrease the perceived separation between classes. The following is hypothesized:

> *Proposition 11*:  Individuals will be less willing to categorize as the perceived separation among available categories decreases.

Lowering the between-category separation weakens the categorization argument.

In the lawyer/engineer problem, one consequence that would be expected from decreasing the between-class separation would be to decrease subjects' reliance on the categorization argument and increase reliance on the more artificial base-rate evidence. In contrast, suppose that instead of engineers and lawyers, the categories were gardeners and nuclear physicists. This would be expected to increase between-class variability, increase use of categorization, and decrease use of the base-rate evidence.

Proposition 11 concerns the readiness of applying the categorization argument at all, vs. other argument approaches. Another effect that is proposed for the categorization argument is in terms of the locus of the categorization that will result:

> *Proposition 12*:  When deciding among two categories for categorization, typicality and perceived variability interact in a multiplicative fashion to affect category selection. If the instance is highly prototypical of the categories, the category with lower perceived variability is preferred. If the instance is atypical of the categories, the category with higher perceived variability is preferred.

We noted earlier how perceived variability may be related to the typicality effect (Shafir, Smith & Osherson, 1990). As a preliminary investigation of Proposition 12, we obtained typicality ratings from undergraduate subjects for a variety of possible occupations for the "Bill" and "Linda" characters from Tversky & Kahneman's (1982) study. Likeness ratings within an occupation category (How alike are category members to each other?) were obtained as indicators of variability. These ratings were used to create stimuli, in the form of the Linda problem described earlier in this chapter, that independently manipulate typicality and variability (e.g. "Linda is a bank teller" vs. "Linda is an accountant").

Our data indicated support for the role of perceived variability in likelihood judgments, as described by Proposition 12. The essence of Proposition 12 is that for instances that are typical of the categories under consideration, the low-variability category provides a stronger argument. For such a category, there is a higher probability for the typical instance to be near the center of the distribution across features. Thus, there is less likelihood of a counter-argument or rebuttal that undermines the categorization argument. In contrast, for instances that are atypical of the categories under consideration, the high variability category provides a stronger argument. High variability increases the likelihood of obtaining the atypical event of the stimulus.

## 7.6 CONCLUDING REMARKS

In general, the reasoning underlying forecasting behavior has not received a great deal of scholarly attention, despite the fact that reasoning is central to beliefs formed about future events of interest (Benson, Curley & Smith, 1995). We have claimed that category knowledge in particular plays a significant role in the beliefs people form, and that the use of category knowledge in argument construction has been an under-studied phenomenon. In particular, we have developed a distributional theory of reasoning with category knowledge. This led to the formulation of a number of testable propositions concerning the role that distributional characteristics, particularly perceptions of the variability within and between categories, play in the domain of probabilistic forecasting. It is hoped that the evidence and propositions presented in this chapter will spur further investigations into this critical area of decision-making behavior.

## NOTES

(1) Browne, Curley and Benson (1997b) and Curley, Browne, Smith and Benson (1994) present other instances of argument forms ("strategies") as applied to probability assessment, aside from the warrant-based forms captured by Table 7.1.

(2)  Brockriede & Ehninger (1960) used the term "classification" to describe this argument. We use the term "individuation" to highlight the movement from general to specific that characterizes the argument. The term "classification" highlights what this argument presumes, i.e. the identification of the relationship between the superset $A$ and the subsets $B_i$. However, to avoid confusion with Brockriede & Ehninger's terminology, we will use the term "categorization" for the next argument type, which centrally concerns this subset–superset relationship.

(3)  Analytic procedure uses log-linear modeling and is described by Fienberg (1977); analysis performed using Systat 3.0 software (see Wilkinson, 1986, Chapter 10).

## REFERENCES

Attneave, A. (1957) Transfer of experience with a class schema to identification learning of patterns and shapes. *Journal of Experimental Psychology*, **54**, 81–8.

Barsalou, L.W. (1985)  Ideals, central tendency, and frequency of instantiation as determinants of graded structure in categories. *Journal of Experimental Psychology: Learning, Memory, and Cognition*, **11**, 629–54.

Barsalou, L.W. (1992) *Cognitive Psychology: An Overview for Cognitive Scientists*. Erlbaum, Hillsdale, NJ.

Benson, P.G., Curley, S.P. & Smith, G.F. (1995)  Belief assessment: an underdeveloped phase of probability elicitation. *Management Science*, **41**, 1639–53.

Billig, M. (1987) *Arguing and Thinking: A Rhetorical Approach to Social Psychology*. Cambridge University Press, Cambridge.

Brockriede, W. & Ehninger, D. (1960)  Toulmin on argument: an interpretation and application. *Quarterly Journal of Speech*, **46**, 44–53.

Browne, G.J., Curley, S.P. & Benson, P.G. (1997a, November)  The effects of subject-defined categories on judgmental accuracy in confidence assessment tasks. Working paper, Texas Tech University, Lubbock, TX.

Browne, G.J., Curley, S.P. & Benson, P.G. (1997b)  Evoking information in probability assessment: knowledge maps and reasoning-based directed questions. *Management Science*, **43**, 1–14.

Collins, A. & Michalski, R. (1989)  The logic of plausible reasoning: a core theory. *Cognitive Science*, **13**, 1–49.

Curley, S.P. & Benson, P.G. (1994)  Applying a cognitive perspective to probability construction. In G. Wright & P. Ayton (eds), *Subjective Probability*. Wiley, Chichester, pp. 185–209.

Curley, S.P., Browne, G.J., Smith, G.F. & Benson, P.G. (1994, January) Practical reasoning in the construction of probability responses. Working paper, University of Minnesota, Minneapolis.

Curley, S.P., Browne, G.J., Smith, G.F. & Benson, P.G. (1995) Arguments in the practical reasoning underlying constructed probability responses. *Journal of Behavioral Decision Making*, **8**, 1–20.

Fienberg, S.E. (1977) *The Analysis of Cross-Classified Categorical Data*. MIT Press, Cambridge, MA.

Fried, L.S. & Holyoak, K.J. (1984) Induction of category distributions: a framework for classification learning. *Journal of Experimental Psychology: Learning, Memory, and Cognition*, **10**, 234–57.

Gigerenzer, G., Hoffrage, U. & Kleinbölting, H. (1991) Probabilistic mental models: a Brunswikian theory of confidence. *Psychological Review*, **98**, 506–28.

Glass, A.L. & Holyoak, K.J. (1986) *Cognition*. Random House, New York.

Golden, J.L., Berquist, G.F. & Coleman, W.E. (1983) *The Rhetoric of Western Thought*. Kendall/Hunt, Dubuque, IA.

Henderson, P.W. & Peterson, R.A. (1992) Mental accounting and categorization. *Organizational Behavior and Human Decision Processes*, **51**, 92–117.

Homa, D. (1984) On the nature of categories. In G.H. Bower, (ed.), *The Psychology of Learning and Motivation: Advances in Research and Theory*, vol. 18. Academic Press, New York, pp. 49–94.

Kahneman, D. & Lovallo, D. (1993) Timid choices and bold forecasts: a cognitive perspective on risk taking. *Management Science*, **39**, 17–31.

Kahneman, D. & Tversky, A. (1972) Subjective probability: a judgment of representativeness. *Cognitive Psychology*, **3**, 430–54.

Kahneman, D. & Tversky, A. (1973) On the psychology of prediction. *Psychological Review*, **80**, 237–51.

Nisbett, R.E., Krantz, D.H., Jepson, C. & Kunda, Z. (1983) The use of statistical heuristics in everyday inductive reasoning. *Psychological Review*, **90**, 339–63.

Quattrone, G.A. & Jones, E.E. (1980) The perception of variability within in-groups and out-groups: implications for the law of small numbers. *Journal of Personality and Social Psychology*, **38**, 141–52.

Schaller, M. (1992) Sample size, aggregation, and statistical reasoning in social inference. *Journal of Experimental Social Psychology*, **28**, 65–85.

Shafir, E.B., Smith, E.E. & Osherson, D.N. (1990) Typicality and reasoning fallacies. *Memory & Cognition*, **18**, 229–39.

Simpson, E.H. (1951) The interpretation of interaction in contingency tables. *Journal of the Royal Statistical Society, Series B*, **13**, 238–41.

Smith, E.E. & Medin, D.L. (1981) *Categories and Concepts*. Harvard University Press, Cambridge, MA.

Smith, G.F., Benson, P.G. & Curley, S.P. (1991) Belief, knowledge, and uncertainty: a cognitive perspective on subjective probability. *Organizational Behavior and Human Decision Processes*, **48**, 291–321.

Sniezek, J.A. & Buckley, T. (1991) Confidence depends on level of aggregation. *Journal of Behavioral Decision Making*, **4**, 263–72.

Thagard, P. & Nisbett, R.E. (1982) Variability and confirmation. *Philosophical Studies*, **42**, 379–94.

Toulmin, S.E. (1958) *The Uses of Argument*. Cambridge University Press, Cambridge.

Tversky, A. & Kahneman, D. (1982) Judgments of and by representativeness. In D. Kahneman, P. Slovic & A. Tversky (eds), *Judgment under Uncertainty: Heuristics and Biases*. Cambridge University Press, Cambridge, pp. 84–98.

Wilkinson, L. (1986) *SYSTAT: The System for Statistics*. SYSTAT, Inc., Evanston, IL.

Yates, J.F. (1982) External correspondence: decompositions of the mean probability score. *Organizational Behavior and Human Performance*, **30**, 132–56.

# The Use of Structured Groups to Improve Judgemental Forecasting

Gene Rowe
*University of Surrey, Guildford, UK*

## SUMMARY

Theoretically, it can be demonstrated that the judgement of a group should be at least as good as, and more often better than, that of an individual from that group. Practically, however, research has shown that group judgements are often sub-optimal as a consequence of a number of processes related to the interactions of group members. One way around such problems is to use structured group procedures such as the Delphi technique. These procedures aim to maintain the positive features of interacting groups (i.e. by combining judgements from a number of individuals) but, through structuring information exchange, aim to preclude the potentially negative processes with which they are often associated. In this chapter, the theoretical rationale behind the use of structured groups will be discussed, and the empirical evidence for their effectiveness will be reviewed. It will be argued that empirical findings have been equivocal regarding the utility of these techniques and their superiority over a variety of other judgement and forecasting procedures.

*Forecasting with Judgment*. Edited by G. Wright and P. Goodwin.

This chapter will then go on to discuss a number of methodological difficulties associated with past research on structured groups. These difficulties include: the lack of appropriate definition of structured group procedures; the over-generalization of findings; the questionable ecological validity of empirical studies; the lack of appreciation of the contingent effectiveness of procedures (contingent on factors related to the judgement/forecasting task and the nature of the panellists); and the problem of the choice of appropriate criteria for evaluating the quality of judgements and forecasts, and hence for assessing the utility of procedures. The chapter will then discuss the future of structured groups in the form of group decision support systems. The problems in evaluating such systems are seen to be even greater than those in evaluating Delphi effectiveness. It will be suggested that only through a re-orientation of research methodology will we gain an increased understanding of the processes in structured groups, and that such understanding is essential before these procedures can be appropriately defined and evaluated.

## 8.1  GROUP DECISION MAKING

### 8.1.1  The Rationale for Using Groups

There are potentially a large number of ways of deriving a forecast for any particular situation. These generally fall into two categories: those entailing some form of mathematical modelling of related historical variables, and those relying upon the judgement of people with relevant knowledge. Generally, research suggests that forecasts made using approaches that are entirely or largely of the former type tend to be in some way better (e.g. more accurate) than the latter. However, there are many situations in which, for example, historical data is absent, and in these cases some form of judgemental forecast may be necessitated. The problem may then be conceptualized as one of manipulating available human resources to increase one's chance of attaining a good or accurate forecast.

One important issue here is whether one should attempt to allocate a single expert to make a particular forecast, or whether one should somehow attempt to gain the opinions of a number of experts and produce some form of aggregate forecast. Intuitively, it seems obvious that a collection of experts should yield a better forecast than an individual. After all, the group must possess *at least* the same amount of information and knowledge as its most knowledgeable member, and will usually possess more. Additionally, the group environment can provide opportunities for the resolution of ambiguous and conflicting knowledge, the facilitation of creativity and the enhancement of individual commitment. Combining individual judgements through the use of groups may therefore lead to "process gain" (Sniezek & Henry, 1989), in which the group actually out-performs its best member in terms of the quality of judgement.

Empirical studies have attempted to determine the relative merits of group vs. individual procedures. These studies generally collect the judgements of individual group members prior to group interaction and use this information to derive two different measures of individual judgement quality. The "individual" benchmark may be represented either by the judgement of a single, randomly-selected individual, *or* by the average of the judgements of all of the individuals—this latter aggregate often being termed a "statistized" group. In comparison to these two benchmarks, group judgement has generally been shown to be better over a wide range of tasks and circumstances, and over both qualitative and quantitative performance criteria (see e.g. Hill, 1982; Ferrell, 1985, for reviews and discussion). Furthermore, a number of studies have found that interacting groups may occasionally perform at the level of their best member and beyond (e.g. Einhorn, Hogarth & Klempner, 1977; Uecker, 1982; Sniezek & Henry, 1989).

### 8.1.2 The Rationale for Not Using Groups

Although performance up to and beyond best-member level has been demonstrated, group judgement has generally been shown to fall short of this standard (again, see Hill, 1982, plus more recent studies, e.g. Miner, 1984; Hastie, 1986). These results suggest that in most circumstances groups fail to use fully the knowledge and expertise of their members and perform below their potential, exhibiting "process loss" (Steiner, 1972). Given the biases and inadequacies in individual judgement demonstrated elsewhere, this should be no surprise. After all, although groups possess at least the same amount of potentially beneficial and appropriate information as their most informed member, they must also possess at least as much misinformation as that of their least informed member. The question becomes: how should group members decide who to listen to? Steiner (1972) conceptualized the problem as a misweighting of individual judgements by group members. This might occur through a mismatch of members' status and the quality of their contributions; through the lack of contribution of proficient yet low-confident members; through the difficulty of evaluating the quality of individual participants; and through the social pressures that may be exerted by an incompetent majority on a competent minority. Process loss might also occur as a consequence of the frequently conflicting motives of the individuals in a group and their need to "win", or at least not to "lose face" (e.g. Hoffman, 1965). Other mechanisms of the group process that might lead to impaired group judgement have also been identified, e.g. in "groupthink" (Janis, 1972; for recent review see Park, 1990) and in group "polarization" (e.g. Lamm & Myers, 1978).

An important issue here concerns the aptness of the model of group judgement and decision making that assumes that it is a logical procedure, unaffected by cognitive biases and limitations, or by factors such as personal prerogatives, social pressures and political necessities. Indeed, in the same way that the subjective expected utility (SEU) theory has been superseded as a descriptive model for individual decision making, so has the view of rational group decision making been superseded by other less idealistic models, such as those of Huber (e.g. 1982), and Janis (e.g. 1992). In such models, constraints to optimal decision making (i.e. cognitive, affiliative and egocentric constraints) are included. What does emerge from this research is that group judgement and decision making is frequently sub-optimal, biased or flawed.

### 8.1.3 Improving Group Performance: Structuring and Instructing Groups

A variety of solutions to the problems associated with interacting groups have been proposed, ranging from simply providing groups with guidelines for behaviour, to the specification of a number of techniques. Eils & John (1980), for example, attempted to instruct groups in good communication strategy by giving them short guide-lines on effective communication. Instructions included, "view initial agreement as suspect" and "avoid changing opinion only to avoid conflict and to reach agreement". They found that groups involved in the judgement of the credit-worthiness of loan applicants that received such guide-lines, performed significantly better than those that were not so instructed. A number of studies have obtained similar results showing the advantage of instructed groups over naturally interacting ones (e.g. Hall & Williams, 1970; Hall & Watson, 1971; Nemiroff & King, 1975; Nemiroff, Passmore & Ford, 1976).

A number of authors have been concerned with identifying good group practice and developing strategies to implement such practice in organizational groups or teams. For example, Belbin (1981) identified a number of common roles that appear to emerge in successful groups during interaction, and has suggested that a similar mix of roles should be encouraged in decision-making groups. Other research has focused on the role of the leader in a group and how their behaviour might influence the judgement and decision-making process (e.g. Adair, 1983). Much of this and similar research has not, however, been rigorously or empirically tested, partly because the models are complex and so controlled evaluation is difficult. As such, the usefulness of these strategies, largely developed as practical management aids, remains unclear, and further consideration of such procedures falls outside the current line of enquiry.

The bulk of research in the area of improving group performance has focused on the development, application and assessment of a number of structured group techniques. Generally, these structure the group environment to limit the possible influence of negative social and group forces, while still allowing some form of interaction to take place between group members in the hope of allowing synthesis of ideas, knowledge and opinions.

The nominal group technique (NGT, also known as the "estimate–talk–estimate" procedure) is one such technique. The idea behind the NGT is that, while interaction among group members may prove dysfunctional during the generation phase of problem solving (due to the inhibition of contributions of unconfident members, the over-influence of dominant individuals, conflicting personal motives, etc.), verbal interaction during the assessment or evaluation phase may be valuable in allowing the clarification and justification of generated items, leading to improved judgement and decision making (Van de Ven & Delbecq, 1971; Delbecq, Van de Ven & Gustafson, 1975). The process begins with each group member writing down ideas concerning the problem scenario and then selecting one of these for presentation to the remainder of the group. This is followed by a group discussion of each point in turn—thereby allowing a degree of interaction—after which the individuals rate or rank-order the presented ideas in isolation (avoiding conformity pressures, etc.). Finally, a mathematical aggregate of the result (usually equal-weighted) is obtained.

Relatively few studies have been conducted on the NGT, although the results from these have been encouraging. For example, Gustafson et al. (1973) evaluated four methods of eliciting subjective likelihood ratio estimates, and found an NGT approach to perform best, outperforming individual estimates (statistically aggregated), interacting groups, and a Delphi-like condition (another mixed aggregation approach that will be considered shortly). Other studies have also reported NGT to perform fairly well in comparison with a variety of alternative techniques, although accuracy improvements have been small (e.g. Fischer, 1981).

A similar technique, variously called the "estimate–feedback–talk" or "consensus after majority vote" procedure (e.g. Holloman & Hendrick, 1972; Reagan-Cirincione & Rohrbaugh, 1992), differs from the NGT only in allowing the final group judgement to be consensually derived rather than based on mathematical aggregation. A number of studies have found that groups using this procedure have significantly outperformed conventionally interacting groups (e.g. Holloman & Hendrick, 1972; Miner, 1984; and Herbert & Yost, 1979—who mistakenly used the term "NGT" to describe a procedure of this type).

## 8.2 THE DELPHI TECHNIQUE

The Delphi technique (e.g. Dalkey & Helmer, 1963) is perhaps the most formalized and studied of the structured group approaches. It was developed during the 1950s by workers at the RAND Corporation while involved on the US Air Force-sponsored Project Delphi. The aim of the project was the application of expert opinion to the selection—from the point of view of a Soviet strategic planner—of an optimal US industrial target system, with a corresponding estimation of the number of atomic bombs required to reduce munitions output by a prescribed amount. More generally, the resultant technique has been seen as a procedure to "obtain the most reliable consensus of opinion of a group of experts... by a series of intensive questionnaires interspersed with controlled opinion feedback" (Dalkey & Helmer, 1963, p. 458). As well as attempting to harness the positive attributes of interacting groups while pre-empting their negative ones, the method has the potential advantage of allowing input from a larger number of participants than can feasibly be included in a normal group or committee meeting.

## 8.2.1 Structure

Four necessary features characterize a Delphi procedure, viz. anonymity, iteration, controlled feedback, and the statistical aggregation of group response. *Anonymity* is achieved through the use of questionnaires. By allowing the individual group members the opportunity to express their opinions and judgements privately, undue social pressures should be avoided. Ideally, this should allow the individual group members to consider each idea on the basis of merit alone, rather than on the basis of spurious and invalid criteria (such as the status of an idea's proponent). Furthermore, with the *iteration* of the questionnaire over a number of rounds, the individuals are given the opportunity to change their opinions and judgements without fear of losing face in the eyes of the (anonymous) others in the group. By aggregating panellists' opinions as *feedback*, the opinions and judgements of all group members are ascertained, and not just those of the most vocal. At the end of the polling of participants, the group judgement is taken as the statistical average (mean/median) of the individuals' estimates on the final round, i.e. effectively an equal weighting of the members of a statistized group.

More precisely, the first round of the *classical* Delphi procedure (Martino, 1983) is unstructured, allowing the individual experts relatively free scope to identify and elaborate on those issues they see as important. The issues are then consolidated by the monitor team into a single set of items requiring quantitative estimates. The resultant structured questionnaire is then sent to panellists on subsequent rounds. After each of these rounds, responses are analysed and statistically summarized (usually into medians plus upper and lower quartiles), which are then presented to the panellists for further consideration. Hence, from the third round onwards panellists are given the opportunity to alter prior estimates on the basis of the provided feedback. Furthermore, if panellists' assessments fall outside the upper or lower quartiles, then they may be asked to give reasons why they believe their selections to be correct against the majority opinion (with all such arguments remaining of anonymous origin). This procedure continues until a certain stability in panellists' responding is achieved—a point that is not specified by the rules of the technique, but which is left entirely at the discretion of the monitor team. The forecast or assessment for each item in the questionnaire is typically represented by the median on the final round, with the degree of disagreement indicated by differences in the quartile figures (i.e. consensus is not entirely forced, since this latter indicator of discontent may be appended to the ultimate response). An important point to note here is that variations from the above Delphi ideal do exist (Martino, 1983). For example, the first round is usually structured, while feedback tends to simply comprise an average figure with no arguments taken from those giving extreme estimates. It will be argued later that these variations have implications for the generalizability of results from Delphi studies.

## 8.2.2   Rationale: A Caveat

There has been some controversy concerning what the Delphi technique is all about, with a number of authors arguing about the appropriate benchmarks for the evaluation of the technique and, indeed, whether it is desirable or even possible to evaluate Delphi effectiveness (e.g. see original critique of Sackman, 1975, and rebuttals of Linstone & Turoff, 1975; Coates, 1975; etc.). Is Delphi a technique for achieving consensus? Is it simply a tool for improving communication effectiveness? Is it nothing more than a procedure of the "last resort"? Is it a procedure for obtaining more accurate forecasts or judgements? What is clear is that Delphi is more than just an instrument for measuring the opinions of dispersed individuals, in that it is fundamentally transformative: it entails an initial statistical average being transformed into a final statistical average through a controlled interaction procedure (e.g. see Parenté & Anderson-Parenté, 1987; and Rowe, Wright & Bolger, 1991, for ideas on the statistical and behavioural nature of transformations). It is to be hoped that the transformation will, in some way, be beneficial. It might be argued that Delphi's fundamental aim is to simply achieve a better consensus, and that would necessitate measuring consensus on the target issue prior to and after the procedure. Most researchers, however, have attempted to evaluate Delphi under the assumption that it is intended to *improve judgement*, and have assessed the efficacy of the technique by comparing final round aggregate judgements, either to aggregate first round judgements (equating to judgements from non-interacting statistical groups) or to judgements derived via comparative procedures, such as interacting groups.

### 8.2.3 Evaluation of Delphi

Most papers involving Delphi relate *applications* concerned with discovering something about a practical issue that is of primary concern to the publications' authors and researchers. In such cases, Delphi is generally presented as an established and valuable tool for aggregating opinions and judgements to develop a policy decision or obtain a prediction. The *applied* use of Delphi is widespread, extending well beyond its origins in the defence and technology forecasting domains. An examination of recent literature, for example, reveals Delphi applications in areas as diverse as those of the health care industry (Hudak et al., 1993), education (Ginsburg, 1992), information systems (Niederman, Brancheau & Wetherbe, 1991), and transportation and engineering (Saito & Sinha, 1991). Evaluations of Delphi are, however, relatively scarce. Details of the majority of published Delphi *evaluative* studies will be presented in Rowe & Wright (in press), and are summarized here.

### 8.2.4 Findings: Delphi Effectiveness

*Consensus*

Empirically, the main way in which "consensus" has been determined is by measuring the variance in responses of Delphi panellists, with a reduction in variance—and hence a convergence in the estimates given by panellists—taken to indicate increased consensus. Results generally suggest that variance does decrease over rounds (e.g. Dalkey & Helmer, 1963; Jolson & Rossow, 1971), although much of the evidence exists in the form of reported-though-analysed trends.

A less common way of attempting to measure consensus considers the extent to which individuals—after the Delphi process has been completed—individually agree with, or accept, the final group aggregate, their own final round estimates, or the estimates of the other panellists. Such measures may be important, given that concern exists as to whether the typical measure of consensus genuinely reflects the intended psychological phenomenon, or whether observed decreases in variance over rounds merely reflect spurious influences more akin to *conformity* than real changes in belief and increased agreement (e.g. Stewart, 1987). Bardecki (1984), for example, has suggested that the measures of central tendency used in Delphi (e.g. medians) may act as powerful anchors that act to narrow the range of responses on subsequent rounds, and that "unless the individual has great assurance and the issue is of considerable importance, there is reason to believe that any consensus will be at least in part a result of assimilative pressure rather than any true education" (p. 283). Bardecki found that respondents with more extreme views were more likely to drop out of a Delphi procedure than those with more moderate views (i.e. nearer the average), suggesting that the impression of consensus may be at least partly due to attrition.

Rohrbaugh (1979) considered consensus using one of these post-procedure assessments, by comparing individuals' post-group responses to their aggregate group responses and to the final responses of their group members. He seemed to show that reduction in "disagreement" in Delphi groups was significantly less than reduction achieved with an alternative technique (social judgement analysis) and, furthermore, found that no significant reduction in disagreement had been achieved in the Delphi groups—suggesting that panellists may have simply been altering their written estimates (conforming) but not their actual opinions (consensus). Erffmeyer & Lane (1984) correlated post-group individual responses to group scores and found there to be significantly more "acceptance" (i.e. significantly higher correlations between these measures) in an alternative structured group technique than in a Delphi procedure, although there were no differences between the extent of acceptance in the Delphi groups and a variety of other group techniques. Unfortunately, no analysis was reported on the difference between the correlations of the post-group individual responses with the first round (0.73) and final round (0.94) group aggregate responses. The high correlation in the latter case does, however, suggest that the various measures of consensus (at least in this study) are related.

What is clear is that further empirical work is needed to determine the extent to which the convergence of those who do not (or cannot) drop out of the typical Delphi procedure are due to either true consensus, or to conformity pressures.

### Delphi vs. statistized groups

The simplest way of gaining a judgement from a collection of individuals is to average their individual estimates without interaction. Such statistized groups have the benefit of increasing the reliability of estimates over those of a randomly selected individual. Furthermore, if one assumes that a "truth plus error" model adequately describes individual estimates for a particular problem, then a statistized group may average out random errors and lead to a response centring upon the true value—which may lead to a judgement that is actually *better* than that of the best individual group member. Unfortunately, systematic bias appears to be more typical of human judgemental performance (e.g. Lichtenstein, Fischhoff & Phillips, 1982), so that a "bias plus error" model is descriptively more apt. In such cases, averaging individual estimates will still result in a judgement with smaller variance than individual estimates (and improved judgement), but will not eliminate the mean error, i.e. the average response will centre upon the mean of the erroneous judgements rather than on the "true" value. As bias increases, the ability of a statistized group to outperform either a randomly selected individual or the best group member decreases (e.g. Sniezek & Henry, 1989).

Because bias is apt to be pervasive, this suggests that there is frequently scope to improve upon the output of the statistized group, and this provides one of the key benchmarks for assessing the effectiveness of Delphi. This benchmark is particularly apt given that the aggregate of estimates from the first round of a Delphi poll is equivalent to that of a non-interacting statistized group. In terms of improvements in accuracy within the Delphi procedure (i.e. comparing final round to first round aggregates), results are not unequivocal, although they are generally supportive. A number of studies have attained significant increases in accuracy over Delphi rounds (Jolson & Rossow, 1971; Best, 1974; Rohrbaugh, 1979; Larreché & Moinpour, 1983, Erffmeyer & Lane, 1984; Sniezek, 1989; Parenté et al. 1984), although a number of others have failed to confirm this relationship (Gustafson et al., 1973; Brockhoff, 1975; Boje & Murnighan, 1982). Reasons for such equivocal results will be considered shortly.

*Delphi vs. interacting groups*

Possibly the most pertinent benchmark for assessing Delphi effectiveness is that provided by interacting groups, since it is concern about process loss factors associated with such groups that provide a rationale for the development and use of structured group techniques. Studies that have compared Delphi to interacting groups have *generally* provided evidence in favour of the additional value of Delphi. The technique was shown to provide more accurate judgement than comparative groups by Riggs (1983), Larreché & Moinpour (1983) and Erffmeyer & Lane (1984), although other studies found no significant differences between the two procedures (Gustafson et al., 1973; Fischer, 1981; Sniezek, 1989, 1990). The only study (of which I am aware) that claimed a converse trend is that of Brockhoff (1975), which found that, although Delphi groups were more accurate than interacting groups on short-term forecasting items, they were less accurate on almanac estimations. There was, however, no analysis of the tabulated results presented in this latter paper.

*Delphi vs. other structured group techniques*

A number of studies have compared Delphi to alternative structured group techniques, such as the NGT. Erffmeyer & Lane (1984) found Delphi to yield significantly greater accuracy than an NGT procedure, although Gustafson et al. (1973) gained results to the contrary, while Fischer (1981), Boje & Murnighan (1982) and Miner (1979) found no significant differences between them. Other studies have compared Delphi to groups in which members were required to argue both for and against their individual judgements (the "Dialectic" procedure; Sniezek, 1989); groups whose judgements were derived from a single, group-selected individual (the "Dictator" or "Best Member" strategy; Sniezek, 1989, 1990); groups that received rules on interaction (Erffmeyer & Lane, 1984); groups whose information exchange was structured according to social judgement analysis (Rohrbaugh, 1979); and to a non-interacting, no-feedback iterative procedure (Boje & Murnighan, 1982). In all of these cases, no significant differences in accuracy emerged between Delphi and any of these procedures, although a study by Larreché & Moinpour (1983) did show Delphi group accuracy to be *inferior* to statistized groups whose members were pre-selected on the basis of a measure of "expertise", while Miner (1979) demonstrated both Delphi and NGT to be significantly less "effective" (a measure combining accuracy and "acceptance of the technique") than a problem centred leadership group approach. Similar to the latter study, Van de Ven & Delbecq (1974) demonstrated Delphi and NGT both to be significantly more "effective" than interacting groups—a measure that was a composite of "quantity of unique ideas generated" and "satisfaction"—but found no difference between these two structured procedures.

In general, then, the above findings suggest that Delphi does lead to higher accuracy than statistized groups and interacting groups, although there is no consistent evidence that it leads to superior accuracy to a variety of other structured interacting and nominal group procedures. Furthermore, Delphi accuracy has occasionally been compared to that of the group's "best member" (an important benchmark, since performance above this level would indicate process gain), with equivocal results: Rohrbaugh (1979) found performance below this level and Parenté et al. (1984) provided some evidence for performance *at* this level. Sniezek (1990) appeared to demonstrate a mediating role of item difficulty, with Delphi performance at best member level on easy items, but inferior on more difficult items.

### 8.2.5 Findings: Processes in Delphi

Although the bulk of evaluative research on Delphi has focused on comparing the technique to other procedures to determine which is "best" (Rowe, Wright & Bolger, 1991), there have been a number of studies that have considered the role of aspects related to the structure of the technique and the nature of the task to see how these impact on judgement change and accuracy.

*The role of feedback*

The role of feedback in Delphi is intended to improve the quality and accuracy of panellist estimates. However, Boje & Murnighan (1982) found that a Delphi-like procedure (with feedback comprising the estimates of panellists, supported by a single reason from each), resulted in judgements that became *less* accurate over rounds, while a procedure that simply required subjects to "think again" about previous estimates (i.e. with no feedback from others) actually resulted in *increased* accuracy. Similarly, Parenté et al. (1984) found—when separating the contributions of polling and feedback in a Delphi-like approach by using a design that allowed an orthogonal decomposition of their effects on accuracy—that "iteration" alone resulted in error reduction for "when" a predicted event would occur, while feedback alone did not. The feedback in this study comprised the percentage of the subjects who thought that each event would occur within a specified time period and, when a majority thought that an event would occur, a median predicted time for this.

If these results are typical of the application of a Delphi procedure, then they imply that the technique might be better constituted by avoiding feedback altogether. An explanation of the rather counter-intuitive results, however, was suggested by Rowe, Wright & Bolger (1991), and considered empirically by Rowe & Wright (1996). They suggested that the kind of feedback presented in Delphi evaluation studies is typically poor and lacking in information, and that its influences, consequently, are difficult to predict. Such feedback generally comprises a single figure, such as a median value, with no additional information in terms of novel ideas or arguments, and hence simply indicates to panellists where the group norm lies. Unfortunately, since most evaluative studies have used student subjects making estimates about non-ecological tasks—often in the form of bizarre almanac questions in which the aim is to guess some quantitatively large figure (such as the diameter of the planet Jupiter)—there is little reason to anticipate any particular panellist expertise, and therefore that the norm figure will be particularly accurate or informed. Rowe & Wright (1996) compared the change in accuracy over rounds of an iterative procedure vs. two Delphi procedures that differed in terms of the nature of the feedback they provided. They found that the accuracy of short-term forecasts increased most, over rounds, for a Delphi condition in which panellist arguments were used as feedback, but that a Delphi condition using simply medians and individual estimates produced no greater degree of improvement than the iterative condition. Best (1974) also found that, for one of two task items, a Delphi group that was given feedback of reasons (in addition to a median and range of estimates) was significantly more accurate than a Delphi group that was simply provided with the latter information.

*Opinion change over rounds*

Parenté & Anderson-Parenté (1987) theoretically demonstrated how the Delphi technique could improve judgemental accuracy over rounds. They elaborated on Dalkey's (1975) theory of errors, suggesting that it is the less expert panellists (the "swingers") who change their estimates to a greater extent in the face of group feedback than the more expert panellists (the "holdouts"). Under this assumption it can be mathematically demonstrated that, over rounds, the median value of the panel, $M$, will move towards the true value, $T$, and hence that accuracy will improve. Evidence for this has come from Rowe & Wright (1996), who found that it was the panellists who were the *least* accurate on the first round of a Delphi poll who were the *most* likely to change their estimates on later rounds (i.e. there was a correlation between the degree of change and objective first round accuracy).

As noted previously, however, there has been some evidence of decreasing accuracy over Delphi rounds, or at least of no significant improvement (e.g. Brockhoff, 1975; Boje & Murnighan, 1982). In such cases, clearly, the above theory cannot be descriptively accurate. In any case, since it is not possible to previously determine objective expertise/accuracy in any situation in which one might wish to practically use the Delphi technique, then it is of interest to discover what other factors might predict the opinion change of panellists over rounds, particularly if such factors correlate to objective expertise. Attempts at identifying such factors, however, have not been particularly successful. Taylor, Pease & Reid (1990) found no evidence of any relationship between the demographic characteristics of panellists (gender, education, etc.) and opinion change. And while Scheibe, Skutsch & Schofer (1975) found some evidence that panellist *confidence* is related to propensity to make judgement changes over rounds (i.e. panellists who gave ratings that suggested they had low confidence exhibited significantly more judgement change from the first to the second round than those of higher confidence), Rowe & Wright (1996) failed to replicate this finding. Mulgrave & Ducanis (1975) considered panellist "dogmatism" and surprisingly found that high levels of dogmatism were related to more opinion change over rounds. The authors could think of no satisfactory explanation for their results.

*Confidence*

In practical group decision-making situations, objective measures for validating decisions rarely exist (and *cannot* exist in forecasting scenarios), and as such it is the confidence of group members that may be the only way of determining whether a decision should or will be implemented (e.g. Sniezek & Henry, 1989). Indeed, it is clear that high confidence can directly affect performance or outcome, as when a group works hard to implement a decision in which it believes, or when a group that expresses high confidence is given additional support that enhances its chance of success (e.g. in self-fulfilling prophecy). It may be argued, then, that enhanced confidence is a desirable outcome in the case of both structured and interacting groups.

Boje & Murnighan (1982) found significant increases, over rounds, in panellist ratings of their confidence in their estimates. In terms of "satisfaction", Van de Ven & Delbecq (1974) found no significant differences between how satisfied members of Delphi and interacting groups were with their procedures, although members of NGT groups were significantly more satisfied than either of these with their technique. Miner (1979), however, found no difference in the degree of "acceptance" of the members of Delphi and NGT groups for the outputs of their techniques. The extent to which *confidence*, *satisfaction* and *acceptance* relate to the same concept is open to debate.

A caveat is required here. Although enhanced confidence would seem to be a desirable outcome from using a technique for a number of *practical* reasons, it is important not to assume that improved confidence equates to improved judgement or decision quality. In the case of the study of Boje & Murnighan (1982), for example, accuracy actually *decreased* over rounds in spite of the increased confidence of panellists. Similarly, Sniezek (1990) found no evidence of a relationship between accuracy and confidence of Delphi panellists, although some evidence for such a correlation has been found by Sniezek (1989) and Rowe & Wright (1996). It is likely that other variables mediate the relationship between confidence and accuracy, and these need to be determined.

*Miscellaneous processes*

A variety of other Delphi processes have been the object of a small number of studies. The impact of group size was considered by Brockhoff (1975) and Boje & Murnighan (1982). The former considered panels of size 5, 7, 9 and 11, and the latter of size 3, 7 and 11. In neither study were any significant effects found for group size. However, for a theoretical treatment of how group size may affect statistical groups, and how this factor may interact with aspects such as the individual validity of the group members, see Hogarth (1978).

A number of studies have considered the nature of Delphi panellists and, in particular, whether self-rating can be used to determine expertise and thus as a basis for selecting a subset of a panel capable of making more accurate aggregate judgements. Results have been somewhat inconsistent, with claims that self-rating is a valid measure of expertise coming from Best (1974), Dalkey, Brown & Cochran (1970), and Rowe & Wright (1996), and evidence against due to Brockhoff (1975) and

Larreché & Moïnpour (1983). It seems likely that the appropriateness of selecting from amongst panellists on the basis of self-rated expertise, in order to increase accuracy, will be highly dependent on the nature of the particular task and the panellists. In the practical implementation of a Delphi poll, the selection of Delphi panellists is, in any case, liable to be more sophisticated. For a review of the expertise issue, see Armstrong (1985) (especially pp. 91–6).

Additional studies have considered aspects such as the effect of item word length on initial panellist consensus (Salancik, Wenger & Helfer, 1971), the number of rounds needed for stability of responses to be achieved (e.g. Brockhoff, 1975; Erffmeyer, Erffmeyer & Lane, 1986), and the way in which the desirability of forecast items relates to accuracy and opinion change over rounds (Rowe & Wright, 1996). Because these topics have not been extensively studied their results will not be laboured here, and the interested reader is invited to consider those references.

## 8.3 PROBLEMS IN RESEARCH ON STRUCTURED GROUP TECHNIQUES

In the following section, problems with *research* on structured group techniques will be considered. The bulk of the criticisms below relate specifically to research on the Delphi technique (the most widespread and formalized of the approaches), although the criticisms *do* apply more generally. The intention of this section is to reveal the extent of caution that is required when considering the apparent findings that have been noted above.

### 8.3.1 Generalizability Problems

*Defining Delphi*

The Delphi technique is a rather loosely defined procedure. In the "classical" example (e.g. Martino, 1983), an unstructured first round is used to elicit ideas from panellists, which are then resolved by the monitor team into a coherent set of scenarios on which numerical estimates are obtained on subsequent rounds; feedback comprises medians *plus* arguments from those panellists whose estimates fall outside the upper and lower quartiles; and the panellists are specifically selected experts. In contrast to this, the Delphis used in experimental studies are much simplified. The first round is invariably structured, the number of rounds rarely exceeds two, the panellists are usually students rather than experts, and feedback generally comprises a simple statistic such as a mean or median value, with no arguments (Rowe, Wright & Bolger, 1991). While these simplifications are understandable and allow Delphi to be examined more easily in a laboratory setting, the question arises as to whether any of these factors are significant predictors of technique efficacy. If they are, then the results obtained from laboratory Delphis may not generalize to the classical prescription: from the results noted in the sections above, and from theoretical work elsewhere, this does appear to be the case.

For example, it has already been noted that some evidence does exist to suggest that the use of *arguments* in feedback can lead to accuracy that is significantly better than that from comparative panels that have received only statistical averages as feedback (e.g. Best, 1974; Rowe & Wright, 1996). This suggests that the classical procedure might be *more* effective than the forms used in the average study.

Further, there has been a considerable amount of research on the issue of expertise and the impact that this might have on judgement and decision quality in Delphi, in interacting groups and more generally (e.g. Armstrong, 1985). Expertise arises as a consequence of an interaction between personal knowledge, and the particular judgement situation. A physicist is only an expert when facing a problem in his/her domain, and student subjects trying to guess the diameter of the planet Jupiter or the tonnage of a certain material shipped from New York in a certain year (for examples of almanac items, see e.g. Gustafson et al., 1973; Boje & Murnighan, 1982), or trying to predict the future price of gold (e.g. Parenté et al., 1984), are no experts at all. Consider, then, how such a panellist might react in the face of feedback that comprises a figure meant to represent the average of the rest of their group. It seems clear that he/she would have no option but to move closer to the norm: they would have no special knowledge or basis to resist this pull, and in any case it would appear to be almost a *task demand* that they give an estimate closer to the average. Increased "consensus" would soon be achieved. But changes in group accuracy would be consequent on the initial level of accuracy, which in this case would be down to luck. And this is problematic, in the sense that a false representation of the Delphi scenario is being made, and results are being generalized to the technique *per se*. The use of proper experts in the technique should lead to better effectiveness of Delphi: the initial aggregate should be more meaningful, and panellists would have the knowledge to resist the pull of any feedback that they felt was misdirected or erroneous. Again, it seems likely that the effectiveness of Delphi, and indeed of other structured group techniques, may well prove greater, in practice, than experimental results would imply.

It is important to understand which of the factors related to the structure of non-interacting group techniques are significant predictors of differential effectiveness. This should lead to more precise definitions of procedures that give less scope for misrepresentation in the laboratory, and lead to more consistent findings. For example, if group size were shown to influence the effectiveness of a Delphi or NGT procedure, then some recommendation about group size should be stated and followed (group sizes in experimental Delphis range from three upwards). It is likely that any derived definition, however, *will* be broad, and that recommendations about the use or otherwise of Delphi will be *contingent* upon situation variables such as the nature of the task.

*Defining tasks*

The importance of *task* was discussed by Hill (1982) in her review on the effectiveness of groups. She noted that "much problem-solving research has indicated that performance was affected by the task involved" and that "...task demands often elicited performance strategies that interacted with characteristics of the group" (p. 520). In the case of Delphi research, the nature of the task used is rarely considered in any depth, and there is rarely any appreciation of how the results obtained might be contingent upon its nature. In the bulk of research on Delphi, the tasks used have tended to be either short-term forecasting tasks, policy-formation tasks (where subjective opinions and views are sought because objective optimal solutions are difficult to specify), or information-poor judgement tasks (typified by studies using almanac-type questions in which unknown values with objectively optimal solutions are assessed). The latter type of tasks have been frequently used (e.g. Dalkey, Brown & Cochran, 1970; Gustafson et al., 1973; Mulgrave & Ducanis, 1975; Brockhoff, 1975; Boje & Murnighan, 1982) because changes in accuracy are easy to verify. Whether results from these tasks should be generalized to forecasting scenarios is, however, uncertain. For example, Wright & Ayton have conducted a variety of studies looking at accuracy and calibration in individuals performing judgemental and forecasting tasks (see Wright & Ayton, 1992, for summary). Not only do they suggest that there are differences in subject performance (and processes) between likelihood estimation and fore-casting tasks, but that forecasting tasks need to be differentiated according to the length of time in the future of the events to be forecast (Wright & Ayton, 1988).

Although the work of Wright & Ayton showed the contingent importance of task nature to individual judgemental performance, and the review of Hill (1982) showed its importance to group judgemental performance, it is clear that structured group performance must also be effected by the nature of the judgemental task, and therefore that any results from a particular study should be considered as appropriate to the particular task or *category* of tasks used. What is needed is a clear categorization of tasks in the same way that we need a clear definition of what is, and is not, Delphi (or NGT, etc.). Some categorizations do exist. For example, McGrath (1984) developed the "circumplex model", which categorized group tasks according to what must be accomplished during the course of a meeting. Thus, generating ideas and actions is associated with planning tasks and creativity tasks; choosing alter-natives is associated with intellective and preference tasks; and solution negotiation is associated with cognitive and mixed-motive tasks. Alternatively, Hill (1982) distinguished tasks into the types: learning/ concept attainment, concept mastery and creativity, abstract problem solving, brainstorming, and complex problem solving. Other attempts at taxonomizing tasks into broad classes also exist (e.g. Davis, 1969; Steiner, 1972). But what characterizes the various and numerous classifications is that they tend not to be based on empirical research, but rather on intuitive bases. Thus, while there is probably some substance behind each and every taxonomy, the broad categories from these also tend to encompass a wide range of tasks that vary in terms of format, time-to-completion, assessment criteria, difficulty of task, instructions, and so on.

This lack of a single, distinct, coherent definition is problematic in that the finer, perhaps more important, features of task types are masked behind the gross and obvious distinctions. It is also problematic because tasks may be inappropriately categorized as a result of definition vagueness, and because effects may be attributed either correctly to the task factor (but for the wrong reasons), or falsely. It would seem that a fundamental understanding of how aspects of tasks effect or relate to behaviour is required—and that this would be of benefit not only to those interested in research on structured group techniques, but to the wider judgement and decision-making domain.

### 8.3.2 Evaluation Problems

Another feature that has served to complicate cross-study generalization concerns the problem of *measurement* of individual and group responses and performance. If the measures used in a particular study are invalid or unreliable, then this calls into question the study's results and their interpretation. In the Delphi field of research, however (and arguably, more widely), there appears to be little debate about whether selected measures do indeed address what they are supposed to address. For example, the concepts of "expertise", "accuracy", and "item difficulty" are often measured post-task according to the proportion of correct answers given by subjects. But are such measures appropriate for assessing the quality of individual/group/structured group performance?

In the case of forecasting, influential forecasters may be able to effect events so that their forecasts are more likely to occur. A post-task measure of forecasting quality might then declare the forecasters to be expert predictors, when their actual skills might lie elsewhere. It is also possible that a good forecast might not be an accurate one. If one considers a hypothetical football match between a premier division side and a third division side, a good forecast might involve predicting victory for the former. Yet if victory were to fall to the latter, as occasionally happens in Cup competitions, then a post-task measure would declare such forecasters to be "inexpert" and their forecasts to be "bad". Indeed, Gigerenzer (e.g. 1993) demonstrated how one set of subjects who might be considered less expert than another can achieve greater accuracy in a judgemental task. That is, he predicted, and subsequently found, that German subjects were "better" than American subjects in terms of achieving a higher proportion of correct choices in sets of items requiring the estimation of which of two US cities is the more populous (for an explanation for this, the reader is referred to Gigerenzer, 1993).

A further problem with regard to the evaluation of the performance of individuals and groups concerns the sheer variety of measures that are often used to assess judgemental quality. For example, in reviewing the performance of groups vs. individuals, Hill (1982) noted that measures of "performance" have included: quantity of solutions; quality of solutions; trials to solution; time to solution; difficulty; and so on. The question arises: is it reasonable to equate and compare these various measures? Since "performance" may be enhanced in one way and not another (e.g. a group may produce more solutions, but of lower quality), this suggests that caution should be exercised. A good discussion of the ways in which performance measures vary, and how they may yield differing conclusions on judgemental performance, may be found in Bolger & Wright (1994). They describe how measures may vary according to the definition or coarseness of the grain of the analysis (i.e. the level at which performance is assessed); the facility or ease with which the judgements measured can be made (i.e. task difficulty); the "hardness" of the measure (e.g. whether it is of the reliability or validity of performance); and the statistical power of the test used (power being the probability of detecting an effect at an acceptable significance level, given that an effect above chance level exists—a phenomenon that depends upon aspects such as sample size and test sensitivity).

Arguably, we need to develop a clearer idea of what we mean by the idea of judgemental or forecasting *quality*, and we need to develop an appropriate classification system of measures. It may be, for example, that measures of *processes* will be more appropriate for assessing the quality of structured group performance (e.g. in terms of number of ideas generated through a procedure) rather than crude measures of the subsequent accuracy of the output. For a discussion of the outcome vs. process debate see e.g. Keren (1992).

## 8.4  THE FUTURE OF STRUCTURED GROUP PROCEDURES

### 8.4.1  Group Decision Support Systems

The idea of extending Delphi beyond a paper-and-pencil questionnaire-based technique through the use of computer technology (allowing the procedure, for example, to be delivered "on-line") has been around for some time (e.g. Hiltz & Turoff, 1978). Similarly, recognition of the opportunities afforded by emerging technology has led to a growing interest in the use of computers to aid in both individual and group judgement and decision-making settings. At the individual level, expert and decision support systems have been developed to model the individual human decision maker. At the "group" level, a variety of techniques have emerged that have been generically referred to as "group decision support systems" (GDSSs). More recently, interest in the ways in which technology may be used to aid groups at work in general—and not only in the domain of decision making—has gained the disciplinary appellation "computer-supported co-operative work" (CSCW).

GDSSs have been defined as systems that "combine communication, computer and decision technologies to support problem formulation and solution in group meetings" (DeSanctis & Gallupe, 1987, p. 589). In particular, such systems aim to remove the communication barriers between group members by directing the pattern, timing and content of discussion and generally, by helping to structure the decision process. The technological components of GDSSs tend to be diverse, from teleconferencing facilities to software that allows decision documenting, vote tabulation and display, and statistical programs like decision analysis. Similarly, a wide range of (behavioural and statistical) techniques may be incorporated within a GDSS, comprising those used to model decisions—such as decision trees, forecasting methods, risk analysis and multi-attribute utility theory (MAUT)—and those used to structure the group process, such as Delphi, the nominal group technique and social judgment analysis. The GDSS concept is best illustrated by a number of examples.

Decision conferencing is one approach that has been practically used to support decision making, and it is perhaps the most formalized. Reagan-Cirincione & Rohrbaugh (1992) describe it as involving intensive computer-supported meetings that typically last 2 days and include every person with a substantial stake in solving the organizational problem. The aim is to allow the group to develop a shared understanding of their problem and to create a clear plan of action through developing a computer-based decision model. This model is built to incorporate the group members' differing perspectives and priorities, with the continuous analysis and updating of the various judgements, estimates, assumptions, etc. that constitute the model, in order to rule out ineffective strategies and focus on the major issues (e.g. McCartt & Rohrbaugh, 1989). Care is taken in the implementation of a decision conference to ensure that every detail that might effect decision making is considered, from the layout of the meeting room and furnishings (to allow effective interpersonal communication) to the provision of materials such as white boards and projection screens to enable the clear presentation of information. The team which supports the conference usually comprises three members, viz. the facilitator, who works with the group to focus discussion, manage disagreement, etc. in order to steadily build up a decision model of the problem; the decision analyst, who is responsible for the group's computer-modelling support, and whose task is to update the model continuously and provide feedback; and the correspondent, who is largely responsible for documenting decisions made by the group.

A second GDSS example, described by DeSanctis, Sambamurthy & Watson (1988), is the software-aided meeting management (SAMM) system. This was designed to promote participative, democratic decision making in groups of 3–16 members. During the procedure, the members sit at a U-shaped table, each with a terminal or personal computer that is networked to a server, and through which they are able to enter individual ideas, messages, ranks, weights, votes, etc. A public screen in front of the group is used to display group ideas, messages and aggregated information on group opinion (averages of weights, votes, etc.). Additionally, a group scratch pad and messaging function are available in the system. The SAMM is controlled by the group itself, so that every member can select from among the available features, which include a brainstorming facility, decision tools (such as problem definition and stakeholder analysis) and voting schemes. A facilitator is also often available to help the group use the system.

Other GDSS examples include GroupSystems, developed at the University of Arizona, Capture Lab at Electronic Data Systems, and COLAB developed at Xerox Park (see e.g. Poole et al., 1993). In spite of the large number of different problem-solving and structuring techniques available for use in groups (Van Grundy, 1981, suggests there are over 70), only a few (such as Delphi and NGT) are regularly employed in GDSSs (e.g. DeSanctis & Gallupe, 1987). As such, there is a degree of similarity between different systems.

The combination in GDSSs of behavioural techniques and computer technology reflects the field's disciplinary origins and interests: the psychological or psychosocial, and the technological. The former stream, according to Kraemer & King (1988), has concentrated on finding out the psychological and cognitive processes of individuals and groups, the nature of small group interaction, and developing ways to facilitate this. Its interest is in how the people involved in a decision-making process think and behave. The latter stream, by contrast, is concentrated on ways of collecting, managing and displaying information that might be useful in the decision situation, and it is dominated by an engineering perspective based on developing tools. Kraemer & King (1988) suggest that it is the latter perspective that has been dominant— an outcome they attribute to uncertainties about the decision-making process. Indeed, the technological dominance is perhaps best illustrated by the attempts that have been made in the literature to taxonomize GDSSs, which have tended to be based on criteria such as the degree and complexity of the technology used in any particular procedure. For example, DeSanctis & Gallupe (1987) describe three levels of systems that are marked by the increasing use of technology and more dramatic intervention in group exchange, while Kraemer & King (1988) classify GDSSs into six types on a similar basis. The dominance of the "technological" camp is important, for it impacts upon the field's ideas on the evaluation of systems.

### 8.4.2 The Evaluation of Complex Systems

The potential of the various GDSSs to aid in judgement, decision making and forecasting is difficult to assess. On paper, the idea of using a variety of complex procedures to improve judgement seems a good one, but the core problem lies in the effective evaluation of procedures. The problems associated with evaluating Delphi are magnified when attempting to evaluate these more complex techniques. For example, the individual GDSSs tend to be fairly loosely defined, with the definitions tending to be little more than rough guidelines that detail the features/resources that are available for the aided group, and that suggest rough timetables or sequences of actions. Such flexibility, it has been argued, is a particularly important feature of GDSSs, given their employment in highly complex and dynamic situations (e.g. DeSanctis & Gallupe, 1987). However, such definitional vagueness (in addition to the similarity of techniques and their overlapping features) would seem to pose problems for researchers interested in evaluating the worth of a *particular* system.

The evaluation of GDSSs has been widely viewed as problematic, and a number of authors have noted the relative paucity of evaluative studies in the area. For example, Reagan-Cirincione & Rohrbaugh (1992) wrote that "no comparative studies of decision conferencing and other approaches have been undertaken as yet" (p. 193) (although more recent work will shortly be discussed), while Kraemer & King (1988) suggested that, as a result of a lack of evaluative research on the qualitative impact of advanced GDSSs, the goal of improving the quality of decisions "has not been demonstrated" (p. 131). Grudin (1989) has made a similar point with regard to the more general field of CSCW.

McCartt & Rohrbaugh (1989), for example, have argued that evaluating the effectiveness of decision conferencing (by linking good decision outcomes to particular types of group decision support) is "extraordinarily difficult", since virtually all real-world GDSS applications provide insufficient base lines of comparison (i.e. tests of alternative techniques or alternative decisions) to satisfy laboratory-based experimental researchers. Similarly, Grudin (1989) has suggested that it is the "extreme difficulty" of evaluating CSCW applications, more generally, that has affected their uptake, and that their evaluation in the field is "remarkably complex owing to the number of people to observe at each site, the wide variability that may be found in group composition, and the range of environmental factors that play a role in determining acceptance" (p. 252). In particular, Grudin points out that evaluation is considerably more difficult for multi-user applications than for single-user ones, as an individual's success with a particular application (e.g. spreadsheet or word processor) is not likely to be affected by "the backgrounds of other group members or by administrative or personality dynamics within the group" (p. 251).

At the heart of the matter is the difficulty of creating a group in the laboratory that will reflect the social, motivational, economic and political dynamics of real work groups, and that will allow complex support procedures to be studied in a more controlled environment. For example, Kiesler & Sproull (1992) note that "... with experience, routines and social norms, established groups may overcome, or create, problems in decision making very differently than experimental groups do (and that) ... organizational practices, structures and technology also can have an impact on group dynamics" (p. 114). Owing to the number of unknown factors influencing use, Grudin (1989) suggests that a full implementation may be required before evaluation is at all possible.

Apart from these research difficulties, the lack of evaluation may also be related to the predominant emphasis of GDSS research and development on technology, rather than on understanding the decision making of people at work. Kraemer & King (1988), for example, have suggested that most products have tended to be "supply pushed", rather than "demand pulled", i.e. that researchers have tended to develop aids that they assume will be needed by decision makers (developed simply because the technology is there), rather than working from the premise of satisfying a current identified demand. (A similar view has been expressed in the CSCW domain; e.g. Bannon & Schmidt, 1991.) One reflection of this is the number of articles in the literature that simply describe some new system, or collection of techniques and technologies, often from the perspective of technical problems solved or potential and theoretical advantages and uses, and which do not substantiate their claims.

A product of the dominance of the technologists' camp is that GDSSs have been criticized for the assumptions they often implicitly make about the human decision maker. For example, Huber (1981, 1982) has suggested that GDSSs make "rational" contributions to decision making—assuming that decision makers use information in a rational manner in order to benefit the organization for which they work, with any lack of success due simply to intellectual or resource constraints. From this perspective, judgement and decision making may be improved by providing participants with *more* information in a *more* *effective* manner. However, humans can only be considered "rational" in a limited sense, and the addition of still greater amounts of information may merely serve to increase the degree of cognitive overload. Furthermore, the rational model of decision making is limited in denying the importance of personal, political and social motives and imperatives—features that alternative decision-making models do not deny (e.g. the "political", "garbage can" and "program" models of Huber, 1982; see also Bannon & Schmidt, 1991; Kling, 1991, for discussions of similar difficulties and issues in the CSCW domain). It is perhaps for such reasons that group support products have not been seen as a great success, with only a few of the numerous prototypes having taken off commercially (e.g. Kraemer & King, 1988; Grudin, 1989; Kling, 1991).

Although the evaluation of systems is not common in the area of complex group support, it is not absent. Most studies have compared computer-supported to unsupported groups, using a variety of performance measures in addition to "accuracy", such as the number of unique ideas generated, decision time, increased participation, etc. For example, Cass, Heintz & Kaiser (1992) conducted a laboratory experiment involving a preference allocation task, in which groups using a GDSS were compared to those that had no access to one, and were evaluated according to the satisfaction of subjects with the process and outcome of their respective meetings. McCartt & Rohrbaugh (1989), accepting that objective measures of effectiveness are usually difficult to obtain, attempted to determine the value of decision conferences according to a number of subjective criteria of participants, such as whether they felt pressure to construct a plan of action, etc. Other evaluative studies that have been conducted include those of Gallupe, DeSanctis & Dickson (1988), Watson, DeSanctis & Poole (1988), Turoff & Hiltz (1982), and Jarvenpaa, Rao & Huber (1988). A more interesting study is that of Poole et al. (1993), which attempted to consider a large number of measures of group behaviour and to relate these to decision outcomes and the nature of the task and group procedure (they considered the SAMM technique).

Perhaps unsurprisingly, and mirroring the pattern of results from Delphi research, the findings from the above studies have ranged from strong support for the effectiveness of computer-supported groups, to evidence that computer support can lead to poorer performance (according to a wide variety of measures). Indeed, according to Rao & Jarvenpaa (1991), "Empirical research in the area of computer support of groups is characterized by inconsistent results across studies" (p. 1347). Rao & Jarvenpaa conclude from this that the "effectiveness" of GDSSs remain an open issue.

There are also a small number of studies that have attempted to consider the *processes* within GDSSs. For example, Connolly, Jessup & Valacich (1990) assessed the influence of anonymity and evaluative comments (critical or supportive) within a GDSS. They used groups of four student subjects, seated at separate terminals, to perform an idea generation problem on a university parking issue. Arguments were received on-screen to aid subjects, and these were either anonymous and critical, anonymous and supportive, identified and critical, or identified and supportive. The authors reported that idea generation was greater under conditions of anonymity than identification; and that critical comments led to more ideas being generated than supportive ones. Furthermore, they also looked at a satisfaction measure, and found that the conditions that led to the least idea generation actually led to the highest participant satisfaction—suggesting that satisfaction (like confidence) may not be highly, or positively, related to a more objective measure of performance quality.

Kiesler & Sproull (1992) have summarized several experiments by themselves and others that have been concerned with the nature of electronic communication interactions. For example, they reported that in comparison to face-to-face groups, technology-mediated groups tend to show a more equal distribution of participation (lesser domination of discussion by high-status people), a longer time to reach decisions, a greater difficulty in reaching consensus (i.e. more "flaming"— expressing rude impulsive views with a loss of concern for politeness), and more risk-seeking behaviour. Furthermore, and interestingly, given the present interest in Delphi, a number of studies have compared responses from paper-and-pencil and electronic mail questionnaires, and found that responses to the latter tend to be more extreme, revealing and less socially desirable (Kiesler & Sproull, 1986; Sproull, 1986). These findings suggest that the medium through which a Delphi questionnaire is delivered might be a further significant factor affecting behaviour, and ultimately, technique effectiveness (for a more comprehensive review of these findings and their implications, see Sproull & Kiesler, 1991; Kiesler & Sproull, 1992).

Other studies have looked at aspects such as how influence patterns change within groups using GDSSs (e.g. Zigurs, Poole & DeSanctis, 1988). The interpretation of this and the above findings is not, for present purposes, important. What is significant, to sum up this section, is that there is a relative lack of debate in the literature on the issue of the evaluation of techniques; that methodologies from empirical psychology and social science (plus software engineering and its related disciplines) appear limited in evaluating systems; and that there is growing concern about the need to research the processes behind judgement and decision making and the reactions of subjects to aspects of complex support systems.

## 8.5  CONCLUSION

In this chapter I have considered the rationale for using structured group techniques to improve judgement, and focused on the most formalized of these, the Delphi technique. Attempts at evaluating the effectiveness of Delphi have been relatively sparse, and results have been somewhat equivocal. The chapter has also considered research on the natural successors to structured group procedures, namely GDSSs. A number of research problems have been identified in both domains. These range from the lack of coherent definitions of procedures and tasks, to variability in measures of effectiveness, to a lack of concern for understanding the processes that underlie the behaviour of individuals taking part in such procedures (see also Rowe, Wright & Bolger, 1991;

Rao & Jarvenpaa, 1991; George, 1992). It is only from careful, well-structured and theoretically-driven research that there is hope of building up an understanding of the influences of group-support procedures and, ultimately, of addressing the critical issue of contingent technique validity.

## REFERENCES

Adair, J. (1983) *Effective Leadership*. Gower, Aldershot.
Armstrong, J.S. (1985) *Long-range Forecasting: From Crystal Ball to Computers*, 2nd edn. Wiley, New York.
Bannon, L.J. & Schmidt, K. (1991) CSCW: Four characters in search of a context. In J.M. Bowers & S.D. Benford (eds), *Studies in Computer Supported Cooperative Work*. Elsevier, North Holland, Amsterdam.
Bardecki, M.J. (1984) Participants' response to the Delphi method: an attitudinal perspective. *Technological Forecasting and Social Change*, **25**, 281–92.
Belbin, R.M. (1981) *Management Teams*. Heinemann, London.
Best, R.J. (1974) An experiment in Delphi estimation in marketing decision making. *Journal of Marketing Research*, **11**, 448–52.
Boje, D.M. & Murnighan, J.K. (1982) Group confidence pressures in iterative decisions. *Management Science*, **28**, 1187–96.
Bolger, F. & Wright, G. (1994) Assessing the quality of expert judgment: issues and analysis. *Decision Support Systems*, **11**, 1–24.
Brockhoff, K. (1975) The Performance of Forecasting Groups in Computer Dialogue and Face to Face Discussions. In H. Linstone & M. Turoff (eds), *The Delphi Method: Techniques and Applications*. Addison-Wesley, London.
Cass, K., Heintz, T.J. & Kaiser, K.M. (1992) An investigation of satisfaction when using a voice-synchronous GDSS in dispersed meetings. *Information and Management*, **23**(4), 173–82.
Coates, J.F. (1975) In defense of Delphi: a review of delphi assessment, expert opinion, forecasting and group process by H. Sackman. *Technological Forecasting and Social Change*, **7**, 193–4.
Connolly, T., Jessup, L.M. & Valacich, J.S. (1990) Effects of anonymity and evaluative tone on idea generation in computer-mediated groups. *Management Science*, **36**(6), 689–703.
Dalkey, N.C. (1975) Towards a theory of group estimation. In H. Linstone & M. Turoff (eds), *The Delphi Method: Techniques and Applications*. Addison-Wesley, London.
Dalkey, N.C., Brown, B. & Cochran, S.W. (1970) The Delphi Method III: Use of self-ratings to improve group estimates. *Technological Forecasting*, **1**, 283–91.

Dalkey, N.C. & Helmer, O. (1963)   An experimental application of the Delphi Method to the use of experts. *Management Science*, **9**, 458–67.

Davis, J.H. (1969)   *Group Performance*. Addison-Wesley, Reading, MA.

Delbecq, A.L., Van de Ven, A.H. & Gustafson, D.H. (1975)   *Group Techniques for Program Planning*. Scott Foresman, Glenview, IL.

DeSanctis, G. & Gallupe, R.B. (1987)   A foundation for the study of group decision support systems. *Management Science*, **33**, 589–606.

DeSanctis, G., Sambamurthy, V. & Watson, R.T. (1988)   Computer-supported meetings: building a research environment. *Large Scale Systems*, **13**, 43–59.

Eils, L.C. & John, R.S. (1980)   A criterion validation of multiattribute utility analysis and of group communication strategy. *Organizational Behavior and Human Performance*, **25**, 268–88.

Einhorn, H.J., Hogarth, R.M. & Klempner, E. (1977)   Quality of group judgment. *Psychological Bulletin*, **84**, 158–72.

Erffmeyer, R.C., Erffmeyer, E.S. & Lane, I.M. (1986)   The Delphi technique: an empirical evaluation of the optimal number of rounds. *Group and Organization Studies*, **11**(1), 120–28.

Erffmeyer, R.C. & Lane, I.M. (1984)   Quality and acceptance of an evaluative task: the effects of four group decision-making formats. *Group and Organization Studies* **9**(4), 509–29.

Ferrell, W.R. (1985)   Combining individual judgments. In G. Wright (ed.), *Behavioural Decision Making*. Plenum, New York.

Fischer, G.W. (1981)   When oracles fail—a comparison of four procedures for aggregating subjective probability forecasts. *Organizational Behavior and Human Performance*, **28**, 96–110.

Gallupe, R.B., DeSanctis, G. & Dickson, G.W. (1988)   The impact of computer-based support on the processes and outcomes of group decision making. *MIS Quarterly*, **12**(2), 277–96.

George, J.F. (1992)   An examination of four GDSS experiments. *Journal of Information Science Principles and Practice*, **18**(2), 149–58.

Gigerenzer, G. (1993)   Probabilistic mental models and bounded rationality. Paper presented to the 14th Conference on Subjective Probability, Utility and Decision Making, Aix-en-Provence, France.

Ginsberg, A. (1992)   Integrating evaluation into decision making. *Public Manager*, **21**(4), 24–5.

Grudin, J. (1989)   Why groupware applications fail: problems in design and evaluation. *Office: Technology and People*, **4**(3), 245–64.

Gustafson, D.H., Shukla, R.K., Delbecq, A. & Walster, G.W. (1973)   A comparison study of differences in subjective likelihood estimates made by individuals, interacting groups, Delphi groups and nominal groups. *Organizational Behavior and Human Performance*, **9**, 280–91.

Hall, J. & Watson, W.H. (1971)   The effects of a normative intervention on group decision-making performance. *Human Relations*, **23**, 299–317.

Hall, J. & Williams, M.S. (1970) Group dynamics training and improved decision making. *The Journal of Applied Behavioral Science*, **6**, 39–68.

Hastie, R. (1986) Experimental evidence on group accuracy. In B. Grafman & G. Owen (eds), *Decision Research*, vol. 2. JAI Press, Greenwich, CT.

Herbert, T.T. & Yost, E.B. (1979) A comparison of decision quality under nominal interacting consensus group formats: the case of the structured problem. *Decision Sciences*, **10**, 358–67.

Hill, G.W. (1982) Group versus individual performance: are $N+1$ heads better than one? *Psychological Bulletin*, **91**(3), 517–39.

Hiltz, S.R. & Turoff, M. (1978) *The Network Nation: Human Communication via Computer*. Addison-Wesley, Reading, MA.

Hoffman, L.R. (1965) Group problem solving. In L. Berkowitz (ed.), *Advances in Experimental Social Psychology*, vol. 2. Academic Press, New York.

Hogarth, R.M. (1978) A note on aggregating opinions. *Organizational Behaviour and Human Performance*, **21**, 40–46.

Holloman, C.R. & Hendrick, H.W. (1972) Adequacy of group decisions as a function of the decision-making process. *Academy of Management Journal*, **8**, 175–84.

Huber, G.P. (1981) The nature of organizational decision making and the design of decision support systems. *MIS QS*, **2** (June), 1–10.

Huber, G.P. (1982) Decision support systems: their present nature and future applications. In G.R. Ungson & D.N. Braunstein (eds), *Decision Making: An Interdisciplinary Inquiry*. Kent, Belmont, CA.

Hudak, R.P., Brooke, P.P., Finstuen, K. & Riley, P. (1993) Health care administration in the year 2000: practitioners' views of future issues and job requirements. *Hospital and Health Services Administration*, **38**(2), 181–95.

Janis, I. (1972) *Victims of Groupthink*. Houghton Mifflin, Boston, MA.

Janis, I.L. (1992) Causes and consequences of defective policy-making. In F. Heller (ed.), *Decision-making and Leadership*. Cambridge University Press, Cambridge.

Jarvenpaa, S.L., Rao, V.S. & Huber, G.P. (1988) Computer support for meetings of groups working on unstructured problems: a field experiment. *MIS Quarterly*, **12**(4), 645–66.

Jolson, M.A. & Rossow, G. (1971) The Delphi process in marketing decision making. *Journal of Marketing Research*, **8**, 443–8.

Keren, G. (1992) Improving decisions and judgments: the desirable versus the feasible. In G. Wright & F. Bolger (eds), *Expertise and Decision Support*. Plenum, New York.

Kiesler, S. & Sproull, L.S. (1986) Response effects in the electronic survey. *Public Opinion Quarterly*, **50**, 402–13.

Kiesler, S. & Sproull, L.S. (1992) Group decision making and communication technology. *Organizational Behavior and Human Decision Processes*, **52**(1), 96–123.

Kling, R. (1991) Cooperation, coordination and control in computer-supported work. *Communications of the ACM*, **34**(12), 83–8.

Kraemer, K.L. & King, J.L. (1988) Computer-based systems for cooperative work and group decision making. *ACM Computing Surveys*, **20**(2), 115–46.

Lamm, H. & Myers, D.G. (1978) Group-induced polarization of attitudes and behavior. In L. Berkowitz (ed.), *Advances in Experimental Social Psychology*, vol. 11. Academic Press, New York.

Larreché, J.C. & Moinpour, R. (1983) Managerial judgment in marketing: the concept of expertise. *Journal of Marketing Research*, **20**, 110–21.

Lichtenstein, S., Fischhoff, B. & Phillips, L.D. (1982) Calibration of probabilities: the state of the art to 1980. In D. Kahneman, P. Slovic & A. Tversky (eds), *Judgment Under Uncertainty: Heuristics and Biases*. Cambridge University Press, Cambridge.

Linstone, H.A. & Turoff, M. (1975) *The Delphi Method: Techniques and Applications*. Addison-Wesley, London.

Martino, J. (1983) *Technological Forecasting for Decision Making*, 2nd edn. American Elsevier, New York.

McCartt, A.T. & Rohrbaugh, J. (1989) Evaluating group decision support system effectiveness: a performance study of decision conferencing. *Decision Support Systems*, **5**, 243–53.

McGrath, J.E. (1984) *Groups: Interaction and Performance*. Prentice Hall, Englewood Cliffs, NJ.

Miner, F.C. (1979) A comparative analysis of three diverse group decision making approaches. *Academy of Management Journal*, **22**(1), 81–93.

Miner, F.C. (1984) Group versus individual decision making: an investigation of performance measures, decision strategies, and process losses/gains. *Organizational Behaviour and Human Performance*, **33**, 112–24.

Mulgrave, N.W. & Ducanis, A.J. (1975) Propensity to change responses in a Delphi round as a function of dogmatism. In H. Linstone & M. Turoff (eds), *The Delphi Method: Techniques and Applications*. Addison-Wesley, London.

Nemiroff, P.M. & King, D.C. (1975) Group decision-making performance as influenced by consensus and self-orientation. *Human Relations*, **28**, 1–21.

Nemiroff, P.M., Passmore, W.A. & Ford, D.L. (1976) The effects of two normative structural interventions on established and *ad hoc* groups: implications for improving decision-making effectiveness. *Decision Sciences*, **7**, 841–55.

Neiderman, F., Brancheau, J.C. & Wetherbe, J.C. (1991) Information systems management issues for the 1990s. *MIS Quarterly*, **15**(4), 474–500.

Parenté, F.J., Anderson, J.K., Myers, P. & O'Brien, T. (1984) An examination of factors contributing to Delphi accuracy. *Journal of Forecasting*, **3**(2), 173–82.

Parenté, F.J. & Anderson-Parenté, J.K. (1987) Delphi inquiry systems. In G. Wright & P. Ayton (eds), *Judgmental Forecasting*. Wiley, Chichester.

Park, W.W. (1990)   A review of research on groupthink. *Journal of Behavioral Decision Making*, **3**, 229–45.

Poole, M.S., Holmes, M., Watson, R. & DeSanctis, G. (1993)   Group decision support systems and group communication. *Communication Research*, **20**(2), 176–213.

Rao, V.S & Jarvenpaa, S.L. (1991)   Computer support of groups: theory-based models for GDSS research. *Management Science*, **37**(10), 1347–62.

Reagan-Cirincione, P. & Rohrbaugh, J. (1992)   Decision conferencing: a unique approach to the behavioral aggregation of expert judgment. In G. Wright & F. Bolger (eds), *Expertise and Decision Support*. Plenum, London.

Riggs, W.E. (1983)   The Delphi method: an experimental evaluation. *Technological Forecasting and Social Change*, **23**, 89–94.

Rohrbaugh, J. (1979)   Improving the quality of group judgment: social judgment analysis and the Delphi technique. *Organizational Behavior and Human Performance*, **24**, 73–92.

Rowe, G., Wright, G. & Bolger, F. (1991)   The Delphi technique: a reevaluation of research and theory. *Technological Forecasting and Social Change*, **39**(3), 235–51.

Rowe, G. & Wright, G. (1996)   The impact of task characteristics on the performance of structured group forecasting techniques. *International Journal of Forecasting*, **12**, 73–89.

Rowe, G. & Wright, G. (in press)   The Delphi technique as a forecasting tool: issues and analysis. *International Journal of Forecasting*.

Sackman, H. (1975)   *Delphi Critique*. Lexington Books, Lexington, MA.

Saito, M. & Sinha, K. (1991)   Delphi study on bridge condition rating and effects of improvements. *Journal of Transport Engineering*, **117**, 320–34.

Salancik, J.R., Wenger, W. & Helfer, E. (1971)   The construction of Delphi event statements. *Technological Forecasting and Social Change*, **3**, 65–73.

Scheibe, M., Skutsch, M. & Schofer, J. (1975)   Experiments in Delphi methodology. In H. Linstone & M. Turoff (eds), *The Delphi Method: Techniques and Applications*. Addison-Wesley, London.

Sniezek, J.A. (1989)   An examination of group process in judgmental forecasting. *International Journal of Forecasting*, **5**, 171–8.

Sniezek, J.A. (1990)   A comparison of techniques for judgmental forecasting by groups with common information. *Group and Organization Studies*, **15**(1), 5–19.

Sniezek, J.A. & Henry, R.A. (1989)   Accuracy and confidence in group judgment. *Organizational Behaviour and Human Decision Processes*, **43**, 1–28.

Sproull, L. (1986)   Using electronic mail for data collection in organizational research. *Academy of Management Journal*, **29**(1), 159–69.

Sproull, L. & Kiesler, S. (1991)   Reducing social context cues: electronic mail in organizational communication. *Management Science*, **32**(11), 1149–512.

Steiner, I.D. (1972) *Group Process and Productivity*. Academic Press, New York.

Stewart, T.R. (1987) The Delphi technique and judgmental forecasting. *Climatic Change*, **11**, 97–113.

Taylor, R.G., Pease, J. & Reid, W.M. (1990) A study of survivability and abandonment of contributions in a chain of Delphi rounds. *Psychology: A Journal of Human Behavior*, **27**, 1–6.

Turoff, M. & Hiltz, S.R. (1982) Computer support for group versus individual decisions. *IEEE Transactions Communications*, **20**(1), 82–90.

Uecker, W.L. (1982) The quality of group performance in simplified information evaluation. *Journal of Accounting Research*, **20**, 388–402.

Van Grundy, A.B. (1981) *Techniques of Structured Problem Solving*. Van Nostrand Reinhold, New York.

Van de Ven, A.H. & Delbecq, A.L. (1971) Nominal versus interacting group processes for committee decision making effectiveness. *Academic Management Journal*, **14**, 203–13.

Van de Ven, A.H. & Delbecq, A.L. (1974) The effectiveness of Nominal, Delphi, and Interacting group decision making processes. *Academy of Management Journal*, **17**(4), 605–21.

Watson, R., DeSanctis, G. & Poole, M.S. (1988) Using a GDSS to facilitate group consensus: some intended and unintended consequences. *MIS Quarterly*, **12**(3), 463–77.

Wright, G. & Ayton, P. (1988) Immediate and short-term judgemental forecasting: personologism, situationism, or interactionism? *Personality and Individual Differences*, **9**, 109–20.

Wright, G. & Ayton, P. (1992) Judgmental probability forecasting in the immediate and medium term. *Organizational Behavior and Human Decision Processes*, **51**(3), 344–63.

Zigurs, I., Poole, M.S. & DeSanctis, G. (1988) A study of influence in computer-mediated communication. *MIS Quarterly*, **12**(4), 625–44.

# Chapter 9

# How Bad Is Human Judgement?

Peter Ayton
*City University, London, UK*

## SUMMARY

Psychological studies of judgemental forecasting can be divided into two general categories. In the first sort of study subjects are presented with some data (often in the form of a time series) and are asked to forecast future points. Studies of this sort are discussed in this volume by O'Connor & Lawrence. This chapter discusses the second sort of study, which can be characterized as memory-based forecasting. In these studies people are asked to predict the occurrence of events, relying on their knowledge of the events to be forecast. Typically people are asked to generate the likelihood of a given event occurring. Asking for probabilities enables researchers to compare judgements with the laws of logic and probability. A common finding has been that human judgement of probability violates the laws of probability. But what should we conclude from that finding? Here I discuss some contrasting images of judgement that emerge from psychological research.

*Forecasting with Judgment*. Edited by G. Wright and P. Goodwin.
© 1998 John Wiley & Sons Ltd.

## 9.1 INTRODUCTION

"Mr Magoo" is an interesting character who stars in a cartoon film series of adventures. For those who are not familiar with him I should describe him. Mr Magoo has very poor eyesight but seems quite oblivious of the fact. He is involved in a number of extraordinary escapades that usually hinge on the fact that he fails to see that he is in great peril. Remarkably, however, no serious harm ever seems to befall him. For example, without realizing it, he might be about to walk out of an office window on the 19th floor of a skyscraper but then a crane will swing past the office just as he steps out and he will stroll up the jib of the crane believing he is walking up the street. Later at home, and unaware of his incredible luck, he can mistake his nephew for a hat-stand *and vice versa* and then complain bitterly about the sullen and unresponsive dumbness of his nephew and the fact that the hat-stand won't stay still.

For some Mr Magoo might well be used as an appropriate metaphor for psychological views of human judgement. One view of human judgement is that people—including experts—not only suffer various forms of myopia but are somewhat oblivious of the fact. For example, the first significant evidence for deficiencies in expert judgement was Meehl's (1954) book which evaluated clinical judgement. Meehl compared the intuitive clinical judgements made by expert psychiatrists (e.g. is this patient schizophrenic?) with those that could be made by a statistical formula using the same information. The statistical decisions were based on a "linear model". A linear model summarizes the relationship between a set of predictor variables and some criterion value—the outcome to be predicted. For example, in predicting the chances of survival from major surgery, relevant predictor variables may be the age, weight and general fitness of the patient. The linear model is constructed in such a way as to maximize the statistical relationship between the predictor variables and the criterion to be predicted. The value of each of the predictor variables is differentially weighted according to the strength of its diagnostic relationship to the criterion and then all the variables are summed.

In approximately 20 studies which compared clinical decisions with statistical decisions, Meehl (1954) found that the statistical model provided more accurate predictions or the two models tied. Over the years since there have been many more studies comparing clinical and statistical judgement in an enormous range of areas of judgement. The superiority of the statistical method over "clinical" judgement has been replicated in all of these studies. Meehl (1986) commented: "There is no controversy in social science which shows such a large body of qualitatively diverse studies coming out so uniformly in the same direction as this one".

Despite this claim, the effect of the research on the practice of clinical judgement has been limited; according to Dawes (1988) it is "almost zilch". Dawes argues that this is because the findings are a challenge to the self-perceptions of experts. It is difficult for highly trained clinicians to accept that they cannot outperform a procedure which simply adds up the cues in favour of each judgement and picks the one with the highest score. This resistance may well be stiffened by the knowledge that the statistical method will not be perfect. There is evidence that resistance to the use of simple decision rules, which—given present knowledge—cannot be outperformed, increases with expertise and the importance of the decision (cf. Yates, McDaniel & Brown, 1991). Given the notion that there is often an illusory degree of control (e.g. Langer, 1982), judges may find it unacceptable to settle for the given number of errors implied by the statistical approach when they feel—erroneously—that their judgement might do better. Arrow (1992) recounts a story that illustrates something of the strength of peoples' fondness for judgement even where its inadequacy is clearly established. Employed as an American air force weather forecaster during the Second World War, Arrow discovered that long-range weather forecasts were no better than numbers pulled from a hat. The forecasters agreed and asked their superiors to be relieved of this task. The reply they received was: "The Commanding General is well aware that the forecasts are no good. However, he needs them for planning purposes".

A further finding from statistical modelling research is the disparity between the nature and complexity of the statistical model and the expert's perception of their own reasoning. Experts appear to have very little insight into their own judgement and typically feel that they are making judgements that are based on more information than the statistical models suggest they consider (Dawes, 1988). Such a state of affairs is rather consistent with our Mr Magoo analogy: the clear suggestion is that people's judgement is poor and, moreover, that they do not realise it. This oblivion in turn might plausibly be responsible for further problems, e.g. over-confidence of forecasts. Over-confidence in forecasting can be described as an unwarranted faith in the reliability of the forecast and has been attributed, at least in part, to a failure to recognize the fallibility of our own judgement. We shall return to over-confidence later.

Although Meehl's research is mute about the mechanisms responsible for judgement, there is no shortage of proposals for mental procedures for judgement. Since the early 1970s Kahneman & Tversky have provided a plethora of demonstrations of human judgemental error and linked these to the operation of a set of mental heuristics. For example, Tversky & Kahneman (1974) claimed that human judgement is over-confident, ignores base rates, is insufficiently regressive, is influenced by arbitrary anchors, induces illusory correlations, and misconceives randomness. The logic of this research is to infer the characteristics of the mental processes used to make judgements by studying the biases which emerge that are not due to inattention or fatigue. The idea, spelled out in Kahneman, Slovic & Tversky (1982), is that, due to limited mental processing capacity, strategies of simplification are required to reduce the complexity of judgement tasks and make them tractable for the kind of mind that people happen to have. Normative decision theory states that *all* information relevant to a decision should be considered. Accordingly, the principal reason for interest in judgemental biases was not merely that subjects made errors but that it supported the notion that people made use of relatively simple but error-prone heuristics for making judgements. This claim has been most strongly made with regard to judgements and decisions made under uncertainty (cf. Kahneman, Slovic & Tversky, 1982) and so naturally lends itself to application to judgemental forecasting.

One such heuristic is *representativeness*. This heuristic determines how likely it is that an event is a member of a category according to how similar or typical the event is to the category. For example, people may judge the likelihood that a given individual is employed as a librarian by the extent to which the individual resembles a typical librarian. This may seem a reasonable strategy but it neglects consideration of the relative prevalence of librarians. Tversky & Kahneman found that when base rates of different categories vary, judgements of the occupations of described people were correspondingly biased—due to base-rate neglect. People using the representativeness heuristic for forecasting were employing a form of stereotyping in which similarity dominates other cues as a basis for judgement and decision making. The impli-cations for forecasting are plain: e.g. a particular sequence of events may be seen as more typical or representative of the set of possible future sequences than other equally likely—but less typical—sequences. As a consequence, it is wrongly judged as more likely to occur.

Judgement by representativeness was invoked by Tversky & Kahneman (1983) to explain evidence for the conjunction fallacy, whereby a conjunction of events is judged more likely than one of its constituents. This is a violation of a perfectly simple principle of probability logic: if A includes B, then the probability of B cannot exceed A. Nevertheless, subjects who read a description of a woman called Linda who had a history of interest in liberal causes gave a higher likelihood to the possibility that she was a feminist bank teller than to the possibility that she was a bank teller—thereby violating the conjunction rule.

Another heuristic used for probabilistic judgement is *availability*. This heuristic is invoked when people estimate likelihood or relative frequency by the ease with which instances can be brought to mind. Instances of frequent events are typically easier to recall than instances of less frequent events, so availability will often be a valid cue for estimates of likelihood. However, availability is affected by factors other than likelihood. For example, recent events and emotionally salient events are more easy to recollect. It is a common experience that the perceived riskiness of air travel rises in the immediate wake of an air disaster. Applications for earthquake insurance in California are apparently higher in the immediate wake of a major quake. Judgements made on the basis of availability then are vulnerable to bias whenever availability and likelihood are uncorrelated.

The *anchor-and-adjust* heuristic is used when people make estimates by starting from an initial value that is adjusted to yield a final value. The claim is that adjustment is typically insufficient. For instance, one experimental task required subjects to estimate various quantities stated in percentages (e.g. the percentage of African countries in the UN). Subjects communicated their answers by using a spinner wheel showing numbers between 0 and 100. For each question the wheel was spun and then subjects were first asked whether the true answer was above or below this arbitrary value. They then gave their estimate of the actual value. Estimates were found to be considerably influenced by the initial (entirely random) starting point (cf. Wilson et al., 1996).

The research into heuristics and biases provided a methodology, a very vivid explanatory framework and a strong suggestion that judgement is not as good as it might be. However, the idea that all of this should be taken for granted was denied by the proponents of the research some time ago. For example, Kahneman & Tversky (1982) made clear that the main goal of the research was to understand the processes that produce both valid and invalid judgements. However, it soon became apparent that: "although errors of judgement are but a method by which some cognitive processes are studied, the method has become a significant part of the message" (Kahneman & Tversky, 1982, p. 124). So how should we regard human judgement?

Ten years ago, when the previous edited volume devoted to judgemental forecasting was published (Wright & Ayton, 1987a), there was considerable discussion concerning the ability of people to make good forecasts. There was discussion of the nature of judgemental heuristics and consideration of the sort of characteristic errors that are associated with them and what, if anything, could be done about it (e.g. Evans, 1987; Wright & Ayton, 1987b). There were also those voices who cautioned against the tempting conclusion that human judgement was a poor basis for making forecasts (Phillips 1987; Beach, Christensen-Szalanski & Barnes, 1987). That debate was well under way then and has continued apace ever since. What lessons are there in this debate to inform understanding the nature of judgemental forecasting?

There has been an enormous amount of discussion of Tversky & Kahneman's findings and claims. It would not be unfair to say that researchers in the heuristics and biases tradition have sometimes generated shock and astonishment that people seem so bad at reasoning with probability despite the fact that we all live in an uncertain world. Not surprisingly, and as a consequence, the claims have been challenged. The basis of the challenges has varied. Some have questioned whether these demonstrations of biases in judgement apply merely to student samples or to experts operating in their domain of expertise. Another argument is that the nature of the tasks set to subjects gives a misleading perspective of their competence. A third argument is that the standards for the assessment of judgement are inappropriate. Consideration of these three types of argument is given below.

## 9.2 EXPERT JUDGEMENT

While there is not the space to review the findings comprehensively here, it is not difficult to find evidence of error and biases in expert judgement (e.g. Ayton, 1992). Estate agents' valuations have been found to be influenced by an irrelevant anchor—information that they deny the relevance of (Northcraft & Neale, 1987); doctors have been found to assess the likelihood of disease according to how representative of the disease the symptoms are—ignoring base rates (Eddy, 1982); experts also violate the conjunction rule—115 delegates at the Second International Symposium on Forecasting (1982) rated the likelihood of "a 30% drop in the consumption of oil in the US in 1983" as higher than "a dramatic increase in the price of oil and a 30% drop in the consumption of oil in the US in 1983" (Tversky & Kahneman, 1983); Wagenaar & Keren (1986) found over-confidence in lawyers' attempts to predict the outcome of court trials in which they represented one side.

## 9.3  JUDGEMENTAL TASKS

Beach, Christensen-Szalanski & Barnes (1987) have discussed the criterion problem for evaluating human judgement. This is the notion that it is not always clear what the proper basis is for the evaluation of judgement. A rather different argument has emerged more recently. In a series of articles, Gigerenzer (e.g. 1991; 1994; 1996) has argued that although people may appear poor at making the judgements required in the problems that have been devised to measure judgement, this may be a misleading picture of judgemental competence. Gigerenzer draws attention to demonstrations of tests of over-confidence, base-rate neglect and the conjunction fallacy where changes in the mode of presentation of the problems produce significant improvements in performance. Each of these sorts of judgemental errors are critical for forecasting and are considered in turn below.

### 9.3.1  Overconfidence

In the 1970s and 1980s a considerable amount of evidence was assembled for the view that people suffer from an over-confidence bias. Typical laboratory studies of calibration ask subjects to answer questions such as:

> Which is the world's longest canal?    (a) Panama
> (b) Suez

Subjects are require to indicate the answer that they think is correct and then state how confident they are on a probability scale ranging from 50% to 100% (as one of the answers is always correct 50% is the probability of guessing correctly). To be well calibrated, assessed probability should equal percentage correct over a number of assessments of equal probability. For example, if you assign a probability of 70% to each of 10 predictions, then you should get seven of those predictions correct. For a full review of this aspect of probabilistic judgement, see McClelland & Bolger (1994).

Over-confidence of judgements made under uncertainty is commonly reported in calibration studies (see Lichtenstein, Fischhoff & Phillips, 1982) and has often been explained as a characteristic of human information processing. Some researchers have implicated the operation of the anchor-and-adjust heuristic (Keren, 1991; Ferrell & McGoey, 1980); ignorance of processing limitations (Pitz, 1974); motivation (Milburn, 1983); cognitive optimism (Dawes, 1980); and response scale effects (Poulton, 1989).

Despite the ubiquity of the over-confidence finding and the rather general explanations for it there were, until recently, no specific testable theories to account for it. Fifteen years ago, in their review of an already vast literature, Lichtenstein, Fischhoff & Phillips (1982) commented that "...a striking aspect of much of the literature reviewed here is its 'dust-bowl empiricism'. Psychological theory is often absent, either as motivation for the research or as explanation of the results" (p. 333). In the last few years theories of judgemental confidence have emerged though as a result and, perhaps rather ironically, the very existence of over-confidence is now in some doubt (e.g. Dawes & Mulford, 1996).

Before describing these theories we should first note that, although over-confidence has been a common finding, there are notable exceptions. The most commonly cited example of well calibrated judgements are weather forecasters' estimates of the likelihood of precipitation (e.g. Murphy & Winkler, 1984), but there are other cases. Keren (1987) found that highly experienced tournament bridge players (although not experienced non-tournament players) made well-calibrated forecasts of the likelihood that a contract, reached during the bidding phase, would be made, and Phillips (1987) reported well-calibrated forecasts of horse races by bookmakers. The studies of good performance rather limit the viability of any explanation that attributes the phenomenon to a general characteristic of human information processing. Plainly, over-confidence is not a fundamental characteristic of human judgement—how, otherwise, is it possible to avoid over-confidence?

"Ecological" theorists (cf. McClelland & Bolger, 1994) claim that over-confidence is essentially an artifact due to the use of artificial experimental tasks and the non-representative sampling of stimulus materials. Gigerenzer, Hoffrage & Kleinbölting (1991) and Juslin (1994) argue that individuals are well adapted to their environments and do not make biased judgements. Over-confidence is observed because the typical general knowledge quiz used in most experiments contains a disproportionate number of misleading items. These authors have found that when knowledge items are randomly (representatively) sampled the over-confidence phenomenon disappears. For example, Gigerenzer, Hoffrage & Kleinbölting (1991) presented their subjects with items consisting of random pairs of the German cities with more than 100 000 inhabitants and asked them to select the biggest and indicate their confidence that they had done so correctly. With this randomly sampled set of items there was no over-confidence. Moreover, even with conventional general knowledge quizzes, subjects *are* aware of how well they are likely to perform overall. Gigerenzer and colleagues found that subjects are really quite accurate at indicating *the proportion of items* that they have correctly answered. Such quizzes are representative of general knowledge quizzes experienced in the past. Thus, even when they appear over-confident with their answers to the individual items, subjects are not over-confident about their performance on the same items as a set. As a corollary, for randomly sampled items, subjects' judgements of overall proportion correct are under-estimates.

Much of the research investigating over-confidence has not studied judgemental forecasts because it is more convenient for researchers to test respondents with general knowledge questions which can be scored immediately. As differences between confidence in general knowledge propositions and future events have been noted before (e.g. Wright & Ayton, 1986), Dilek Önkal and I examined the ability of sports writers to forecast football matches and found that, for a representative sample of matches, they were not over-confident (Ayton & Önkal, 1996).

Another idea relevant to the interpretation of the evidence of over-confidence comes from Erev, Wallsten & Budescu (1994), who have suggested that over-confidence may, to some degree, reflect an underlying stochastic component of judgement. Any degree of error variance in judgement would create a regression that appears as over-confidence in the typical calibration analysis of judgement. When any two variables are not perfectly correlated—and confidence and accuracy are not perfectly correlated—there will be a regression effect. Imagine two variables, $X$ and $Y$, that are imperfectly correlated: the average value for the $X$s at a given value of $Y$ will be closer to the mean of the $X$s than will $Y$; at the same time, the average value for the $Y$s at any given value of $X$ will be closer to the mean of the $Y$s than the $X$ itself. So it is that sons of very tall fathers are on average shorter than their fathers, *and* the fathers of very tall sons are shorter than their sons.

Developing this idea, Budescu, Erev & Wallsten (1997) have presented a generalization of the results from the Erev, Wallsten & Budescu (1994) paper, which shows that over-confidence and its apparent opposite, under-confidence, can be observed *simultaneously* in one study, depending upon whether probabilistic judgements are analysed by conditionalizing accuracy as a function of confidence (the usual method showing over-confidence) or *vice versa*. Budescu, Erev & Wallsten (1997) presented evidence from simulations that simultaneous over- and under-confidence can be attributed to random error in probability judgements coupled with the method of analysis. Pfeifer (1994) has also illustrated that perfectly calibrated judges can appear to be over-confident because of such effects.

So, could it be that all the evidence for over-confidence is merely an illusion created by regression and inappropriate sampling of test items? In the first study to try to answer this question empirically, Budescu, Wallsten & Au (1997) attempted to measure and allow for the effects of random error by presenting the same items (random pairs of large American cities) several times to their subjects. These authors provide evidence to suggest that the vast majority of the individuals (87%) in their study were biased towards over-confidence, even after the effects of random error in their judgements had been taken into account. It should also be noted that they used a representative sample of items which should eliminate over-confidence—other than that attributable to error variance.

### 9.3.2 Base-rate Neglect

Research following Tversky & Kahneman's original demonstration of base-rate neglect established that base rates might be attended to more (although usually not sufficiently) if they were perceived as relevant (Bar-Hillel, 1980) had a causal role (Kahneman & Tversky 1982b) or were "vivid" rather than "pallid" (Nisbett & Ross, 1980). However, Gigerenzer, Hell & Blank (1988) have argued that the real reason for variations in base-rate neglect is nothing to do with any of these factors *per se*, but because the different tasks may to varying degrees encourage the subject to represent the problem as a Bayesian revision problem. They claimed that there are few inferences in real life that correspond directly to Bayesian revision where a known base rate is revised on the basis of new information. Just because the experimenter assumes that he has defined a Bayesian revision problem does not imply that the subject will see it the same way. In particular, the subjects may not take the base rate asserted by the experimenter as their subjective prior probability. In Kahneman & Tversky's original experiments, the descriptions were not actually randomly sampled (as the subjects were told) but especially selected to be "representative" of the professions. To the extent that the subjects suspected that this was the case, then they would be entitled to ignore the offered base rate and replace it with one of their own perception.

In an experiment, Gigerenzer, Hell & Blank (1988) found that when they let the subjects experience the sampling themselves, base-rate neglect "disappeared". In the experiment their subjects could examine 10 pieces of paper, each marked "lawyer" or "engineer" in accord to the base rates. Subjects then drew one of the pieces of paper from an urn and unfolded it so they could read a description of an individual without being able to see the mark defining it as being of a lawyer or engineer. In these circumstances, subjects clearly used the base rates in a proper fashion. However, in a replication of the verbal presentation where base rates were asserted, rather than sampled, Kahneman & Tversky's base-rate neglect was replicated.

Kahneman & Tversky (1996) have argued that a fair summary of the research would be that explicitly presented base rates are generally under-weighted but not ignored. They have also pointed out that in Gigerenzer, Hell & Blank's (1988) experiment, subjects who sampled the information themselves still produced judgements that deviated from the Bayesian solution in the direction predicted by representativeness. Plainly then, representativeness is useful for predicting judgements. However, to the extent that base rates are not entirely ignored (see Koehler, 1995), the heuristic rationale for representativeness is limited. Recall that the original explanation for base-rate neglect was the operation of a simple heuristic that reduced the need for integration of information. If judgements in these experiments reflect base rates—even to a limited extent—it is hard to account for by the operation of the representativeness heuristic.

**Conjunction Errors**

Tversky & Kahneman (1983) reported evidence that violations of the conjunction rule largely disappeared when subjects were requested to assess the relative frequency of events, rather than the probability of a single event. Thus, instead of being asked about likelihood for a particular individual, subjects were requested to assess how many people in a survey of 100 adult males had had heart attacks, and then were asked to assess the number who were both over 55 years old *and* had had heart attacks. Only 25% of subjects violated the conjunction rule by giving higher values to the latter than to the former. When asked about likelihoods for single events it is typically the vast majority of subjects who violate the rule.

Gigerenzer (e.g. 1994; 1996) has suggested that people are naturally adapted to reasoning with information in the form of frequencies and that the conjunction fallacy "disappears" if reasoning is in the form of frequencies, for this reason. This suggests that the difficulties that people experience in solving probability problems can be reduced if the problems require subjects to assess relative frequency for a class of events rather than the probability of a single event. Thus, it follows that if judgements are elicited with frequency formats there would be no biases. Kahneman & Tversky (1996) disagree, and argue that the frequency format serves to provide subjects with a powerful cue to the relation of inclusion between sets that are explicitly compared, or evaluated in immediate succession. When the structure of the conjunction is made more apparent, then subjects who appreciate the constraint supplied by the rule will be less likely to violate it. Salient cues to set inclusion prompt subjects to adjust their judgement.

To test this explanation, Kahneman & Tversky (1996) reported a new variation of the conjunction problem experiment, where subjects made judgements of frequencies but the cues to set inclusion were removed. They presented subjects with the description of Linda and then asked their subjects to suppose that there were 1000 women who fit the description. They then asked one group of subjects to estimate how many of them would be bank tellers; a second *independent* group of subjects were asked how many were bank tellers and active feminists; a third group made evaluations for both categories. As predicted, those subjects who evaluated both categories mostly conformed to the conjunction rule. However, in a between-groups comparison of the other two groups, the estimates for "bank tellers and active feminists" were found to be significantly higher than the estimates for bank tellers. Kahneman & Tversky argue that these results show that subjects use the representativeness heuristic to generate their judgements and then edit their responses to respect class inclusion where they detect cues to that relation. Thus, they concluded that the key variable controlling adherence to the conjunction rule is not the relative frequency format *per se* but the opportunity to detect the relation of class inclusion.

Hertwig (1997) has challenged this interpretation, arguing that in Kahneman & Tversky's (1996) experiment there was an ambiguity in the wording of the categories. Subjects asked to assess the numbers of people who are bank tellers and active feminists might have read this to mean "how many are *both* bank tellers and active feminists" (the intended conjunction) or "how many are feminists *or* bank tellers" (the union of these two categories). Hertwig conducted an experiment similar to Kahneman & Tversky's, only he included a reworded definition of the conjunction category designed to remove this ambiguity—"bank tellers who are active in the feminist movement". Whilst he replicated the finding reported by Kahneman & Tversky with their wording of the conjunction category, the reworded description of the conjunction category produced mean frequencies that were lower than those for the "bank teller" category. Thus, Kahneman & Tversky's finding, that conjunction violations can be found with frequency judgements where cues to the inclusion relation are removed, was not replicated.

Of course, Hertwig's experiment does not establish that Kahneman and Tversky's explanation of their experiment is incorrect—even if the wording was interpreted as he suggests. Conformity to the conjunction rule does not mean that judgements could not be made by representativeness. However, the fact that conjunction errors are common with single-event judgements, and that the effect that Kahneman & Tversky (1996) reported with independent groups could not be replicated by Hertwig's re-wording of the categories, is consistent with the argument that judgements made with frequencies may not exhibit the biases reliably found for probabilities for single events. We need to understand more of the reasons underlying the limiting conditions of cognitive biases—how it is that seemingly inconsequential changes in the format of information can so radically alter the quality of judgement. Biases that can be cured so simply cannot be held to reveal fundamental characteristics of the processes of judgement—but why then is it that they occur at all, and what are the implications for forecasting practice? We consider these questions in the next two sections.

## 9.4 STANDARDS FOR JUDGEMENT

Kahneman & Tversky (1982a) wrote: "The presence of an error of judgement is demonstrated by comparing people's responses either with an established fact ... or with an accepted rule of arithmetic, logic or statistics. However, not every response that appears to contradict an established fact or an accepted rule is a judgemental error ... The student of judgement should avoid overly strict interpretations, which treat reasonable answers as errors..." (pp. 493–4). As this quotation makes clear, the method adopted by Kahneman & Tversky and many others is to compare human judgement with accepted rules of arithmetic, logic and statistics—normative rules. In one sense, the normative status of these rules is beyond reproach—the rules of logic and statistics represent human understanding of what it is to reason. It follows, therefore, that human thought should correspond to these rules if it is to prove effective. Judgements that violate normative rules cannot be valid (e.g. Wright & Ayton, 1987). Nonetheless, the relative (in)effectiveness of non-optimal heuristic strategies remains an open question.

### 9.4.1 Fast and Frugal Judgements

A rare attempt to measure the relative efficacy of simple mental strategies for judgement is reported by Gigerenzer & Goldstein (1996), who ran a competition to evaluate the performance of a set of different strategies. Gigerenzer & Goldstein produced a measure of the efficacy of simple mental strategies for judgement by measuring the number of correct inferences that different strategies made, rather than by focusing on violations of normative rules. The class of simple models that Gigerenzer & Goldstein tested were what they called "fast and frugal" algorithms. To make a judgement, they neither considered all the information nor attempted any sort of integration of information prescribed by such normative procedures as multiple regression or Bayes' theorem. The "fast and frugal" procedures relied on just one piece of information in order to make predictions. By the standards of classical rationality enshrined in normative rules, the mental strategies that Gigerenzer & Goldstein considered look very stupid indeed. Indeed, Gigerenzer & Goldstein are quite explicit about the fact that the simple algorithms that they tested violate basic axioms such as transitivity—one of the cornerstones of classical rationality (McClennan, 1990). Nevertheless, the proof of the pudding is in the eating.

The motivation for this apparently futile exercise is Simon's (1956) idea of bounded rationality. Simon emphasized that, due to its limited capacity, human information processing would be obliged to use "satisficing" methods for problem solving. Satisficing procedures are not normatively optimal but reflect the constraints supplied by human information processing and the constraints—and opportunities—provided by the nature of the environment. Most of the research on human judgement has focused on the non-optimal nature of simple human information-processing strategies—the importance of the environment structure in determining performance has not received the same degree of attention. Nevertheless, we have already seen how ecological psychologists have attacked the evidence for over-confidence by considering how mental strategies might exploit the way information is structured in the natural environment. But how could judgement strategies that violate normative rules and utilize just one piece of information possibly be of effective service?

In their simulation, the properties of a set of German cities were used as information in order to make predictions as to which city was the biggest. Commonly known correlates of city size, such as whether it has a university, a soccer club in the top division or an Inter-City rail station, were the information that the algorithms had to rely on. One of the algorithms that Gigerenzer & Goldstein tested was termed the "Take the Best" algorithm—so called because it simply looked up the most diagnostic feature that discriminated between two cities and then responded accordingly. Thus, if the two cities under consideration cannot be discriminated on the basis of the most diagnostic cue (e.g. whether it is the National capital or not), the search through memory continues. The search for discriminatory cue values proceeds in order of their relative diagnosticity until a cue is found that discriminates the two cities (e.g. one has an Intercity rail station and the other does not), whereupon information retrieval is stopped and the judgement made according to this single cue.

Gigerenzer & Goldstein's simulation compared simple algorithms, such as "Take the Best", with other more familiar decision rules that integrate information, such as multiple regression for various states of imperfect knowledge (information about cue values). Surprisingly, they found that "Take the Best" did as well as any of the other algorithms and considerably better than some. Also, as it only uses one piece of information, it will be much faster than any model that retrieves more information and attempts integration. The result is important for demonstrating that, although adherence to normative rules may be sufficient for good judgement, it is not necessary. Simple mental rules— we could even call them heuristics—*can* exploit the structure of information in the environment to make good inferences. As a consequence of this finding, one feels drawn to question the present pre-eminent status of normative rules for defining rationality and for serving as a bench-mark for judgemental performance.

Of course, the Gigerenzer & Goldstein study is a simulation demonstrating the potential of simple strategies—it did not investigate judgements actually made by humans. In a test of real human judgements, Dilek Önkal and I (Ayton & Önkal, 1996) examined the ability of Turkish business studies students to forecast 32 English football matches after rating their familiarity with the team names. Although these subjects could not be expected to know much about the intricacies of English football, they might be able to respond on the basis of familiarity of the place names. Many, though not all, English clubs include the name of the town or city in their names. One will tend to hear about the bigger cities of a country more than the smaller ones; bigger cities tend to have better supported and hence stronger teams and stronger teams are somewhat more likely to win. We analysed the Turkish business students' use of familiarity as a cue for forecasting. Forty-seven per cent of the time, subjects gave equal familiarity ratings to both of the participating teams. Omitting those cases, we found that our subjects chose the team to win the game as the team with the higher familiarity rating 93% of the time. The Turkish students correctly predicted 62.5% of the games. This was only marginally lower than the forecast accuracy of far more knowledgeable British football fans, who predicted 65.6% of the games. Plainly, in this real forecasting task, people with very little knowledge and who principally relied on one piece of information could forecast almost as well as those with a lot of knowledge.

### 9.4.2 Support Theory

A contrast to this approach to studying judgement can be found in Tversky & Koehler's (1994) development of support theory. Support theory can be viewed as an elaboration of the heuristics and biases research program. The theory predicts and seeks to account for systematic incoherence in subjective probabilities attributable to the mental processes responsible for judgement. The theory is designed to predict and explain under what sort of circumstances—and why—people's judgements violate the tenets of probability theory. The benchmark for the empirical investigations of support theory is the logic of probability. Plainly, judgements of likelihood that violate axioms of probability cannot, by definition, be normatively valid judgements. Not only are such judgements not valid, but notice how, in the tradition of heuristics and biases research, one can use the laws of probability as a means of identifying the process of judgement. The laws of probability can serve as a basis for a kind of figure-ground segregation; the figure—judgement—can be "seen" against the background of probability theory. Thus, support theory is not a theory that attempts to account for how well people might perform when coping with uncertainty with sub-optimal reasoning.

Support theory proposes that different descriptions of the same event can lead to different evoked subjective probabilities. In particular, the theory implies that the more explicitly the description of an event or hypothesis is characterized, the more support will be associated with it, resulting in a higher subjective probability. So, for example, one might consider the likelihood of an event such as dying of unnatural causes. Alternatively, one could subdivide this general hypothesis into an exhaustive disjunction of more specific components—such as accident, homicide, or all other unnatural causes—and consider the likelihood of dying from each of these rather more explicit sorts of natural causes separately.

Tversky & Koehler hypothesized that people assess the degree of support for a general event by contemplating the most available or representative cases. Because people do not typically assess the degree of support for a more general description by considering the support for each of the constituent parts, they would tend to find less support for, and hence give a lower probability to, a general description than they would for a decomposition of the same hypothesis described in terms of its more explicit constituents. A more explicit description could remind people of relevant cases that might otherwise escape their attention, leading to an increase in evidence and hence perceived likelihood. Even where no new cases or evidence are retrieved, a more explicit description could increase the relative salience of evidence already retrieved. According to the theory, increased salience would result in increased judgements of likelihood.

Empirically, Tversky & Koehler found that if subjects were asked to evaluate the likelihood of a general hypothesis, then they tended to give lower likelihoods than they gave to the sum of the likelihoods given to an exhaustive set of constituents of the same hypothesis. For example, subjects estimated the likelihood of dying from unnatural causes to be 32%. However, other subjects asked to assess the likelihoods of dying from accident, homicide or other unnatural causes gave judgements of 32%, 10% and 11% respectively. These sum to 53%—considerably higher than 32%. Thereby it can be seen that *implicit* disjunctions of events (general descriptions) attract less support than their explicitly decomposed equivalents—a phenomenon that Tversky & Koehler labelled "*sub-additivity*".

Tversky & Koehler proposed that the degree of sub-additivity should increase with the number of components in the explicit disjunction. They found that "unpacking" implicit disjunctions into a larger number of constituents increased the amount of sub-additivity that they found. Accordingly, when subjects assessed the likelihoods for seven constituents of a general hypothesis, the amount of sub-additivity was even greater than for the three-component case described above.

The unpacking principle is used by Tversky & Koehler to explain a broad range of findings in judgement research. For example, we have already considered evidence for the conjunction effect, whereby a conjunction of events, *AB*, is judged more likely than one of its constituents, *A*. Tversky & Koehler suggested that, when considering *AB*, subjects failed to retrieve evidence for *A* that was available when considering *AB*. Thus, the delegates at the forecasting conference described earlier who violated the conjunction rule in their forecasts for a 30% drop in US oil consumption may not have fully unpacked this hypothesis. The possibility of a 30% drop in consumption caused by a dramatic price increase is an implicit component of the more general 30% drop in consumption hypothesis—but may not be unpacked when considering the likelihood of a drop in consumption.

Several studies using "fault trees" have demonstrated what has been termed an "out of sight, out of mind" bias, such that when people are asked to judge the likelihood of different causes for a problem, such as why a car might not start (Fischhoff, Slovic & Lichtenstein, 1978) or a restaurant fail (Dube-Rioux & Russo, 1988), their judgements are determined by the specificity of descriptions given in the fault tree. Fischhoff, Slovic & Lichtenstein (1978) found that car mechanics judged that "the cause of failure is something other than the battery, the fuel system or the engine" increased from 0.22 to 0.44 when this hypothesis was broken up to refer to more specific components (e.g. the starting system, the ignition system).

A similar argument can explain why Johnson et al. (1993) found that subjects who were offered (hypothetical) health insurance that covered hospitalization for any disease or accident were willing to pay a higher premium than subjects who were offered health insurance that covered hospitalization for any reason. Explicit mention of disease and accident increased the perceived chances of hospitalization and so increased the attractiveness of insurance.

Fox, Rogers & Tversky (1996) studied professional options traders and asked them to make a number of probability judgements regarding the price of Microsoft stock on a given future date (e.g. that it would be greater than $88 per share and less than $94). They found that, although these traders were experienced in predicting the value of Microsoft stock, their judgements showed marked sub-additivity.

While the unpacking principle of support theory predicts sub-additivity for implicit disjunctions, it also requires that the probabilities for explicit disjunctions should be additive. Thus, where distinguishable elements of a hypothesis are made explicit, they should sum to the value of the hypothesis. Tversky & Koehler (1994) asked subjects to estimate the percentage of US married couples with "less than 3"; "3 or more"; "less than 5" or "5 or more" children. Each subject considered exactly one of the four hypotheses, which they assumed are always evaluated by subjects in relation to their complement as if it was also explicitly evaluated. The estimates added to 97.5% for the first pair of hypotheses and 96.3% for the second pair of hypotheses—in sharp contrast to the sub-additivity observed earlier, the estimates for the complementary pairs of hypotheses were approximately additive. This finding is important for support theory because it excludes an alternative account for sub-additivity in implicit disjunctions, according to which the evaluation of evidence is biased in favour of the focal hypothesis. If subjects simply gave higher probabilities to any hypothesis that they were considering, perhaps because of a confirmation bias in evidence search, then the unpacking principle would not be necessary to account for sub-additivity in implicit disjunctions.

However, there is evidence for failure of explicit disjunctions to adhere to additivity. For example Wright & Whalley (1983) found, in their study that asked people to make judgements of probability for a list of explicitly disjunctive hypotheses (e.g. which of a set of horses will win the race), that as the number of events explicitly listed in a set of mutually exclusive and exhaustive events was increased, student subjects gave judgements of the likelihood of these events that summed to a larger value. When the number of events in a set was held constant more subjects gave judgements that summed to greater than one—and to a greater degree—when individuating information was introduced (e.g. the past form for race horses). The explicitness or implicitness of a hypothesis does not determine whether judgements will be additive or not. Consequently, unpacking does not fully account for the biases. It seems merely sufficient to assume that judgements of a longer list of mutually exclusive events will produce greater violations of the additivity principle.

Recently Macchi, Osherson & Krantz (1996) have found evidence for the opposite of sub-additivity—super-additivity—in judgements of complementary propositions. They reasoned that, in cases where people have very little knowledge relevant to an evaluation of the truth of a proposition, they will be unable to retrieve much evidence for it—or its complement. They predicted and found that for some pairs of complementary propositions (e.g. "The height of the Duomo in Milan is greater than that of Notre Dame in Paris" and "The height of the Notre Dame in Paris is greater than that of the Duomo in Milan"[1]) subjective probabilities consistently added to less than one.

Note that the exceptions to support theory that we consider are also examples of violations of laws of probability—it seems that violations of probability theory are more general than the current version of support theory explains (further examples are given in Ayton, in press). It is also worth noting here that non-additivity is also excluded for complementary pairs of propositions by one other non-Bayesian model of judgement. Gigerenzer, Hoffrage & Kleinbölting (1991) argue that people use ecologically valid cues to evaluate likelihoods. Although, as we have seen, this model anticipates over-confidence where test items may have been sampled unrepresentatively of the natural environment, additivity of judgement is a guaranteed consequence of using the same cue(s) for a given proposition and its complement. Whatever the status of the theory, one should note the clear implication from the evidence that judgements of likelihood fail to adhere to the normative requirements of probability theory. By this reckoning judgement fails. What can we do about it?

## 9.5   CAN WE HAVE A PRACTICAL REMEDY FOR JUDGEMENTAL BIASES?

Kahneman & Tversky (1979) argued that one way to avoid the biases of subjective probability implied by the heuristic account was to take an external rather than an internal view, by contemplating the target event in relation to a reference class of similar events and considering the distribution of likelihoods for the whole class of events. Although the strategy looks rather like a way of attempting to invoke a frequentist set for judging likelihood, which Gigerenzer argues eliminates biases, the rationale is rather different. The claim is that cues to extensionality will assist people to avoid making non-extensional judgements. This analysis has been amplified and extended by Kahneman & Lovallo (1993), who argue that people have a strong tendency to see problems as unique when they would be more advantageously viewed as instances of a broader class. They claim that the natural tendency in thinking about a particular problem, such as the likelihood of success of a business venture, is to take the "inside" rather than the "outside" view. People will pay particular attention to the distinguishing features of a particular case and reject analogies to other instances of the same general type as crudely superficial and unappealing. Consequently, they will fall prey to fallacies of planning—ignoring base rates and anchoring their estimates on present values or extrapolations of current trends.

Kahneman & Lovallo argue that once a forecaster takes the inside view, he/she will not seek out relevant statistical knowledge, neglect base rates and so be less likely to formulate a realistic estimate, and then will be over-confident about his/her forecasts. This is plainly a somewhat disconcerting view of human judgement of likelihood. However, in advising that anyone attempting to assess probabilities should take an "outside view", it also seems that there is very little in practical terms that separates the advocates of the heuristic and the frequentist approaches in terms of their recommendations for improving the quality of subjective probabilities. For example, Kahneman & Lovallo review evidence which suggests that, because they take an inside view, people can be unrealistically optimistic (or, if failure is easier to imagine, pessimistic). They cite a study by Cooper, Woo & Dunkelberger (1988) of entrepreneurs interviewed about their chances of business success. The entrepreneurs' assessments were unrelated to objective predictors of business success, such as college education, prior super-visory experience and initial capital. Moreover, more than 80% of them described their chances as 70% or better, whilst simultaneously perceiving the survival rate for new businesses of their type as low as 33%. Such findings can be taken as evidence for poor judgement under uncertainty—or alternatively as evidence that people are better off not attempting to assess probabilities for single events.

Instead of concluding that, for whatever reason, biases are less evident when judgements are assessed in frequencies, we could ask ourselves why it is that when subjects are asked to assess likelihoods for single events they produce responses that are so well predicted by the heuristics approach. For example, in one of their studies Kahneman & Tversky (1982b) asked one group of subjects to judge the representativeness of personality descriptions with respect to a whole series of different professions. A separate group of subjects rated the likelihood that each of the described individuals really was a member of each of the listed professions. The correlation between the two was 0.96; plainly, the judgements of likelihood were quite indistinguishable from those of representativeness. It would seem that there is a danger that when asked to assess subjective probabilities for single events, subjects will report a measure of representativeness or availability.

There are also occasions when there will be single events for which no obvious reference class exists, and then one will plainly be unable to assess likelihood by adopting an outside view, or by taking the frequentist approach. Consider, for example, the possibility, in 1991, that Saddam Hussein would attack Israel. How could the Israeli government have gone about assessing a subjective probability for this unique proposition? No doubt a number could be produced but what would it be worth? One might perfectly well be able to account for the (no doubt varying) subjective probabilities offered by a sample of people by referring to various judgemental heuristics. But, note that, without any reference class, we have no means of evaluating the validity of any judgements that might be offered. A single probability that is unconstrained by reference to any parent distribution admits no standard for evaluation. Consequently, the probability of unique events remains something of a mystery.

According to von Mises (1957), Hartmann (1869) somehow derived mathematical formulae for evaluating the probability that natural events are due to spiritual causes and calculated that it is 0.5904. Elsewhere the argument has been made that, for any practical application, under these circumstances one ought to abandon any attempt to produce quantitative forecasts and instead use more qualitative techniques, such as scenario planning (e.g. Schoemaker, 1991, 1995; van der Heijden 1994) or argumentation (Fox, 1994; Hardman & Ayton, 1997).

Tversky & Koehler (1994) argue that it is practically impossible for probability judgements to adhere to additivity. Although any given complete set of judgements could be checked for additivity, judges cannot be expected to imagine all possible relevant unpackings of hypotheses or generate all relevant future scenarios and so additivity could be violated by future refinement. However, Tversky & Koehler argue that although one might be tempted to infer that, in general, judgements of likelihood should be eschewed, there is often no viable alternative. While physical properties such as weight, length and illumination have objective methods for their measurement, there are no objective means for assessing the probability of such things as the success of a business plan or the guilt of a suspect. Even a highly developed understanding of probability theory would be of little avail.

An alternative is to abandon the attempt to use the calculus of probability altogether, as indeed has happened in the field of risk assessment for certain novel hazards where there is very little in the way of historical data (cf. Hardman and Ayton, 1997). For example, the United Kingdom Department of Health's Committee on Carcinogenicity of Chemicals in Food (Carter, 1991) concludes:

> The committee does not support the routine use of quantitative risk assessment for chemical carcinogens. This is because the present models are not validated, are often based on incomplete or inappropriate data, are derived more from mathematical assumptions than from a knowledge of biological mechanisms and, at least at present, demonstrate a disturbingly wide variation in risk estimates depending on the model adopted.

In recounting the investigation into the *Challenger* space shuttle disaster, Richard Feynman (1990) reports that the risk estimates of NASA management and engineers differed by a factor of more than 300. The more remote estimate provided by the management led Feynman (1990) to comment "If a guy tells me the probability of failure is 1 in $10^5$, I know he's full of crap".

On 26 March 1996, following the revelation that the consumption of BSE-infected[2] beef was the likeliest cause of a new strain of Creuzfeldt–Jacob Disease,[3] the UK government's Spongiform Encephalopathy Advisory Committee issued a statement to British newspapers concerning the risks associated with British beef. This statement explicitly avoided mention of any quantification of the risk of BSE infecting beef-eating humans: "The committee has carefully considered whether a quantitative risk assessment can provide an estimate of the absolute risk in relation to BSE. In its judgement a precise measure is impossible because of a number of interacting uncertainties". However, in the same report it does say "The risk is likely to be extremely small".

Although experimental subjects seem to be quite happy to produce quantitative estimates of likelihood for virtually anything that they are asked, this may not reflect the way that people must deal with uncertainty or indeed even the way that they already naturally deal with uncertainty. The practice of quantifying uncertainty with numbers is a very recent development in the history of human thought (cf. Hacking, 1975). Since most of our knowledge about probabilistic judgement has been derived from laboratory studies, the documentation of the heuristics and biases implicated in the assessment of probability may be valid but unrelated to the way in which people may choose to deal with uncertainty, given a free choice. In particular, people may find ways of judgementally dealing with uncertainty other than by attempting to evaluate probabilities.

Of course, there is no simple panacea for these problems; just because you do not ask people to evaluate numerical probabilities does not mean that they are no longer vulnerable to judgemental bias. If judgements are the basis for actions then, if judgement is poor, those actions may well be sub-optimal. DeBondt & Thaler (1986) reported findings indicating that the stock market over-reacts to recent news. They examined the performance of a large number of stocks over 3-year intervals from 1926 to 1982. They found that those stocks that did worse than average in one 3-year period tended to do better than average in the next 3-year period and *vice versa*. Thus, high-performing stocks tended to be over-valued and low-performing stocks tended to be under-valued. These findings suggest that there is an over-reaction to news—short-term surges in earnings are unsustainable and companies faced with difficulties try hard to solve them. As a consequence, a regression to the mean will occur but investors seem insensitive to it—otherwise the performance of stocks would not have been predictable in this fashion. Insensitivity to regression was one of the biases in judgement that Tversky & Kahneman (1974) took to be indicative of heuristic judgement. (Note, though, that there is some evidence for the opposite effect. For example, some studies have shown that investors will invest significantly more money in failing than in successful investments. This behaviour has been labelled "an escalation bias": cf. Staw & Ross, 1989.)

Thaler (quoted in Fuerbringer, 1997) claims that the high volume of trade is "... the single most embarrassing fact for an efficient market ... People are supposed to be buying and holding". That the volume of trade is inappropriately high is shown in a study by Odean (in press), who has uncovered further evidence of over-confidence and insensitivity to regression in his study of trading. Examining 10 000 accounts at a brokerage firm from 1987 to 1993, Odean found that individual investors had an average annual turnover rate of 78% in the securities they owned. However, the stocks that they sold outperformed the ones they bought by about 3 percentage points, before commissions, in the year after the sale. According to Fuerbringer (1997), such under-achievement can be held to be the price that investors pay for over-confidence about their own investment forecasts.

Both of these studies of apparently sub-optimal stock market forecasting are also possibly attributable to the role of emotions such as decision regret (Loomes & Sugden, 1982). Stock market investors might be driven more by fear of missing out on investment opportunities than by over-confidence or judgemental error *per se*. Given that investors cannot hope to select the best-performing stocks every day, they will be surrounded by examples of all sorts of investments that they could have bought—but didn't—which performed better than the investments that they did select. This may well generate an experience of regret for not switching stocks; thoughts of foregone gains may be irresistible to some. Although these studies have the advantage of demonstrating the real consequences of non-optimal behaviour, it is hard to be precise about the cause of the non-optimal decisions.

One possibility is that such apparently anomalous behaviours are grounded in successful adaptation to other circumstances—just as the presence of sweetness in foods was, historically, a valid cue to nutritiousness before manufacturing exploited it to increase profits and obesity. This sort of argument has been made with respect to the tendency for the finding that judgements can be "conservative" (Winkler & Murphy, 1973). "Conservatism" is the term used to describe the once commonly reported experimental result that judgements are insufficiently influenced by new information. This is quite the opposite of base-rate neglect and, perhaps because it is now in something of a theoretical wilderness (cf. Fischhoff & Beyth-Marom, 1983), is now a finding rather neglected itself.

## 9.6 CONCLUDING COMMENT

The issues surrounding the evaluation of human judgement are complex and are not going to be resolved easily or, in my judgement, in the near future. Nevertheless, there has been some progress in understanding judgement. It seems clear (to all but some economists) that people cannot conceivably represent all the information that normative models demand we utilize for judgement: "Who could design a brain that could perform the way this model mandates? Every single one of us would have to know and *understand* everything completely, and at once" (Daniel Kahneman, quoted by Bernstein, 1996).

To make more progress in understanding judgement we will need further studies that do more than merely knock down the straw man defined by the normative rules of statistics and rational choice theory. The theory of probability can define the probabilities at the gaming wheel or at the casino—there is no need to spin the wheel or roll the dice to estimate the likelihood of the outcome, but real life is different. Here information is essential. Whether you want to bet on horses, invest in a pension or decide whether to take an umbrella to work, it would be sensible to contemplate something other than the laws of probability theory to inform your judgement. As many people appear to spend their lives happily enough without ever contemplating such rules (consciously at least), it seems that satisficing strategies may well often work well enough. Quite how it is that people are able to respond as effectively as they are using non-normative mental strategies and the very limited amount of information that they can cope with remains to be fully explored and explained. A better understanding of the value of limited information may, I suspect, help to answer the question posed by Bernstein (1996) who, after reviewing evidence for bias in stockbrokers' judgements, wondered: "If people are so dumb, how come more of us smart people don't get rich?". Even Mr Magoo gets by.

## NOTES

(1)   Subjects were also explicitly told in each case that the two buildings were not the same height.

(2)   BSE refers to bovine spongiform encephalopathy, a degenerative brain disease in cattle, popularly known as "mad cow disease".

(3) Creuzfeldt–Jacob Disease (CJD) is a degenerative brain disease in humans, often referred to as the human equivalent of mad cow disease. At the time of writing there is a strong (but unproven) possibility that contact with BSE-infected material can cause certain types of CJD.

# REFERENCES

Arrow, K.J. (1992)  I know a hawk from a handsaw. In M. Szenberg (ed.), *Eminent Economists: Their Life and Philosophies.* Cambridge University Press, Cambridge and New York.

Ayton, P. (1992)  On the competence and incompetence of experts. In G. Wright & F. Bolger, (eds), *Expertise and Decision Support*, Plenum, London.

Ayton, P. (in press)  How to be incoherent *and* seductive: bookmakers' odds and support theory. *Organizational Behavior and Human Decision Processes.*

Ayton, P. & Önkal, D. (1996)  Effects of expertise on confidence in forecasts. Paper presented to the *International Symposium on Forecasting*, Istanbul, Turkey.

Bar-Hillel, M. (1980)  The base-rate fallacy in probability judgements. *Acta Psychologica*, **44**, 211–33.

Beach, L.R., Christensen-Szalanski, J. & Barnes, V. (1987)  Assessing human judgment: has it been done, can it be done, should it be done? In G. Wright & P. Ayton (eds), *Judgemental Forecasting*. Wiley, Chichester.

Bernstein, P.L. (1996)  *Against the Gods: The Remarkable Story of Risk.* Wiley, New York.

Budescu, D.V., Erev, I. & Wallsten, T.S. (1997)  On the importance of random error in the study of probabilistic judgment. Part I: New theoretical developments. *Journal of Behavioral Decision Making*, **10**, 157–71.

Budescu, D., Wallsten, T.S. & Au, W.T. (1997)  On the importance of random error in the study of probabilistic judgment. Part II: Applying the stochastic judgment model to detect systematic trends. *Journal of Behavioral Decision Making*, **10**, 173–88.

Carter, R.L. (Chairman) (1991)  Guidelines for the evaluation of chemicals for carcinogenicity. In *Department of Health Report on Health and Social Subjects*. HMSO, London.

Cooper, A., Woo, C. & Dunkelberger, W. (1988)  Entrepreneurs' perceived chances for success. *Journal of Business Venturing*, **3**, 97–108.

Dawes, R.M. (1980)  Confidence in intellectual judgments. In E.D. Lantermann & H. Feger (eds), *Similarity and Choice*. Hans Huber, Bern.

Dawes, R.M. (1988)  *Rational Choice in an Uncertain World*. Harcourt, Orlando, FL.

Dawes, R.M. & Mulford, M. (1996) The false consensus effect and overconfidence: flaws in judgment or flaws in the way we study judgment? *Organizational Behavior and Human Decision Processes*, **65**, 201–11.

DeBondt, W.F.M. & Thaler, R.H. (1986) Does the stockmarket over-react to information? *Journal of Finance*, **40**, 793–808.

Dube-Rioux, L. & Russo, J.E. (1988) An availability bias in professional judgment. *Journal of Behavioral Decision Making*, **1**, 223–37.

Eddy, D.M. (1982) Probabilistic reasoning in clinical medicine: problems and opportunities. In D. Kahneman, P. Slovic & A. Tversky (eds), *Judgement Under Uncertainty: Heuristics and Biases*. Cambridge University Press, Cambridge.

Erev, I., Wallsten, T.S. & Budescu, D.V. (1994) Simultaneous overconfidence and underconfidence—the role of error in judgment processes. *Psychological Review*, **101**, 519–27.

Evans, J. St B.T. (1987) Beliefs and expectations as causes of judgmental bias. In G. Wright & P. Ayton (eds), *Judgmental Forecasting*. Wiley, Chichester.

Ferrell, W.R & McGoey, P.J. (1980) A model of calibration for subjective probabilities. *Organizational Behavior and Human Performance*, **26**, 32–53.

Feynman, R.P. (1990) *What Do You Care What Other People Think? Further Adventures of a Curious Character*. Unwin Hyman, London.

Fischhoff, B. & Beyth-Marom, R. (1983) Hypothesis evaluation from a Bayesian perspective. *Psychological Review*, **90**, 239–60.

Fischhoff, B., Slovic, P. & Lichtenstein, S. (1978) Fault trees: sensitivity of estimated failure probabilities to problem representation. *Journal of Experimental Psychology: Human Perception and Performance*, **4**, 330–44.

Fox, J. (1994) On the necessity of probability: reasons to believe and grounds for doubt. In G. Wright & P. Ayton (eds), *Subjective Probability*. Wiley, Chichester.

Fox, C.R. Rogers, B.A. & Tversky, A. (1996) Options traders exhibit subadditive decision weights. *Journal of Risk and Uncertainty*, **13**, 5–17.

Fuerbringer, J. (1997) Why both bulls and bears are often so bird-brained. *New York Times*, March 30.

Gigerenzer, G. (1991) How to make cognitive illusions disappear: beyond "Heuristics and Biases". In W. Stroebe & M. Hewstone (eds), *European Review of Social Psychology*, vol. 2, pp. 83–115. Wiley, Chichester.

Gigerenzer, G. (1994) Why the distinction between single event probabilities and frequencies is important for psychology and *vice versa*. In G. Wright & P. Ayton (eds), *Subjective Probability*. Wiley, Chichester.

Gigerenzer, G. (1996) On narrow norms and vague heuristics: a rebuttal to Kahneman and Tversky. *Psychological Review*, **103**, 592–6.

Gigerenzer, G. & Goldstein, D. (1996) Reasoning the fast and frugal way: models of bounded rationality. *Psychological Review*, **103**, 650–69.

Gigerenzer, G., Hell, W. & Blank, H. (1988) Presentation and content: the use of base rates as a continuous variable. *Journal of Experimental Psychology: Human Perception and Performance*, **14**, 513–25.

Gigerenzer, G., Hoffrage, U. & Kleinbölting, H. (1991) Probabilistic mental models: a Brunswikian theory of confidence. *Psychological Review*, **98**, 506–28.

Hacking, I. (1975) *The Emergence of Probability*. Cambridge University Press, Cambridge.

Hardman, D.K. & Ayton, P. (1997) Arguments for qualitative risk assessment: the StAR risk adviser. *Expert Systems*, **14**, 24–36.

von Hartmann, E. (1869) *Philosophie des Unbewussten*. Leipzig.

Hertwig, R. (1997) Judgment under uncertainty: beyond probabilities. Unpublished manuscript, Max Planck Institute for Psychological Research, Munich, Germany.

Johnson, E.J., Hershey, J., Meszaros, J. & Kunreuther, H. (1993) Framing, probability distortions and insurance decisions. *Journal of Risk and Uncertainty*, **7**, 35–51.

Juslin, P. (1994) The overconfidence phenomenon as a consequence of informal experimenter-guided selection of almanac items. *Organizational Behavior and Human Decision Processes*, **57**, 226–46.

Kahneman, D. & Lovallo, D. (1993) Timid choices and bold forecasts. A cognitive perspective on risk taking. *Management Science*, **39**, 17–31.

Kahneman, D., Slovic, P. & Tversky, A. (eds) (1982) *Judgement under Uncertainty: Heuristics and Biases*. Cambridge University Press, Cambridge.

Kahneman, D. & Tversky, A. (1979) Intuitive prediction: biases and corrective procedures. *Management Science*, **12**, 313–27.

Kahneman, D. & Tversky, A. (1982a) On the study of statistical intuitions. In D. Kahneman, P. Slovic & A. Tversky (eds), *Judgement under Uncertainty: Heuristics and Biases*. Cambridge University Press, Cambridge.

Kahneman, D. & Tversky, A. (1982b) Judgements of and by representativeness. In D. Kahneman, P. Slovic & A. Tversky (eds), *Judgement under Uncertainty: Heuristics and Biases*. Cambridge University Press, Cambridge.

Kahneman, D. & Tversky, A. (1996) On the reality of cognitive illusions: a reply to Gigerenzer's critique. *Psychological Review*, **103**, 582–91.

Keren, G.B. (1987) Facing uncertainty in the game of bridge: a calibration study. *Organizational Behavior and Human Decision Processes*, **39**, 98–114.

Keren, G. (1991) Calibration and probability judgments: conceptual and methodological issues. *Acta Psychologica*, **77**, 217–73.

Koehler, J.J.J. (1995) The base-rate fallacy reconsidered—descriptive, normative, and methodological challenges. *Behavioral and Brain Sciences*, **19**, 1–55.

Langer, E.J. (1982) The illusion of control. In D. Kahneman, P. Slovic & A. Tversky (eds), *Judgement under Uncertainty: Heuristics and Biases*. Cambridge University Press, Cambridge.

Lichtenstein, S., Fischhoff, B. & Phillips, L.D. (1982) Calibration of probabilities: the state of the art to 1980. In D. Kahneman, P. Slovic & A. Tversky (eds), *Judgement under Uncertainty: Heuristics and Biases.* Cambridge University Press, Cambridge.

Loomes, G. & Sugden, R (1982) Regret theory: an alternative theory of rational choice under uncertainty. *Economic Journal*, **92**, 805–24.

Macchi, L., Osherson, D. & Krantz, D.H. (1996) Superadditive probability judgment. Unpublished paper, Department of Psychology, Columbia University.

McClelland, A.G.R & Bolger, F. (1994) The calibration of subjective probabilities: theories and models 1980–1994. In G. Wright & P. Ayton (eds), *Subjective Probability*. Wiley, New York.

McClennan, E.F. (1990) *Rationality and Dynamic Choice*. Cambridge University Press, Cambridge.

Meehl, P.E. (1954) *Clinical versus Statistical Prediction: A Theoretical Analysis and a Review of the Evidence*. University of Minnesota Press, Minneapolis.

Meehl, P.E. (1986) Causes and effects of my disturbing little book. *Journal of Personality Assessment*, **50**, 370–75.

Milburn, M.A. (1983) Sources of bias in the prediction of future events. *Organizational Behavior and Human Performance*, **21**, 17–26.

Murphy, A.H. & Winkler, R.L. (1984) Probability forecasting in meteorology. *Journal of the American Statistical Association*, **79**, 489–500.

Nisbett, R. & Ross, L. (1980) *Human Inference: Strategies and Shortcomings*. Prentice Hall, Englewood Cliffs, NJ.

Northcraft, G.B. & Neale, M.A. (1987) Experts, amateurs, and real-estate: an anchoring-and-adjustment perspective on property pricing decisions. *Organizational Behavior and Human Decision Processes*, **39**, 84–97.

O'Dean, T. (in press) Are investors reluctant to realise their losses? *Journal of Finance*.

Pfeifer, P.E. (1994) Are we overconfident in the belief that probability forecasters are overconfident? *Organizational Behavior and Human Decision Processes*, **58**, 203–13.

Phillips, L.D. (1987) On the adequacy of judgmental probability forecasts. In G. Wright & P. Ayton (eds), *Judgmental Forecasting*. Wiley, Chichester.

Pitz, G.F. (1974) Subjective probability distributions for imperfectly known quantities. In L.W. Gregg (ed.), *Knowledge and Cognition*. Erlbaum, Hillsdale, NJ.

Poulton, E.C. (1989) *Bias in Quantifying Judgments*. Erlbaum, New York.

Schoemaker, P.J.H. (1991) When and how to use scenario planning: a heuristic approach with illustration. *Journal of Forecasting*, **10**, 549–64.

Schoemaker, P.J.H. (1995) Scenario planning: a tool for strategic thinking. *Sloan Management Review*, **36**, 25–40.

Simon, H. A. (1956) Rational choice and the structure of the environment. *Psychological Review*, **63**, 129–38.

Staw, B.M. & Ross, J. (1989) Understanding behavior in escalation situations. *Science*, **246**, 216–20.

Tversky, A. & Kahneman, D. (1974) Judgment under uncertainty: heuristics and biases. *Science*, **185**, 1124–31.

Tversky, A. & Kahneman, D. (1983) Extensional versus intuitive reasoning: the conjunction fallacy in probability judgment. *Psychological Review*, **90**, 293–315.

Tversky, A. & Koehler, D. (1994) Support theory: a non-extensional representation of subjective probability. *Psychological Review*, **101**, 547–67.

van der Heijden, C. (1994) Probabilistic planning and scenario planning. In G. Wright & P. Ayton (eds), *Subjective Probability*. Wiley, Chichester.

von Mises, R. (1957) *Probability, Statistics and Truth*. Dover, New York.

Wagenaar, W.-A. & Keren, G.B. (1986) Does the expert know? The reliability of predictions and confidence ratings of experts. In E. Hollnagel, G. Mancini & D.D. Woods (eds), *Intelligent Decision Support in Process Environments*. Springer-Verlag, Berlin.

Wilson, T.D., Houston, C.E., Etling, K.M. & Brekke, N. (1996) A new look at anchoring effects: basic anchoring and its antecedents. *Journal of Experimental Psychology: General*, **125**, 387–402.

Winkler, R.L. & Murphy, A.M. (1973) Experiments in the laboratory and the real world. *Organizational Behavior and Human Performance*, **20**, 252–70.

Wright, G. & Ayton, P. (1986) Subjective confidence in forecasts: a response to Fischhoff and MacGregor. *Journal of Forecasting*, **5**, 117–23.

Wright, G. & Ayton, P. (eds) (1987a) *Judgemental Forecasting*. Wiley, Chichester.

Wright, G. & Ayton, P. (1987b) The psychology of forecasting. In G. Wright & P. Ayton (eds), *Judgemental Forecasting*. Wiley, Chichester.

Wright, G. & Whalley, P. (1983) The supra-additivity of subjective probability. In B.P. Stigum & F. Wenstøp (eds), *Foundations of Utility and Risk Theory with Applications*. D. Reidel Publishing Company, Dordrecht.

Yates, J.F., McDaniel, L.S. & Brown, E.S. (1991) Probabilistic forecasts of stock prices and earnings: the hazards of nascent expertise. *Organizational Behavior and Human Decision Processes*, **40**, 60–79.

# Integration of Statistical Methods and Judgment for Time Series Forecasting: Principles from Empirical Research

J. Scott Armstrong* and Fred Collopy**
*University of Pennsylvania, Philadelphia, and
**Case Western Reserve University, Cleveland, USA

## SUMMARY

We consider how judgment and statistical methods should be integrated for time-series forecasting. Our review of published empirical research identified 47 studies, all but four published since 1985. Five procedures were identified: revising judgment; combining forecasts; revising extrapolations; rule-based forecasting; and econometric forecasting. This literature suggests that integration generally improves accuracy when the experts have domain knowledge and when significant trends are involved. Integration is valuable to the extent that judgments are used as inputs to the statistical methods, that they contain additional relevant information, and that the integration scheme is well structured. The choice of an integration approach can have a substantial impact on

_Forecasting with Judgment_. Edited by G. Wright and P. Goodwin.
© 1998 John Wiley & Sons Ltd.

the accuracy of the resulting forecasts. Integration harms accuracy when judgment is biased or its use is unstructured. Equal-weights combining should be regarded as the benchmark and it is especially appropriate where series have high uncertainty or high instability. When the historical data involve high uncertainty or high instability, we recommend revising judgment, revising extrapolations, or combining. When good domain knowledge is available for the future as well as for the past, we recommend rule-based forecasting or econometric methods.

## 10.1   INTRODUCTION

Assume that you need to make forecasts for time-series, such as the prices of natural resources. Should you use judgment or statistical methods? As an example, the historical series for the price of chromium is shown in Figure 10.1. The historical data would seem to be valuable and statistical methods can make use of this information. Expert judgment also uses knowledge about the factors influencing the prices of natural resources? Each approach has advantages and disadvantages, so one might also consider integrating statistical methods and judgment.

Judgment is useful because domain experts often have knowledge of recent events whose effects have not yet been observed in a time series,

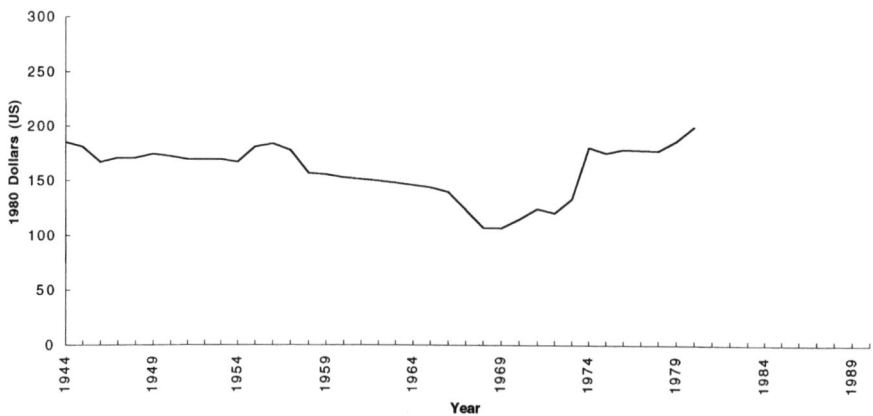

**Figure 10.1**   Chromium prices

of events that have occurred in the past but are not expected to recur in the future, or of events that have not occurred in the past but are expected for the future. For example, they may know about policy changes that are likely to cause substantial changes over the forecast horizon. While these types of information should be valuable for forecasting, there are also risks in using unaided judgment. Experts may see more in the data than is warranted. And they are subject to a variety of biases such as anchoring, double counting, and optimism.

Statistical methods are less prone to biases and can make efficient use of prior data. Statistical methods are reliable; given the same data, they will produce the same forecast whether the series relates to costs or revenues, to good news or bad. However, statistical procedures are myopic, knowing only about the data that are presented to them.

Given the relative advantages of judgment and statistical forecasts, it seems sensible to integrate them.[1] As we will show, integration of judgment and statistical methods can lead to substantial gains in accuracy under certain conditions (in comparison to using either of them alone). But when incorrectly applied, as often happens, integration can harm accuracy.

Our conclusions are based on a review of prior literature. The review was aided by previous reviews on judgmental and statistical forecasting by Bunn & Wright (1991), Goodwin & Wright (1993, 1994), and Webby & O'Connor (1996). To ensure that our interpretations of prior research are accurate, we circulated a draft of this chapter to those whose work we cited.[2] We asked them to examine our interpretation of their work, and to indicate if we had misinterpreted their work or if they were aware of additional studies that should be included. Responses were received from eight authors. This led to revisions and to the identification of additional studies.

In all, our review includes 47 relevant empirical studies. Note that research on the integration of judgment and statistical methods is generally recent; all but three of these studies have been published since 1985.[3]

In this chapter, we examine when you are likely to gain from integrating statistical methods and judgment, and how best to achieve such integration. In the next section, we describe the components that can be integrated. We then propose screening criteria to identify the conditions under which integration is feasible and useful. Most of the chapter is devoted to describing research findings related to various procedures for integrating judgment and statistical methods. These lead to some principles for integration. We conclude with a discussion of the conditions related to the choice of an integration procedure.

## 10.2   COMPONENTS FOR INTEGRATION: JUDGMENT AND STATISTICAL METHODS

We consider three ways that judgment can be integrated into time series forecasting.[4] First, there is judgment about what data are relevant to the forecasting task. Second, the judgment of forecasting experts can be used to determine the approach to be used (e.g. "If you expect that automobile sales will continue to grow, the best way to forecast them over the next 12 months is to use seasonally adjusted exponential smoothing"). Third, experts can incorporate domain knowledge into the forecasts (e.g. "Based on the state of the economy and considering the marketing plan, we expect that Ford's unit automobile sales will increase by 5% over the next 12 months").

The first judgment task facing a forecaster has to do with what data are to be used. By "data" we mean the series of interest (typically called the time series) and any available time series on causal factors. Data can be based on objective or subjective inputs (such as surveys). Exactly what series to use will depend upon the problem being addressed. For example, when studying airline passenger behavior, should one count the number of people who fly, the number of trips they take, the number of segments they fly, the number of airplane embarkations they make, or something else? Should the data be collected by days, weeks, months, quarters or years? These are not trivial issues. They depend on the decisions to be made, the costs of and kinds of data available and the rate at which things are changing. Once a time series is selected, one must decide whether it should be forecast directly or decomposed.

Judgment is needed to decide what statistical procedures to use in a given situation. These statistical procedures can be classified based on the data they use. Extrapolation uses only the historical values of the time series whose future value is of interest. Regression methods estimate the effects of causal variables as well.

Domain experts make judgments based on their knowledge about the product/market, and on their expectations about patterns in the data. This domain knowledge can be used to define the variable of interest, to make revisions in the time series observations, or to adjust for unusual events such as strikes, stockouts or drought. Experts can use their domain knowledge directly to make forecasts, or to estimate starting values and smoothing parameters for models that specify expectations about future effects of causal variables. They can use it to select analogous or related series, which can aid in estimating trends (e.g. Duncan, Gorr & Szczypula, 1993). Domain knowledge can be used to identify the causal factors acting on the series and to make estimates about how they will change over the forecast horizon (e.g. by anticipating a major change in price or a change in product characteristics). It can also be used to specify expectations about future effects, such as price becoming less important to consumers.

It seems to be commonly believed that the more information experts have about a series, the better judgmental forecasts they will be able to make. However, laboratory studies have concluded that additional information can harm accuracy. Further, in some circumstances at least, confidence grows even as accuracy declines (e.g. Davis, Lohse & Kottemann 1994). To avoid this, decision support systems can be used to structure domain knowledge.

## 10.3 FEASIBILITY CONDITIONS

To integrate judgment with statistical forecasts, one must be able to produce statistical forecasts. This means that there must be quantitative data available and these must have some relevance for the future. Such data are not always available. For example, when launching a highly innovative product, one often lacks data, even on similar products. In other cases, large discontinuities (new laws, wars, new products, etc.) can render prior data irrelevant for predictions about the future.

To be useful, judgments should incorporate information that is not captured by the statistical forecast and *vice versa*. To a large extent, time series capture the effects of all of the changes in the past, so it is primarily when domain knowledge provides information about recent or pending changes that it may be useful. For example, if management were to decide to phase out a product by removing all marketing support, this knowledge would be useful. Another example would be if substantial price changes are planned for a product that has sold at a constant price in the past. Still another example is when those who are doing the forecasting have good knowledge of the historical data and also much control over the series, such as for management's 1-year forecasts of corporate earnings (Armstrong 1983). On the other hand, if time series are, themselves, the result of many unbiased judgments (as in markets), there may be little benefit from integration.

One problem with human judgment is that it is easily biased. An upturn in sales for one of the company's products can be seen by the product manager as an early indicator of a period of sustained growth, while a downturn of similar magnitude might be dismissed as a transient slump. When the forecasters have motivations for a particular outcome, inclusion of their judgmental forecasts is likely to add bias to the forecast. This tends to make forecasts less accurate than those produced by a statistical method.

While these conditions might seem obvious, they are sometimes ignored. This is especially so for the condition related to bias. A failure to meet any one of these conditions might cause integration to be of little value or even to harm accuracy.

## 10.4   PROCEDURES FOR INTEGRATION

Assuming that the above conditions are met, integration should be considered. All of the methods we will discuss involve integrating *structured* judgment. A variety of decision support procedures can be used to structure judgment. At the simplest level, they may involve ensuring that the arithmetic is done correctly. MacGregor, Lichtenstein & Slovic (1988) concluded that experts often make arithmetic errors when using judgmental decomposition.

Another way to structure judgment is to organize historical data for presentation to experts. While it is often assumed that a picture is worth a thousand words, research findings suggest that graphics help only under certain conditions and can sometimes even harm forecast accuracy. Harvey & Bolger (1996) reviewed the research and conducted experiments. They found that graphs led to more accurate judgmental forecasts when the series contained trends, but that otherwise, tables yielded more accurate forecasts. They concluded that the use of graphs of trended series reduced the tendency to underestimate the steepness of the trends when judges used tables. On the other hand, graphs reduced their ability to estimate the level of untrended data due to inconsistency and an overforecasting bias, which were both greater with graphs.

A comprehensive approach to aiding judgment was developed by Edmundson (1990). Using a computer-aided approach, judges decomposed judgments about the level, trend and seasonality of a series. This approach proved superior to the use of statistical methods alone.

The various ways in which statistical methods and domain knowledge can be integrated for time series forecasting are illustrated in Figure 10.2. The five procedures to integrate judgment and statistical methods are shown in the shaded boxes. They include revising judgmental forecasts after seeing statistical extrapolations, combining judgmental and extrapolation forecasts, using judgment to revise extrapolations, rule-based forecasting and econometric methods.

Integration procedures are expected to be successful to the extent that the judgments and the statistical forecasts are independent. Such

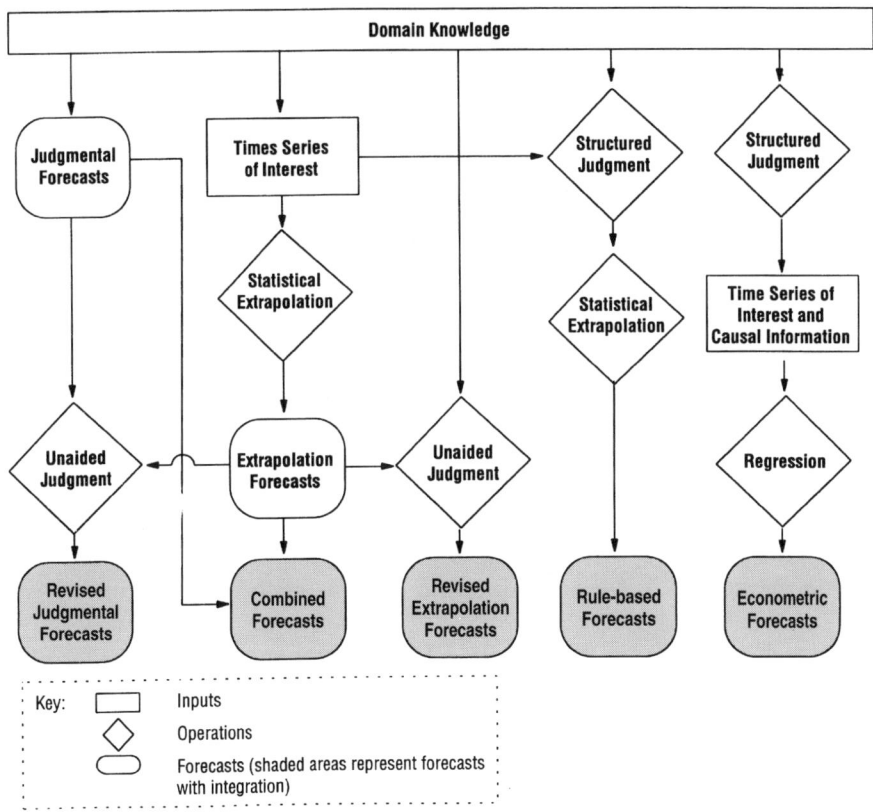

**Figure 10.2** Integration of judgment and statistical methods

independence can be achieved by carefully structuring the procedures used for integration, such as by specifying any weighting in advance of seeing the statistical forecasts. A review of evidence supporting this is provided in Armstrong (1985, pp. 52–7). The methods on the right side of the Figure, econometric methods in particular, are the most highly structured.

### 10.4.1   Revised Judgmental Forecasts[5]

One way to integrate judgment and statistical methods is for experts to make judgmental forecasts, and then revise them based on statistical extrapolations. Carbone & Gorr (1985) asked 14 subjects to make judgmental forecasts for 10 time series from the M-competition data (Makridakis et al., 1982). Subjects were then allowed to make extrapolation forecasts and use these to revise their judgmental forecasts. These revised forecasts were more accurate.

Lim & O'Connor (1996b) suggest that decision makers get overwhelmed by information, but if the information is structured it improves performance. Using simulated data, Lim & O'Connor (1996a) asked subjects to make judgmental extrapolations and then provided them with forecasts from a damped trend exponential smoothing model. The subjects' adjustments improved accuracy. This gain was enhanced if they were also provided with relevant causal information. Thus, accuracy was improved when the forecaster followed a structured procedure in which a preliminary forecast was made, the data were reviewed and the forecast was then revised.

Judges may be resistant to new information provided by statistical forecasts. Lim & O'Connor (1995) found that subjects presented with statistical forecasts (after having made a judgmental forecast) put too much weight on their initial judgmental forecast when combining the two. This persisted even when they were presented with information about the reliability of the statistical forecasts and the inaccuracy of their initial forecasts.

Consider again the time series showing the price of chromium. Experts would be asked to make a judgmental forecast. Following this, they would be provided with a statistical extrapolation like that in Figure 10.3, which is based on Holt's exponential smoothing, and asked to adjust their initial forecast. The evidence suggests that the adjusted forecasts would be superior if the time series adds information beyond what is in the judgments.

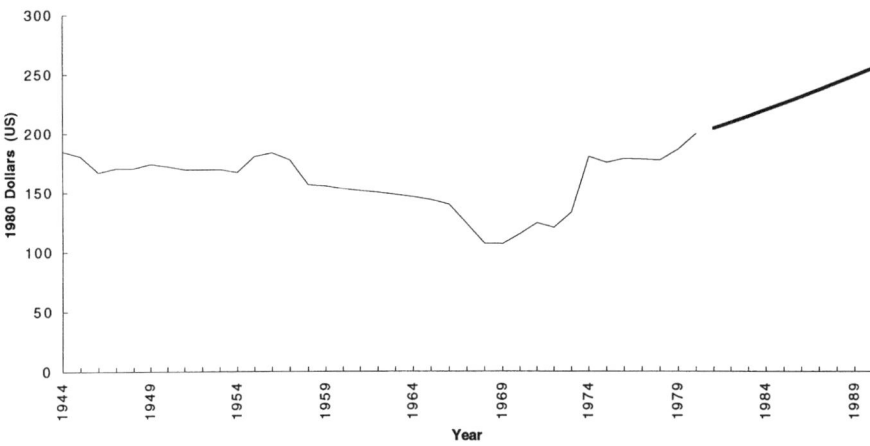

**Figure 10.3**  Chromium prices: Holt's forecast

### 10.4.2  Combined Forecasts

If one could know which method, statistical or judgmental, would produce the more accurate forecast, then that method should probably be used, or at least weighed more heavily. In practice, alternative forecasts nearly always contain some added information. Combining them aids accuracy to the extent that the added information is valid and reliable but different.

*Mechanical* combinations have at least three advantages. First, they are more objective, avoiding the introduction of biases or political manipulation. Second, it is easier to disclose fully the process that produced them. Third, they tend to be more accurate because they use knowledge more effectively. These conclusions about combining are drawn partly from Clemen's (1989) review of over 200 empirical studies on combining statistical forecasts. Similar conclusions have been obtained from research on combining judgmental forecasts (Armstrong 1985, pp. 91–6). Below we review the evidence that these conclusions apply as well to combinations of statistical and judgmental forecasts. Such combinations seem especially useful because they may have different biases that cancel one another.

Lawrence, Edmundson & O'Connor (1986), using 68 monthly series from the M-competition (Makridakis et al., 1982), combined eyeball judgmental extrapolations with statistical extrapolations from exponential smoothing. The judges had no domain knowledge. Alternative presentations of the data (tables vs. graphs) and various combinations of the forecasts were compared. Overall, combining reduced the mean absolute percentage error (MAPE) by about 7% (compared with the accuracy of the average component forecast), with a tendency for more improvement for shorter horizons (an 8.9% gain for 1–6 months ahead forecasts) than for longer-term (6.2% for 13–18 months ahead). This gain was slightly better than the gain for equal-weights combining of six statistical extrapolation forecasts for these series (6.1% gain on average).

Lobo & Nair (1990) examined combinations of judgmental and statistical extrapolations of corporate earnings for eight years for 96 firms. Judgmental forecasts were made by two groups with domain knowledge (security analysts who specialized in those stocks) and two statistical forecasts were made (one using random walk with drift and one using ARIMA). We reanalyzed results from their Table 1 and concluded that, on average, the combination of judgmental and statistical forecasts led to a 5.2% reduction in MAPE. This exceeds the gain from combining their two statistical methods (2.1%) or their two judgmental methods (0.6%).

Blattberg & Hoch (1990) combined judgmental and statistical forecasts and achieved statistically significant gains in accuracy (tested using $R^2$). They did not, however, estimate the magnitude of the error reduction.

Sanders & Ritzman (1989, 1990, 1992), studied judgmental forecasts by warehouse planners. The experts had much domain knowledge and the forecast horizon was short (1 day ahead). The conditions, then, were ideal for the use of judgment. They concluded that the combination of judgmental and extrapolation forecasts led to improved accuracy when applied to series of medium to low variability. Otherwise, it was best to rely on judgmental forecasts alone. Overall, however, their combined forecasts were about 15.8% more accurate than the typical component forecasts (based on our analysis of Table 1 in Sanders & Ritzman, 1989).

Lim & O'Connor (1995) conducted an experiment where judges had a decision support system that provided feedback on the relative accuracy of judgment and statistical procedures. Subjects placed too much weight on their own judgment, so that the forecasts were not as accurate as they might have been. One might expect this to harm accuracy. Indeed, Bretschneider et al. (1989), in a field study of revenue forecasting by state governments, concluded that state governments in the USA that used formal procedures for combining had more accurate forecasts than states that used subjective weighting.

A reasonable starting point for combined forecasts would be to use equal weights (Clemen, 1989). In some conditions, however, it may help to use differential weights. For example, because experts are relatively good at estimating current levels, it makes sense to weight judgment more heavily for levels. Consistent with this, Webby & O'Connor's (1996, pp. 97–9) review concluded that judgmental forecasts were superior to statistical ones, especially for short-term forecasts (where the level estimate is most important) and when the experts had good domain knowledge.

If differential weights are used, they should be developed in advance and should be based on research findings, not on the opinions of experts involved in the forecasting task. The weights should also be recorded so that analyses may determine how to improve the weighting scheme.

### 10.4.3 Revised Extrapolation Forecasts

The most common way to integrate statistical methods and domain knowledge is to revise extrapolations. According to Sanders & Manrodt's (1994) survey of forecasters at 96 US corporations, about 45% of the respondents claimed that they always made judgmental adjustments to statistical forecasts, while only 9% said that they never did. The main reasons they gave for revising quantitative forecasts were to "incorporate knowledge of the environment" (39%), "incorporate product knowledge" (30%) and "incorporate past experience" (26%). While these reasons seem sensible, there is a problem in that adjustments are often made by biased experts. In a survey of members of the International Institute of Forecasters, 269 respondents were asked whether they agreed with the following statement: "Too often, company forecasts are modified because of political considerations".[6] On a scale from 1 = "disagree strongly" to 7 = "agree strongly," the mean response was 5.4. Fildes & Hastings (1994), using a survey of 45 managers in a large conglomerate, found that 64% of them believed that "forecasts are frequently politically motivated".

Judgmental revisions might improve accuracy if the forecaster is able to identify patterns that are missed by the statistical procedure. Most extrapolation methods do not, for example, deal with discontinuities (Collopy & Armstrong, 1992b). This might also be true for other important pattern changes. A number of studies have examined subjective adjustments where subjects did not have relevant domain knowledge, suggesting that the improvements were due to their ability to recognize pattern changes that were not handled by the extrapolation methods. Willemain (1989) showed that subjective adjustments led to improvements in the accuracy of extrapolation for artificial time series; however, in another study involving 24 series from the M-Competition, he found no advantage for subjective adjustments (Willemain, 1991). Sanders (1992), in a study involving simulated data, concluded that judgmental revisions of extrapolation forecasts led to some gains in accuracy for series that had low noise, especially when there was a step function in the historical series. Carbone et al. (1983) had subjects make revisions for 25 time series from the M-competition (where subjects had only the title and dates of the series in addition to the series itself). In general, these adjustments tended to harm accuracy.

Judgmental revisions might also improve accuracy if the forecaster were able to take advantage of causal information that the statistical method had not used. Wolfe & Flores (1990) and Flores, Olson & Wolfe (1992) found improvements when judgmental adjustments were made to corporate earnings series that had high variability. However, experts were no more accurate than non-experts, suggesting that these improvements had more to do with the patterns of data than with the causal information.

Based on their study of a situation where the judges had domain knowledge, Mathews & Diamantopoulos (1989) concluded that judgmental revisions of quantitative forecasts led to improved accuracy. These adjustments were made by individual experts.

It seems appealing to make subjective adjustments. Consider the forecast of chromium prices. In Figure 10.3, we provided an extrapolation produced by Holt's exponential smoothing. One could start with the forecast, then revise it judgmentally. Given good domain knowledge and a structured process, judgmental revisions are likely be useful.

Subjective adjustments contradict our advice that judgment should be used as an input to statistical methods, rather than to revise the statistical forecasts. The exceptions that one might consider, such as correcting errors, adjusting for interventions or failure to include an important variable, are better dealt with by producing a new forecast than by revising the old one.

Judgmental revisions are risky. Given the danger of double counting and the difficulty of avoiding biases, one way to make subjective adjustments would be to have experts decide what adjustments would be appropriate for the model (e.g. add 2% to the forecast for each horizon) *before seeing the forecasts*. We are unaware of any tests of this approach.

In summary, revisions of extrapolation forecasts seem most relevant where forecasters have good domain knowledge and the revisions are based on structured judgment. Lacking such conditions, judgmental revisions might harm accuracy. Given that the research findings to date are limited and difficult to interpret, other factors might be involved, adding to the risk of judgmental revisions.

### 10.4.4   Rule-based Forecasts

Rule-based forecasting uses structured judgmental inputs to statistical procedures. Rule-based forecasts depend upon an assessment of the conditions faced in the forecasting task. The basic idea is that the forecasting methods must be tailored to the situation and that a key aspect of this is domain knowledge. Domain knowledge can help to identify the direction of causal forces on the series of interest, the functional form that the time series is likely to follow, and the presence of any unusual patterns or observations.

The rules are instructions on how to weight the forecasts from a set of simple forecasting methods, and the weights vary according to features of the series. The rules for weighting the forecasts are derived from experts and from prior research. Rule-based forecasting uses expert judgments about the characteristics of series and about causal forces as inputs to extrapolation methods.

Collopy & Armstrong (1992a) found that rule-based forecasting was more accurate than the use of equal weights in 1 to 6-year forecasts for 126 annual economic time series from the M-competition. The gains were greater for series that involved good domain knowledge, significant long-term trends, low instability and low uncertainty. In an extension using the same 126 series, Vokurka, Flores & Pearce (1996) assessed some of the characteristics automatically. They achieved substantial improvement over using statistical procedures alone, although not quite as large as those in Collopy & Armstrong (1992a). This suggests that at least some of the gain from using judgment can be incorporated into the statistical forecasting procedures. Vokurka, Flores

& Pearce found further improvements when they used a decision support system. It had a graphical interface that allowed the user to view a graph of the time series, the forecast method selected by the system, and forecasts from alternative methods. Users had the capability to change the forecasting method or the forecasted values. Adya, Collopy & Kennedy (1997) used rules to identify the presence of many of the features for the series examined in Collopy & Armstrong (1992a) and obtained similar results.

The chromium series that we have been using as illustration was part of a 1980 challenge that Julian Simon posed to ecologists: "Pick any natural resource and any future date. I'll bet the [real] price will not rise" (Tierney 1990). He based this on long-term trends, and the reasoning that there had been no major changes in the long-term causal factors. Paul Ehrlich, an ecologist from Stanford University, accepted the challenge; he selected five metals (copper, chromium, nickel, tin, and tungsten) and 10 years. The prices for these metals had been rising over the recent past. In general, the causal forces for the prices of resources are "decay". This is due to improved procedures for prospecting, more efficient extraction procedures, lower energy costs, reduced transportation costs, development of substitutes, more efficient recycling methods, and more open trade among nations. A proposed force that might lead to increased prices is that the resource is exhaustible; however, this seldom has a strong effect because new sources are found. With respect to petroleum reserves, for example, Ascher (1978, pp. 139–41) showed that forecasts of the ultimate available petroleum reserves *increased* from the late 1940s to the mid-1970s. Such changes seem common for resources because of improvements in exploration technology. Thus, the overall long-term causal force seems to be decay, and prices of metals would be expected to decrease.

Rule-based forecasting is especially useful when domain knowledge indicates that recent trends may not persist. In the case of metals prices, Ehrlich assumed that recent price trends would continue. We had implemented Ehrlich's assumption in Figure 10.3 by using Holt's exponential smoothing to extrapolate recent trends for one of his five metals, chromium. This led to a forecast of sharply rising prices. In contrast, although the rule-based forecast initially forecasts an increase in prices (because it allows that short-term trends might continue), over the 10-year horizon the forecasts become dominated by the long-term trend, which is downward and consistent with the causal forces. This same pattern was found for each of the five metals forecasts made in

1980.[7] A rule-based forecast for chromium prices is shown in Figure 10.4. This forecast resulted from specifying the causal forces acting on the series as decay and the functional form as additive. The actual data for 1981–1990 are also shown in this Figure. Simon won the bet on the price of chromium as well as for the other four metals.

### 10.4.5 Econometric Forecasts

When judgmental inputs are used to identify a model and regression is used to obtain estimates for the coefficients of this model, we refer to the integration as an econometric model. Econometric models provide the most highly structured approach to integrating judgment. In addition to functional form, judgment is used to select causal variables and to specify the directions of effects (Dawes & Corrigan, 1974). Prior research (summarized by Armstrong, 1985, and Fildes, 1985) indicates that, when judgment is based on good domain knowledge, econometric models are typically more accurate than alternative procedures when large changes are involved.

Stepwise regression is an approach in which statistical procedures are used to identify the model. It does not call for integration with judgment, so we exclude it from our discussion of econometric methods. In fact, given that it ignores domain knowledge, we recommend that stepwise regression should not be used in forecasting. Indeed, there is little support for its use (Armstrong 1985, pp. 52–7).

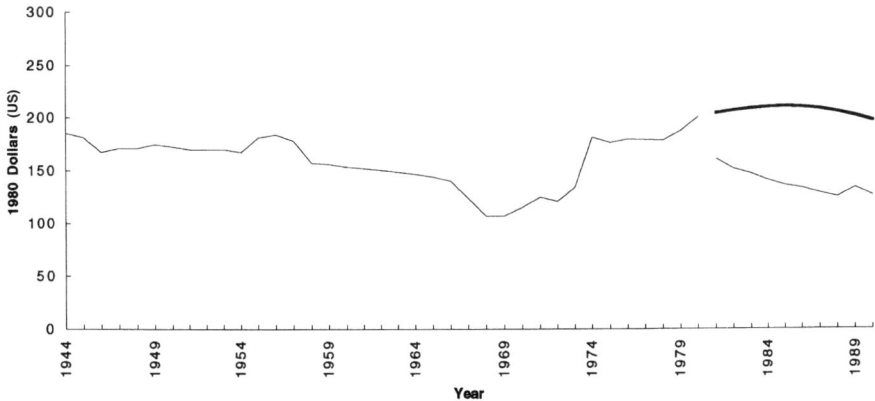

**Figure 10.4**  Chromium prices: rule-based forecast (bold) and actuals

Econometric models are more accurate than judgment for cross-sectional forecasts. Gove & Meehl (1996) reached this conclusion after a review of 136 comparative empirical studies; 64 studies found the model's forecasts to be superior to the experts, there were 64 ties, and the experts were superior in eight studies. No similar analysis has been done for time series forecasts, but our impression is that judgment is superior to econometric forecasts under certain conditions, such as for short-range forecasts.

Studies involving cross-sectional forecasts have found that subjective revisions are of little benefit and they tend to harm accuracy. For example, Griffith & Wellman (1979) found that subjective adjustments of quantitative forecasts reduced accuracy for six hospitals during the period 1967–1971. In Harris (1963), experts' revisions of football forecasts from an econometric model reduced their accuracy. Weinberg (1986) found that judgmental revisions of forecasts for arts performances did not improve accuracy.

In contrast, subjective adjustments to econometric models often improve the accuracy of short-term time series forecasts (McNees, 1990). Armstrong (1985, pp. 237–8) reviewed four empirical studies and concluded that subjective revisions will be useful primarily to the extent that they adjust for recent changes in the current level. Comparable gains can be made by mechanical adjustments based on the most recent error of the model. For example, one useful procedure is to take half of the error in forecasting the latest period, and add that to the forecast for the next period. (In effect, this adjusts the current status or level.) Vere & Griffith (1995) and Donihue (1993) provided additional evidence on this issue. However, McNees (1990) concluded that subjective adjustments are superior to mechanical adjustments.

Forecasters may be biased and they may put too much emphasis on their opinions. For example, Weinberg (1986) found that experts were correct about the direction of the revisions on 12 of 15 arts performances, but they were too aggressive, such that on average there was no improvement. McNees (1990) found that economic experts were too aggressive and that this harmed accuracy. To address these problems, adjustment factors should be independent of the forecasts. This could be done by asking experts what adjustments they would make for a given model before they see the forecasts. These would be used to adjust the level and the trend estimates; these revisions would be recorded for further evaluation.

Another problem with judgmental revisions is that record keeping is often poor (Turner, 1990). The lack of a record means that forecasters are unlikely to get well-summarized feedback of the effect of their adjustments, and, as a result, they will have difficulties learning how to improve them. To address this, judgmental revisions should be done in a structured and fully disclosed manner.

## 10.6  PRINCIPLES FOR INTEGRATION

Although much research has been done recently, the number of studies does not yet allow for a quantitative integration of their results. Furthermore, the failure of many of the studies to specify conditions has compounded the problem. Nevertheless, we draw some conclusions about principles for integrating judgment and statistical methods.

One generalization is that judgment is most effective if used as an input to statistical forecasting, less effective if used independently, and least effective if used to revise quantitative forecasts. Another generalization is that structure helps; the more structured the inputs and the more structured the integration procedures, the more accurate the forecasts.

Equal weighting of statistical and judgmental forecasts is a good starting point. Departures from an equal weighting of judgment and statistical models should be based on good domain knowledge. When uncertain about which forecasting procedure will be most accurate, use equal weights on judgment and statistical forecasts. However, in cases where one method can be expected to do better than the other, it should be weighted more heavily. For example, in cases where there have been substantial recent disruptions for reasons that are known to the experts, and where the experts have received good feedback on the accuracy of their forecasts, one might put more weight on the judgmental forecasts. On the other hand, as the amount of high quality and relevant data is increased, more emphasis should be given to statistical methods. As domain knowledge increases, put more weight on judgement relative to statistical forecasts. When the amount and quality of the data improves, more weight should be placed on statistical forecasts.

Experts are not effective in integrating large amounts of information that might be relevant to forecasting changes. This implies that judgment is more effective for estimating where one is now than for predicting change. Another way of saying this is that experts are better at "nowcasting" than at forecasting. Evidence supporting this position is summarized in Armstrong (1985, p. 237). As a result, it may help to decompose the forecasting problem into level and change. Judgment would be weighted more heavily for estimating levels. With increases in the amount of change anticipated, it is advisable to place more weight on the statistical methods relative to judgment (Armstrong, 1985, pp. 393–402).

Judgmental revisions of forecasts are likely to harm accuracy if done by biased experts. Furthermore, revision does not appear to be the most effective way to use judgment. It is distressing that software developers have been making it easier for forecasters to make unstructured judgmental adjustments. Instead, software should encourage prior inputs of judgment and describe how to structure this information (e.g. information about levels or about causal forces). If judgmental revisions are used, they should be carefully monitored (what revisions were made, when, by whom, and why). The evaluation should compare the accuracy of the forecasts with and without the revisions.

Our discussion has focused on forecasting expected values. We have not addressed the issue of estimating the uncertainty associated with prediction intervals. To date, little research has been done on the integration of judgment and statistical methods to estimate prediction intervals. However, Armstrong & Collopy ( 1997) found that judgment could be valuable in the estimation of prediction intervals; in particular, the use of causal forces helped to identify series where the log errors were expected to be asymmetric.

## 10.7 CONDITIONS UNDER WHICH INTEGRATION PROCEDURES ARE EFFECTIVE

Assuming that the feasibility conditions have been satisfied (quantitative data available, time series and judgment each contribute different information, and judgment is not obviously biased), one might conclude that some form of integration is relevant. But which? While our recommendations focus on accuracy, other criteria, such as ease of understanding the forecasting method, might be as important as accuracy (Yokum & Armstrong, 1995).

The choice of an integration procedure is dependent upon the conditions. Time series conditions can be separated into those related to domain knowledge and those related to the historical time series, and the interaction of these:

(1) Domain knowledge
- Unusual past event (e.g. knowledge about when a strike occurred).
- Planned intervention.
(2) Historical time-series
- Significant long-term trend.
- Uncertainty (e.g. coefficient of variation about the trend; differences in direction of long- and short-term trends).
- Instability (e.g. discontinuities or last observation unusual).
(3) Conflicts between domain knowledge and time series
- Contrary series (when the expected direction of the trend conflicts with the short-term extrapolation).

The determination of these conditions can be done judgmentally, although some of the historical conditions can also be done statistically, as shown in Collopy & Armstrong (1992a), and extended by Adya, Collopy & Kennedy (1997) and by Vokurka, Flores & Pearce (1996).

Research has provided little direct evidence on how these conditions affect the accuracy of various methods, except for rule-based forecasting, where the conditions are an integral part of the procedure. Applying general principles from above, however, permits us to speculate about the relative effectiveness of the various integration methods.

For situations where little historical domain knowledge exists, the selection of an integration approach is not critical. But if there is good domain knowledge, econometric forecasting can permit it to be modelled, and thereby integrated effectively with the statistical data from the time series itself. Rule-based forecasting can also integrate domain knowledge, although not as well.

If experts have up-to-date information that has not been integrated into the historical data, then their information should be used in the forecasts. This can occur with respect to recent events whose effects have not been fully incorporated into the data or with respect to planned interventions, such as a major price change.

For situations involving high degrees of uncertainty or instability, revisions and simple combinations can be helpful. In these conditions the methods on the left hand side of Figure 10.2 are likely to do at least as well as the more sophisticated methods. Since they will generally be easier to implement, they should be favored.

When there is knowledge of future changes, structured approaches to integration are likely to have a particularly high payoff. When contrary trends are encountered, their extrapolation is dangerous (Armstrong & Collopy, 1993). In such cases, econometric methods offer a more promising approach. Although not directly tested, we also expect that econometric forecasts will be more accurate than rule-based forecasting if one has good information about the causal relationships, and if the causal factors can be accurately forecast, or if they can be set by decision makers. Econometric forecasts are likely to be superior to rule-based forecasts because they give explicit attention to the effects of each causal variable. Of course, one must also consider cost as a factor, especially for situations requiring thousands of forecasts.

If experts have knowledge about large recent changes, judgmental adjustments of the current status are likely to improve accuracy. These judgements should be made by unbiased experts and they should be fully disclosed.

## 10.8  CONCLUSIONS

We have presented three conditions under which the integration of judgment and statistical methods should be considered. The conditions involve having relevant quantitative data, judgmental inputs that provide different information, and unbiased judgments.

Given those three conditions and uncertainty about which method is likely to produce the best forecast, integration is expected to improve accuracy, although the improvements in accuracy will depend upon the extent to which the judgmental inputs are well structured. Of particular importance is that judgment be used as an input to the statistical methods, rather than to revise their output.

In general, equal-weights combining provides a good way to integrate and it should be viewed as the benchmark. To the extent that the historical series involve good domain knowledge, significant trends, low uncertainty and low instability, we recommend the use of rule-based forecasting. If, in addition, the future conditions involve interventions and contrary trends, we recommend econometric methods.

While the recent surge of interest in the integration of judgment and statistical methods is promising, we expect that our ability to draw generalizations will continue to be limited unless researchers report on the conditions involved in their studies. We have proposed some historical and future conditions that we think will be helpful in organizing and testing knowledge in this area, but suspect that they can be expanded upon. Given the importance to decision makers of incorporating judgment into their forecasts, and the importance to businesses and society of unbiased and accurate forecasts, this seems to be a most promising area for further research. We believe that a research program should be oriented to identifying the conditions under which a given type of integration should be used.

## ACKNOWLEDGMENTS

Paul Goodwin, Nigel Harvey, Stephen Hoch, Marcus O'Connor, Nada Sanders and Thomas Willemain provided useful comments on early versions of this paper. Monica Adya contributed to the analysis. Editorial assistance was provided by Colleen Gepperth.

## NOTES

(1)   We do not include procedures that manipulate judgmental forecasts statistically, such as judgmental bootstrapping procedures.

(2)   According to a study by Eichorn & Yankauer (1987), authors frequently make mistakes in their summaries of prior research.

(3)   This overstates currency somewhat, in that some of the review papers cited works that had been published before 1985.

(4)   We do not address the use of judgment as data. For example, intentions surveys involve people's judgments of people about how they will behave.

(5)   We recognize that when forecasts are used for decision making, managers may make adjustments. For example, given a sales forecast of 100 units per month, the manager might initially produce 110 units per month in order to build up inventory. Our concern in this chapter is only with the forecast, in this case the 100 units per month, so we do not examine decision-making adjustments. Such adjustments might be useful, of course, as is discussed by Goodwin (1996).

(6)   This survey was conducted in 1989 by Thomas Yokum and Scott Armstrong. The responses to this question were analyzed depending on whether the respondent was a decision maker, practitioner, educator or researcher. While the practitioners stated the strongest agreement, there were no statistically significant differences among these groups.

(7) The forecasts were prepared by Monica Adya, using a version of rule-based forecasting that is described in Adya, Collopy & Kennedy (1997). The data were obtained from *Metals Week*.


# REFERENCES

Adya, M., Collopy, F. & Kennedy, M. (1997) Heuristic identification of time series features: an extension of rule-based forecasting. Working paper available from Monica Adya (adya@umbc.edu).

Armstrong, J.S. (1983) Relative accuracy of judgmental and extrapolative methods in forecasting annual earnings. *Journal of Forecasting*, **2**, 437–47.

Armstrong, J.S. (1985) *Long-range Forecasting*, 2nd edn. Wiley, New York.

Armstrong, J.S. & Collopy, F. (1993) Causal forces: structuring knowledge for time series extrapolation. *Journal of Forecasting*, **10**, 147–9.

Armstrong, J.S. & Collopy, F. (1997) Prediction intervals for extrapolation of annual economic data: evidence on asymmetry corrections. Working paper.

Ascher, W. (1978) *Forecasting: An Appraisal for Policy Makers and Planners*. Johns Hopkins University Press, Baltimore.

Blattberg, R.C. & Hoch, S.J. (1990) Database models and managerial intuition: 50% model + 50% manager. *Management Science*, **36**, 887–99.

Bretschneider, S.I., Gorr, W.L., Grizzle, G. & Klay, E. (1989) Political and organizational influences on the accuracy of forecasting state government revenues. *International Journal of Forecasting*, **5**, 307–19.

Bunn, D. & Wright, G. (1991) Interaction of judgmental and statistical forecasting methods: issues and analysis. *Management Science*, **37**, 501–18.

Carbone, R., Andersen, A., Corriveau, Y. & Corson, P.P. (1983) Comparing for different time series methods the value of technical expertise, individualized analysis and judgmental adjustment. *Management Science*, **29**, 559–66.

Carbone, R. & Gorr, W.L. (1985) Accuracy of judgmental forecasting of time series. *Decision Sciences*, **16**, 153–60.

Clemen, R. (1989) Combining forecasts: a review and annotated bibliography. *International Journal of Forecasting*, **5**, 559–83.

Collopy, F. & Armstrong, J.S. (1992a) Rule-based forecasting: development and validation of an expert systems approach to combining time series extrapolations. *Management Science*, **38**, 1394–414.

Collopy, F. & Armstrong, J.S. (1992b) Expert opinions about extrapolation and the mystery of the overlooked discontinuities. *International Journal of Forecasting*, **8**, 575–82.

Davis, F.D., Lohse, G.L. & Kottemann, J.E. (1994) Harmful effects of seemingly helpful information on forecasts of stock earnings. *Journal of Economic Psychology*, **15**, 253–67.

Dawes, R. & Corrigan, B. (1974) Linear models in decision making. *Psychological Bulletin*, **81**, 95–106.

Donihue, M.R. (1993) Evaluating the role judgment plays in forecast accuracy. *Journal of Forecasting*, **12**, 81–92.

Duncan, G., Gorr, W.L. & Szczypula, J. (1993) Bayesian forecasting for seemingly unrelated time series: application to local government revenue forecasting. *Management Science*, **39**, 275–93.

Edmundson, R.H. (1990) Decomposition: a strategy for judgmental forecasting. *Journal of Forecasting*, **9**, 301–14.

Eichorn, P. & Yankhauer, A. (1987) Do authors check their references? A survey of the accuracy of references in three public health journals. *American Journal of Public Health*, **77**, 1011–12.

Fildes, R. (1985) The state of the art: econometric models. *Journal of the Operational Research Society*, **36**, 549–86.

Fildes, R. & Hastings, R. (1994) The organization and improvement of market forecasting. *Journal of the Operational Research Society*, **45**, 1–16.

Flores, B.E., Olson, D.L. & Wolfe, C. (1992) Judgmental adjustment of forecasts: a comparison of methods. *International Journal of Forecasting*, 7, 421–33.

Goodwin, P. (1996) Statistical correction of judgmental point forecasts and decisions. *Omega*, **24**, 551–9.

Goodwin, P. & Wright, G. (1993) Improving judgmental time series forecasting: a review of guidance provided by research. *International Journal of Forecasting*, **9**, 147–61.

Goodwin, P. & Wright, G. (1994) Heuristics, biases and improvement strategies in judgmental time series forecasting. *Omega*, **22**, 553–68.

Gove, W.M. & Meehl, P. (1996) Comparative efficiency of informal (subjective, impressionistic) and formal (mechanical, algorithmic) prediction procedures: the clinical–statistical controversy. *Psychology, Public Policy, and Law*, **2**, 293–323.

Griffith, J.R. & Wellman, B.T. (1979) Forecasting bed needs and recommending facilities plans for community hospitals: a review of past performance. *Medical Care*, **17**, 293–303.

Harris, J.G. Jr (1963) Judgmental vs. mathematical prediction: an investigation by analogy of the clinical vs. statistical controversy. *Behavioral Science*, **8**, 324–35.

Harvey, N. & Bolger, F. (1996) Graphs versus tables: effects of data presentation format on judgmental forecasting. *International Journal of Forecasting*, **12**, 119–37.

Lawrence, M.J., Edmundson, R.H. & O'Connor, M.J. (1986) The accuracy of combining judgmental and statistical forecasts. *Management Science*, **32**, 1521–32.

Lim, J.S. & O'Connor, M. (1995) Judgmental adjustment of initial forecasts: its effectiveness and biases. *Journal of Behavioral Decision Making*, **8**, 149–68.

Lim, J.S. & O'Connor, M. (1996a) Judgmental forecasting with time series and causal information. *International Journal of Forecasting*, **12**, 139–53.

Lim, J.S. & O'Connor, M. (1996b) Judgmental forecasting with interactive forecasting support systems. *Decision Support Systems*, **16**, 339–57.

Lobo, G.J. & Nair, R.D. (1990) Combining judgmental and statistical forecasts: an application to earnings forecasts. *Decision Sciences*, **21**, 446–60.

MacGregor, D., Lichtenstein, S. & Slovic, P. (1988) Structuring knowledge retrieval: an analysis of decomposed quantitative judgments. *Organizational Behavior and Human Decision Processes*, **42**, 303–23.

Makridakis, S., Anderson, A., Carbone, R., Fildes, R., Hibon, M., Newton, J., Parzen, E. & Winkler, R. (1982) The accuracy of extrapolation (time series) methods: results of a forecasting competition. *Journal of Forecasting*, **1**, 111–53.

Mathews, B.P. & Diamantopoulos, A. (1989) Judgmental revision of sales forecasts: a longitudinal extension. *Journal of Forecasting*, **8**, 129–40.

McNees, S.K. (1990) The role of judgment in macroeconomic forecasting accuracy. *International Journal of Forecasting*, **6**, 287–99.

Sanders, N.R. (1992) Accuracy of judgmental forecasts: a comparison. *Omega*, **20**, 353–64.

Sanders, N.R. & Manrodt, K.B. (1994) Forecasting practices in US corporations: survey results. *Interfaces*, **24**(2), 92–100.

Sanders, N.R. & Ritzman, L.P. (1989) Some empirical findings on short-term forecasting: technique complexity and combinations. *Decision Sciences*, **20**, 635–40.

Sanders, N.R. & Ritzman, L.P. (1990) Improving short-term forecasts. *Omega*, **18**, 365–73.

Sanders, N.R. & Ritzman, L.P. (1992) The need for contextual and technical knowledge in judgmental forecasting. *Journal of Behavioral Decision Making*, **5**, 39–52.

Tierney, J. (1990) Betting the planet. *New York Times Magazine*, December 2, p. 52.

Turner, D.S. (1990) The role of judgment in macroeconomic forecasting. *Journal of Forecasting*, **9**, 315–45.

Vere, D.T. & Griffith, G.R. (1995) Modifying quantitative forecasts of livestock production using expert judgments. *Journal of Forecasting*, **14**, 453–64.

Vokurka, R.J., Flores, B.E. & Pearce, S.L. (1996) Automatic feature identification and graphical support in rule-based forecasting: a comparison. *International Journal of Forecasting*, **12**, 495–512.

Webby, R. & O'Connor, M. (1996) Judgmental and statistical time series forecasting: a review of the literature. *International Journal of Forecasting*, **12**, 91–118.

Weinberg, C.B. (1986) Arts plan: implementation, evolution, and usage. *Marketing Science*, **5**, 143–58.

Willemain, T.R. (1989) Graphical adjustment of statistical forecasts. *International Journal of Forecasting*, **5**, 179–85.

Willemain, T.R. (1991) The effect of graphical adjustment on forecast accuracy. *International Journal of Forecasting*, **7**, 151–4.

Wolfe, C. & Flores, B. (1990) Judgmental adjustment of earnings forecasts. *Journal of Forecasting*, **9**, 389–405.

Yokum, J.T. & Armstrong, J.S. (1995) Beyond accuracy: comparison of criteria used to select forecasting methods. *International Journal of Forecasting*, **11**, 591–7.

# Index